NATO AND THE QUEST FOR POST-COLD WAR
SECURITY

Also by Clay Clemens

RELUCTANT REALISTS: The CDU/CSU and West German Ostpolitik

NATO and the Quest for Post-Cold War Security

Edited by

Clay Clemens
Associate Professor of Government
College of William and Mary
Williamsburg
Virginia, USA

Foreword by Baroness Thatcher

First published in Great Britain 1997 by
MACMILLAN PRESS LTD
Houndmills, Basingstoke, Hampshire RG21 6XS and London
Companies and representatives throughout the world

A catalogue record for this book is available from the British Library.

ISBN 0–333–71641–8

First published in the United States of America 1997 by
ST. MARTIN'S PRESS, INC.,
Scholarly and Reference Division,
175 Fifth Avenue, New York, N.Y. 10010

ISBN 0–312–17603–1

Library of Congress Cataloging-in-Publication Data
NATO and the quest for post-cold war security / edited by Clay
Clemens.
p.   cm.
Includes bibliographical references (p.   ) and index.
ISBN 0–312–17603–1 (cloth)
1. North Atlantic Treaty Organization.   2. National security–
–Europe.   I. Clemens, Clay, 1958–
UA646.3.N229 1997
355'.031091821—dc21   97–3274
                                                         CIP

This book is printed on paper suitable for recycling and made from fully managed and
sustained forest sources.

10   9   8   7   6   5   4   3   2   1
06   05   04   03   02   01   00   99   98   97

Printed in Great Britain by
The Ipswich Book Company Ltd
Ipswich, Suffolk

To the memory of Michael C. Coon

Contents

Foreword
Baroness Thatcher

It is an honour to introduce this volume resulting from an important conference on NATO sponsored by the College of William and Mary and the Alliance's Atlantic Command (SACLANT). What follows are my own views. Some may be reflected by other contributors to this collection; some may agree with me, others may not. I leave the readers to judge who is right.

Thatcher's First Law of Politics is that the unexpected happens, and when it does, you had better be prepared. And you had better be decisive. I have learned that lesson from quite a long time in the front line. Thatcher's Second Law of Politics is that, when viewing the future and deciding what to do at any given moment, you must have learned from history so that you do not repeat past mistakes. You might not necessarily think this observation should come from a politician, but it does: the deepest things in politics are the enduring principles. The deepest policies are those that will last through different times, different administrations, and will always be necessary to safeguard the future.

My first Law of Politics – the unexpected happens and when it does you had better be prepared – came from the times when I was very young, because such times leave a lasting impression. I still remember the atmosphere of the 1930s. At our school, we all had to correspond with someone in a different language. All of a sudden, we had a *cri de coeur* from the father of my sister's Austrian correspondent. Hitler had marched in, and they were Jewish. If Edith could be got out, could we possibly take her in? We did. That brought these terrible events home to us in a way that nothing else could. And we learned a very great deal of that period. I had also learned from being a voracious reader of the newspapers, and – as the youngest in the family – by listening ardently to the conversation of my elders, hearing of some of the difficulties, the doubts, and of the rise of Hitler.

But I also heard sentiments that were perhaps heard in other countries. For there had been World War I. We had lost hundreds of thousands of young men. A whole generation. We never expected to have to go to war again. After all, we were great idealists. We believed in fundamental principles. No one, we thought, could ever be so mad as to go to war again – to stop this great development, the great increase in standards of living, the great hopes for the future. No one would be so mad as to go to war again. And, therefore, there was some idea that because we were right, because we had the right ideas, because we had the right principles, this of itself was an armour against fate. Of course it was not: ideals have never stopped a dictator. Only stronger weaponry will deter him.

But during that time, during the 1930s there was resistance to rearmament. There was a peace ballot. And I remember very vividly some people coming back from holiday in Nazi Germany telling us what was happening. We were slow to rearm. When Hitler marched into Czechoslovakia – first, into Sudeten Czechoslovakia where there was a German minority – we were alerted. But we could not do very much because we had not really rearmed. Neville Chamberlain had to go to negotiate with the dictator to get the best deal he could, and was assured that this was the last request for extra territory, the last claim Hitler had. He came back with an agreement called Munich. We were a little bit ashamed, but the point is this: the unexpected had happened, and we were not prepared.

Neville Chamberlain could not have done anything else at the time. Between that year of 1938 and 1939, we had to rearm as fast as we could. Because, of course, this was not Hitler's last claim. The following March, he marched into Prague. The following September, he marched into Warsaw. By that time, Chamberlain had given him a warning that if he continued, we would be at war. We were. All this is etched on my memory.

After World War II, things were different – very different We had learned the lessons. We had learned that we could not disarm, much as we wished to after six years of war. NATO was formed in 1948 – the greatest defensive alliance in the world. It was a marvellous decision. It kept America in Europe, which was vital. To be certain of peace required not only an alliance of surrounding countries, but one country of much greater power, the greatest democracy in the world – the United States of America.

So the formation of NATO was quite different from what had happened after World War I. We had learned the lessons of history: never appease an aggressor, because he will only get more and more demanding, better and better equipped. So we must at all times keep our defences strong, because the unexpected does happen. That is why I am the greatest supporter of the continuation of NATO in its present role, its first role – collective security against possible attack. We know not from where, but we must always be prepared. And that role must continue.

Yes, NATO will have other roles, as it may have with Russia, a kind of partnership for peace. But I myself would not include Russia in NATO at all. She has a very long way to go before becoming a stable democracy, and indeed, is having very great difficulty. A country which had no rule of law and had known no freedom for a very long time is not easily able to become a stable society.

What about Poland, Czechoslovakia, Hungary? Here I have had no doubt for some time. We should have taken action already. I do not know what has happened to some politicians; they do not like taking decisions quickly at the right time. Why, when the Iron Curtain came down; why, when the Soviet Union collapsed and they became free nations again – why did we not take Poland, Czechoslovakia, and Hungary into NATO, or promise to take them into NATO as soon as they were able to have the requisite equipment to do so? It is for me something of a mystery. But, then, my generation always felt rather guilty because we had not been able to save them before. Certainly, when these countries became free, it seemed that they should be taken in. There were various people who said, 'Oh no, don't do anything like that yet. It might provoke Russia'. But defence policy based on the fact that something might provoke Russia will never be sound or sure. You must not let other people determine your defence policy.

When I have been to visit Poland, people have said to me something like this: 'Don't you understand, Mrs. Thatcher, what it is like sitting here in the crossroads of Europe? We were attacked by Hitler. He marched in, and then in came Stalin.' They have said, 'On one side we had one enemy, and on another side another. Don't you understand that we need the security of NATO?' And I have said 'yes'. I also understood in Czechoslovakia too. There they are, knowing their history, and seeing that NATO will not take them in. It is a disgrace.

Thirdly, NATO should be able to extend its operations to other areas. The current area is drawn really rather rigidly. When the Bosnian terror came up, that was technically 'out-of- area', which is absolutely absurd. We must extend our operations. It does not mean that the whole of NATO would have to go abroad; selected countries would go, but under the NATO banner. And that should be done fairly quickly.

Bosnia, for example, was not a question of lack of military means. We had them all. It was lack of resolve. We had seen what had happened in Croatia. There had been a peace deal, and unfortunately after that peace the weaponry had been moved into Bosnia, which was asking for trouble. The Serbs were the clear aggressors in Bosnia. We saw what was happening on our television screens. It was very different from World War II, when we did not know what was going on in the concentration camps until afterwards. Here we saw the concentration camps, we saw some of the terrible things that were happening. We had heard from Vukovar, and elsewhere in Croatia, about the awful massacres and the mass graves. Yet in Bosnia we did not take firm action.

Eventually, of course, there were people who were starting to arm Croatia, and also starting to arm Bosnia. But that left the Serb aggressor openly making attacks and, of course, terrible things were happening – the massacres, the mass graves. The United Nations decided, therefore, to have a resolution on safe havens and some NATO forces in Bosnia with authority from the UN to defend them, including by going outside in order to stop an attack. They also had the authority to defend with force of arms the humanitarian convoys, to see that they got through.

What happened was very strange indeed. Those powers were not fully used. The safe havens were not safe, and there were not sufficient soldiers allocated to them. So the very thing people had gone there for, safety, was denied them. At the last one, Srebrenica, there are thus mass graves. Again, it was a case of the United Nations letting people down. I feel deeply about this: it should never have happened.

The Dayton Accord is not a model of clarity. It has provided for NATO armed forces to try to keep the peace, but only for two years. What is going to happen afterwards? If they pull out and there is no fundamental peace, it is a great mishmash of ethnic hatred that people cannot forget. Whereas they all lived among one another before the war took hold there, they are now in separate enclaves, and we are going to have a new situation.

There are other very considerable problems facing the West. One of the worst since the collapse of Russia is the massive increase in nuclear proliferation. Many nuclear weapons seem to be available in the former Soviet Union for sale outside. An increasing concern to NATO is a fear of sponsored terrorism, whereby small nuclear devices or chemical warfare weapons might be used to blackmail. Iraq and Iran could build a nuclear bomb by getting hold of some of the weapons-grade plutonium. There are undoubtedly a large number of transactions taking place, some from North Korea, some from Russia. Add some of that nuclear material to the ease of getting missiles and the absence of an anti-ballistic missile defence, and you can see the very great difficulties. Some of these states, rogue states – Iran and Iraq and Syria – would not have anything like the scruples about using a nuclear weapon that the nuclear powers have had all of these years. Another real danger is from fanatical Islamic groups which, after the collapse of the Soviet Union, started to destabilize the orthodox Islamic states.

In a nuclear age, international terrorism has taken on an increased strategic importance. In bygone days, Russia would keep a tight hold on her client states like Iran, Iraq, and Syria. When it collapsed, that hold no longer pertained, and so there are far many more local wars and local hostilities and local terrorism than in the past. Saddam Hussein only invaded from Iraq after the collapse of the Soviet Union. This, I am afraid, is not really very cheerful for anyone, but is something that we have to face in the modern world. We also have to reckon that the advance of science is constantly putting more powerful weapons than ever before in the hands of evil men.

And so, where does that leave us? There is but little comfort, except that we have kept a major war from starting and have been able to put out a number of local wars – or could have done, had action been taken quickly enough.

True, there will always be conflict. This is very difficult for idealistic people to accept. But the good Lord put evil into the hands of men. It is part of human nature, part of the eternal battle between good and evil. There will always be those who are prepared to use force to obtain their objectives. Dictators will not suddenly become an extinct species. Our experience in the Gulf War taught us a vital lesson: never appease an aggressor, and keep our defences strong. It is vital that democracies maintain their military strength and keep up their technological lead. Strength does not cause wars, but weakness attracts an aggressor.

It is not a bad recipe that I started with: Thatcher's First Law of Politics. The unexpected will happen. Better by far to keep up defence to prevent war than to lack strong defences and to attract war. We owe at least that to the future generation.

Acknowledgements

Contributions to this volume began as presentations at a symposium on the future of NATO, co-sponsored by The Thomas Jefferson Program in Public Policy at The College of William and Mary, and the Supreme Allied Command, Atlantic (SACLANT). Held in April, 1996, the meeting brought together military officials and diplomats, politicians and journalists, scholars and think-tank analysts, students and local citizens – all for the purpose of discussing complicated issues that will have a major bearing on international security well into the next century.

This book thus reflects the efforts of two different organizations and numerous individuals. The symposium was made possible above all by the leadership and support of SACLANT, under Supreme Allied Commander, Atlantic, General John J. Sheehan, USMC, and his deputy, Vice-Admiral Ian D.G. Garnett, as well as by the commitment of The College of William and Mary, under President Timothy J. Sullivan and Provost Gillian T. Cell. Their shared desire for public dialogue on NATO's future paved the way for this uniquely successful collaborative enterprise between an allied joint military command and an American university.

Officials and staff members at both organizations laboured long and hard to ensure the success of the final product. From the SACLANT side, Director of Analysis and Research Ralph Nahra, as well as LCDR Dennis Gallagher, provided invaluable input and support. At William and Mary, those to whom gratitude is due include, above all, Professor David Finifter, Director of the College's Thomas Jefferson Program in Public Policy, who worked for over a year in preparing the NATO symposium. His efforts benefited greatly from the leadership and hard work of Ambassador Robert Fritts, as well as excellent assistance from their staff – Karen Dolan, Linda McCauley, Karen Schifrin and Elaine McBeth, as well as Kimberly Holloway and Alison Spock – and other College officials including Stewart Gamage, Bill Walker, Cindy Bagley, Lillian Kelly, Joyce Laughlin and Sue Peterson.

For their help in preparing the papers for publication, the editor would also like to thank Jane Fogarty, Tess Owens, and Karen Hammer, as well as Rhonda Newsom.

Among its other aims, the SACLANT/William and Mary symposium sought to help student participants think about ways of resolving complex issues, for members of their generation will have to work at preserving peace and security in the new century. This volume is dedicated to the memory of one young man who was ready for such a commitment and would surely have made his contribution.

Chapter 7, 'Reviving the West', by Charles Kupchan, is reprinted by permission of *Foreign Affairs*, 75 no. 3 May–June 1996. Copyright 1996 by the Council on Foreign Relations, Inc.

Notes on Contributors

Ronald D. Asmus is a senior researcher for RAND Corporation. Prior to joining RAND in 1988, he was a research associate at the Free University in Berlin and a senior researcher at Radio Free Europe/ Radio Liberty. Dr Asmus has written widely on Central European politics and U.S.–European relations, and – most recently – a book entitled *Germany's New Geopolitics*.

Ted Galen Carpenter is vice-president for defence and foreign-policy studies at the Cato Institute in Washington, D.C. Along with book chapters, edited collections, and journal articles, Dr Carpenter's publications include *Beyond NATO: Staying Out of Europe's Wars* (1994) and *A Search for Enemies: America's Alliances After the Cold War* (1992).

Clay Clemens teaches Government at the College of William and Mary. His articles have most recently appeared in *West European Politics*, *German Politics*, and *Armed Forces and Society*.

Susan Eisenhower is President of The Eisenhower Group, Inc., an international consulting firm, as well as founder and chair of The Center for Political and Strategic Studies. Along with articles, she has authored *Breaking Free: A Memoir of Love and Rebellion* (1995) and *Mrs Ike: Memories and Reflections on the Life of Mamie Eisenhower* (1996).

William G. Hyland is now Research Professor of International Relations at Georgetown University's School of Foreign Service. He edited *Foreign Affairs* from 1984 to 1992. Prior to that Mr Hyland was Deputy National Security Advisor (1975–77) and Assistant Secretary of State for Intelligence and Research (1973–75). His books include *The Fall of Khrushchev* (1968), *Mortal Rivals* (1987), *The Cold War* (1990) and *The Song is Ended* (1995).

Charles A. Kupchan is Senior Fellow for Europe at the Council of Foreign Relations and Research Associate Professor at Georgetown University. Dr Kupchan served in the Clinton Administration as Director for European Affairs at the National Security Council. His publications include *The Persian Gulf and the West* (1987), *The Vulnerability of Empire* (1994) and *Nationalism and Nationalities in the New Europe* (1995).

F. Stephen Larrabee is a senior analyst with RAND's International Policy Department. He is author of *East European Security After the Cold War* (1994) and edited *The Volatile Powderkeg: Balkan Security After the Cold War* (1994). He was a member of the National Security Council staff (1978–81), and spent ten years at the Institute of East-West Security Studies in New York City

Gale A. Mattox is a Professor of Political Science at the U.S. Naval Academy. She has served with the State Department's Policy Planning Staff (1994–95) and Bureau of European and Canadian Affairs (1985–86). Dr Mattox has co-authored *Evolving European Defense Policies* (1987), and co-edited *Germany at the Crossroads* (1992) and *Germany Through American Eyes* (1989).

Simon Serfaty is Professor of International Politics at Old Dominion University and Senior Associate and Director of European Studies for the Center for Strategic and International Studies. His publications include over forty-five major essays in leading professional journals and books such as *New Thinking and Old Realities: America, Russia, and Europe* (1991) and *Taking Europe Seriously* (1992). He is co-founder of the journal *Géopolitique*.

Stephen F. Szabo is Associate Dean for Academic Affairs at Johns Hopkins University's Paul H. Nitze School of Advanced International Studies. He has served at the State Department's Foreign Service Institute and the National War College. Dr Szabo's publications include *The Changing Politics of German Security* (1990) and *The Diplomacy of German Unification* (1992).

Introduction

NATO's history reads like a record of continuous internal debate over its own future. Scepticism and uncertainty accompanied the establishment of a North Atlantic Alliance. Subsequent decades brought new crises – over nuclear strategy, the distribution of responsibilities, or the balance of burdens. Library shelves sag under the weight of books on controversies that loomed large in their day, with words like 'challenge', 'troubled', 'quandary', 'dilemma', and 'uncertainty' in the titles – volumes often distinguishable mainly by publication date and cover art. And then NATO almost become a victim of its own success. For helping achieve its ultimate aim – to end Europe's Cold War division – raised doubt about the need for an Atlantic Alliance at all: critics and even old fans asked if preserving NATO made sense now that the Soviet bloc no longer existed.

That debate has ended with a fairly unambiguous 'yes'. But quick on its heels has come a fresh controversy over whether NATO should serve not only as a framework for the collective defence of its members but as a major instrument of security for all of Europe and even regions beyond. To use Ronald Asmus's term, 'double enlargement' would mean expanding Alliance involvement in non-traditional missions, like international peacekeeping or peace enforcement, and extending its frontiers to embrace states of the former Soviet bloc. NATO leaders are formally committed to both steps, yet each remains contested, a subject of often heated discussion among experts on both sides of the Atlantic, as well as among other policy-makers and, increasingly, politicians.

A PREVIEW OF THE ISSUES

Contributors to this volume analyse the need for and prospects of an Alliance more deeply involved in missions other than those falling under the North Atlantic Treaty's Article 5 – collective defence of member states. One issue addressed is possible centres of instability that might affect allied interests or simply evoke concern: long defined as the Middle East, Africa or conceivably (if implausibly) beyond,

1

'out-of- area' for NATO now includes the Balkans, even possibly parts of the former USSR. Yet as the authors note, risks or humanitarian problems arising in any of these regions promise to grow more diverse, making it difficult to arrive at a common concept of interests even among allies accustomed to cooperating.

Equally unclear is how prepared many member states are to send troops on *any* future non-traditional missions outside Western Europe. Such ventures would often require major political and resource commitments. To the extent they are ready, there is the question of rival frameworks and possible divisions of labour. Do member states agree that NATO is best-equipped to manage joint 'out-of-area' action? After all, for years the European Union's defence arm, the West European Union (WEU), seemed to be the consensus choice for such work. Are NATO's Implementation Force (IFOR) and Stabilization Force (SFOR) in Bosnia now models for future missions? Does the answer lie in the 1996 Berlin decision, which envisages WEU members of the Alliance deploying forces out-of-area in Combined Joint Task Forces (CJTF) with US help and infrastructure, even if America itself decides not to take part? And is France as prepared to make its peace with an increasingly, even globally active NATO as events in the mid-1990s suggested?

Even greater controversy centres on partly-related proposals to admit new members from the former Soviet bloc, most notably the Visegrad states of East Central Europe – Poland, Hungary, and the Czech Republic, as well as possibly Slovakia; some Balkan countries, namely Slovenia and Romania; and at some point the small Baltic republics of Latvia, Estonia and Lithuania. In late 1996, Alliance leaders decided to make their first offers at a summit meeting in Madrid set for the following summer, with membership to take effect a few years later. In some ways, geographic enlargement has become to NATO in the 1990s what deployment of medium-range nuclear forces was a decade earlier – an issue that, for better or worse, fans and foes alike believe may shape, even overshadow, the Alliance's future and define its role. Each contributor to this volume deals with at least some aspect of this issue – its relevance or lack thereof to Western security; its effect on democracy and economic reform in Eastern Europe; its possible role in 'completing' the continent's unity; its connection to and impact upon plans for EU expansion; its implications for military planning, including the now dormant but always potentially-volatile nuclear issue; and – above all – its repercussions for events in and relations with Russia.

A PREVIEW OF THE CONTRIBUTIONS

Section I examines the changing context of Western security, as well as NATO's evolving response and relationship with other regional organizations, above all the EU and WEU.

Simon Serfaty sets current discussions of NATO and its post-Cold War direction in a historical and geopolitical context. He offers a reminder that even new issues have antecedents, yet warns against becoming a prisoner of past parallels. Despite praising Europe's progress towards integration, Serfaty views the persistence of national identity and other problems in a process that 'promised too much and delivered too little' as reasons for doubt that the EU will handle security on its own. Thus he sees continuing US leadership as essential, even while wondering if Americans are ready for, or have even focused upon, that task. When it comes to organizing European security, he contends that 'institutional blueprints' drawn up decades ago for the EU and NATO remain relevant, yet adds that reforming and enlarging both structures eastward will require time, care and coordination.

Enhancing this 'European security identity' is the focus of Gale Mattox's chapter. As old as the Alliance itself, the call to encourage or allow a greater military role by members other than the United States is being answered in several ways. Mattox assesses the potential for a more active WEU and uses for or limits on NATO CJTFs. She assesses prospects that the Organization for Security and Cooperation in Europe (OSCE) could play a larger part – and thus promote a European identity – in providing for security through political or diplomatic means. She concludes that NATO remains the flagship of European security but continues to require support from a fleet of other organizations, even some without direct US participation.

Stephen Szabo points out that the collapse of a hegemonic threat, along with proposals for making enlargement palatable by limiting NATO's military dimension, are reducing the priority of collective defence, even as the need for crisis management grows ever more acute. Such changes, he notes, will increasingly raise questions among many American leaders about the necessity for and nature of a US role in the old world, making a European security identity appear all the more vital. Yet doubting that the American contribution can be supplanted altogether, Szabo suggests the need for further steps towards reforming the Alliance while preserving its basic transatlantic structure.

Contributors to Section II make the case for enlargement, both functional and geographic. An early and ardent advocate of those policies, Ronald Asmus, treats them as mutually reinforcing. Warning of a potential 'disconnect' between 'what [the Alliance] is best geared to do and the most pressing strategic challenges facing the Western world', he contends that Washington's partners must help move NATO towards a broad out-of- area agenda, partly in order to help assure Americans of its continuing relevance. At the same time, Asmus labels extending Western security guarantees eastward a moral, political and even economic imperative. This step, he adds, would guard against another disconnect – this one between an expanding EU and the Alliance. Asmus sees enlargement to East Central Europe as likely to be less costly or troublesome than critics suggest, especially if NATO could simultaneously succeed in working out a strategic partnership with Russia.

Taking up where Asmus leaves off, Stephen Larrabee assesses Eastern Europe's case and readiness for entry into the Alliance. Larrabee analyses economic, political and military reform efforts in Poland, Hungary and the Czech Republic, as well as co-operation between them, concluding that the balance – despite unevenness and setbacks – is positive. Though fear of Russia did not generate the desire of these states for NATO membership, he argues, Moscow's resistance has given them new cause for co-operation with the West. They likewise have a 'strong stake in the continued survival of an independent, stable, democratic Ukraine'. And, he contends, while eager for EU membership, East European states see it as a complement to, not a substitute for, inclusion in NATO.

In the final chapter of Section II, representatives from two countries that figure prominently in Asmus and Larrabee's analysis – Hungary and the Czech Republic – make their own case. So too do officials from states further east: Slovakia and Lithuania. Each stresses that exclusion of his land would leave NATO and Europe incomplete. Their Ukrainian counterpart voices his government's view that enlargement could enhance stability if it avoids 'new dividing lines' and fully takes into account 'the primary national security interests of all interested nations'.

That caution is amplified considerably in Section III, which reflects the wide, varied array of arguments against current plans for enlargement. Charles Kupchan does not oppose reaching out to Europe's post-Communist countries, but claims that since 'NATO's formality and the rigour of its territorial guarantees' are outdated, extending them eastward will not prove feasible, just as expanding a federalizing EU will 'founder as states resist further attempts to whittle away their sovereignty'. Kupchan claims that trying to expand both organizations will weaken them, 'as member states attempt to escape unwanted responsibilities'. He proposes scaling back the vision of enlargement by subsuming both NATO and the EU in a broader but considerably looser transatlantic union.

Susan Eisenhower's concern lies with the impact of enlargement on the evolution of democratic stability in Russia. Chronicling the growth of disenchantment with the West among reformers in Moscow, those who – given a string of Kremlin concessions that ended the Cold War – dreamed of genuine partnership, she contends that they will see an Alliance pushed to their nation's borders as the final betrayal. Such humiliation, she warns, could also mean grist for the mills of anti-Western, anti-democratic forces. Eisenhower calls for a new frame-work of relations with both Russia on the one hand, and countries that lie between NATO and that faded superpower on the other: 'an innovative structure, reflecting the most crucial current political, social and economic challenge of our time: the integration of the former communist world into the West'.

William Hyland has similar reservations about enlargement, a plan he depicts as the result of confused, even illusory efforts to grapple with complex post-Cold War realities by inventing a new 'contain-ment' mission for the Atlantic Alliance. Such a step, he contends, is poorly timed and 'puts the cart before the horse': the West's aim should be to stabilize Russian democracy.

A far broader critique of the plan for enlargement comes from Ted Galen Carpenter, who calls it deceitful, risky or both. While extending the Alliance eastward means much more than merely welcoming new members to a diplomatic club, he warns, advocates downplay the major new security obligations involved because they know the West is not ready or able to honour such commitments. And yet if the step causes an uneasy Russia to lash out, he adds, NATO could find itself facing a crisis – one that even revives the risk of nuclear tension. In his view, this 'desperate effort to find a new mission' for the Atlantic Alliance thus does not serve, but in fact greatly endangers, US security interests.

One point grows steadily clearer chapter by chapter: the diversity, indeed even at times the incompatibility, of arguments both for and against granting NATO new roles. To some extent, these dissonances among security policy specialists are matched by and compound (as yet) low-key but mounting discord over the Alliance's future among politicians and public opinion on both sides of the Atlantic. Thus the book's conclusion surveys evolving attitudes in key West European countries, as well as in the United States itself, assessing options and obstacles that may lie ahead for NATO as it ventures into uncharted territory.

I
Rethinking Western Security Structures

1 NATO at Sixty: Quests for Western Security in a Changed Europe

Simon Serfaty

Much has happened in Europe since the Cold War ended and this century's last decade began: the war in the Persian Gulf, the unification of Germany, the collapse of the Soviet Union, the Maastricht treaty, the conflicts that have accompanied the disintegration of Yugoslavia and the rise of new states elsewhere in the continent, and even the resurgence of a neo-communist political leadership that had been assumed dead when the 1990s opened. Initially, the states of Europe and the European Union (EU) – to which fifteen of them belong – had claimed that their time had come. 'This is the hour of Europe', it was said, 'not the hour of the Americans'.[1] Events, however, have proven otherwise.

Clearly, the quest for security in Europe did not end with the Cold War. Beyond the single-issue polemics of the moment, the post-Cold War years suggest four general lessons that were or should have been known, but remained largely ignored:

– the inherent instabilities of every postwar international configuration;
– Europe's unpreparedness for attending to security issues that require a credible amount of military force;
– the indispensability of American leadership and American power; and, accordingly,
– the continued relevance of the complementary institutions built during the Cold War – the North Atlantic Treaty and its military Organization (NATO), and the European Union and its associated organizations, including the Western European Union (WEU).

BEYOND BOSNIA

Predictably enough, the end of the Cold War gave rise to much hope for a new international order: after each war, it is customary for the victorious states to celebrate, for the vanquished states to complain, and for all to dismiss the likely possibility of a reprise.[2] It should not have required the war in Bosnia as a reminder that the birth of such a new order, grandly announced by President George Bush in the immediate aftermath of the Gulf War, would take time. Every postwar period is a period of global uncertainty and local instabilities. So it had been after both world wars. In fact, compared to 1919 and to 1945, the years since the fall of the Berlin Wall in 1989, or since the disintegration of the Soviet Union in 1991, have been relatively orderly. No part of a defeated state, and no province of a former ally, was invaded by the triumphant states, as was the case in 1919–1923. There has been no new hegemonial bid – no coup, no blockade, no externally-sponsored revolt against the state, as was the case in 1945–1948. If anything, Europe has been returning to the relative moderation of the nineteenth century, when limited wars prevailed, rather than to the organized insanities of the twentieth century, when total wars erupted.

Remembering how slowly the postwar order unfolded after 1945 can help. Some, to be sure, prefer to remember instead a vision that emerged spontaneously and was enforced decisively in a few weeks. But a vision is what is imagined after everything has worked. After World War II, there were so many 'visions' as to threaten incoherence.[3] Before these visions could be reconciled, there were many setbacks, many turning points that led nowhere, agreements that decided nothing, policy reversals and public anxieties, charges and countercharges among emerging allies and adversaries alike. A painfully-built Western 'coalition of the willing' fought with and within itself nearly as much and as often as with others. From 1945 to 1957, the postwar order took a dozen years to emerge; a dozen years during which the wartime alliance collapsed and a new Grand Alliance was conceived, established, organized, enlarged, and strengthened – from the Washington Treaty signed in April 1949 to Germany's entry in NATO in May 1955; a dozen years during which the effectiveness of European reconstruction preceded and shaped the fact of reconciliation between the states of Europe, starting with the Organization for European Economic Cooperation (OEEC) as the institutional conduit for Marshall aid; and a dozen years during which, after many false starts (including an ill-fated Defence Community), the Rome Treaties signed in March 1957 launched a small Europe based on a modest undertaking known as the Common Market, which few states wanted to join and even fewer expected to succeed.

The war in the Balkans and other territorial and ethnic conflicts elsewhere should be placed in this unpredictable postwar context of predictable instabilities – the broad context, that is, of (dis)order resulting from the dramatic transformation of the two largest European states: Germany, now unified, and Russia, now unhinged. Yet these postwar instabilities have been viewed instead in a prewar context – pre-Cold War and/or pre-world wars – as the ghosts of Europe's earlier history, haunting judgments about the present and policies for the future.

Clichés about the temptations of appeasement and the spread of nationalism provide the policies they suggest with an historical weight that cannot be ignored lightly. Who would dispute Margaret Thatcher's eloquent voice against the shame of Western appeasement in the 1930s, heard in the context of her criticism of Western policies in Bosnia, which she challenged before anyone else? Who would object to the late French president, François Mitterrand, making his farewell message a warning against nationalism as a cause for war in order to urge his EU partners to pursue, past the Cold War, the quest *communautaire* started after World War II?[4]

But however justified these concerns may be generally, they fail to apply specifically. In Bosnia or elsewhere, charges of appeasement aimed at America's and, by implication, NATO's resistance to using military force (and accepting related casualties) rest on the unverifiable assumption that earlier intervention would have had not only different results, but also markedly better results, than those faced in the absence of any such intervention. Who is to say? An American military intervention in Bosnia during the waning months of the Bush administration or the first year of the Clinton presidency might have caused such high levels of casualties as to force a prolonged escalation of the war, à la Lebanon, with an ever-higher level of US involvement and the ever-present risk of escalation in the region. Conversely, or subsequently, increasing US casualties might have precipitated a sudden withdrawal, à la Somalia, thereby paving the way for new calls for a dissolution of NATO and a possible political *sauve-qui-peut* in Europe. In either case, such an intervention might have launched a debate in the United States of the 'no more Bosnias' variety. If anything, missed opportunities in the Balkans grew out of errors made earlier: before the brutal use of force revived ancient ethnic hatreds, and when more effective diplomatic action by Europe, with the explicit support of the United States, could have soothed tensions and might even have prevented such fateful decisions as Germany's premature recognition of Croatia; or, after the war began, when European peace plans were hastily dismissed in the United States as a matter of principle but without alternative policies that could credibly enforce the lofty principles of denying the aggressor's gains – with the participation, that is, of US ground troops.[5] In other words, the case for an earlier use of American force in Bosnia should have been based on interests rather than on principles alone – and it should have been centred on a realistic appraisal of the state of post-Cold War Europe rather than on vague memories of Europe's ill-defined prewar years.

Similarly, events in Europe since 1991 have raised apprehensions about a resurgence of nationalism which are exaggerated both because of their scope and because of their implications. Whose nationalism and what kinds of war, where and relative to when? Paradoxically, the war in Bosnia confirms that the nationalisms of the past have been tamed, compared to fifty or one hundred years ago. To be sure, killing in the Balkans resumed with a ferocity that violates our sense of humanity. But it could no longer escalate as easily, and for as long, as it did during the earlier half of the century. From the Sarajevo learned about in earlier schooldays to the Sarajevo watched on television, the geography of past conflicts seems to have remained the same. But the history of these European conflicts has been changing, nevertheless. Faced with the prospects of another war in the Balkans, the countries of Europe did not quite revert to their past confrontational instincts: they agreed on a policy, even if that policy failed to satisfy all of them equally. As to the two superpowers of Cold War years, US efforts to pretend that the Balkans war was not immediately relevant to its interests were ultimately abandoned, and the ambitions of Russian forces to enter the Balkans were placed in a remarkable NATO framework. The point is not to argue for complacency: this is not the time for taking a time-out from history, but the time for trying even harder to master it. With the mythical period of postwar transition used to explain every crisis and justify every delay, decisions are awaited in one critical moment that will shape the security order in Europe during the initial part of the coming century.

The first signs of this defining moment are still in Bosnia, where three unforgiving communities endowed with their own armies and protectors must learn to live with the territorial and constitutional arrangements imposed upon them by the United States and its NATO partners. In the summer of 1995, a Western consensus was achieved only when a likely departure of United Nations forces raised the spectre of US-led NATO forces protecting a bloody retreat under the devastating glare of nearly-live television. Faced with two bad interventionist options – to enforce peace or to protect extraction – President Clinton gambled on the option that seemed clearly more honourable and possibly less costly (especially after Croatia's offensive had exposed the myth of Serbia's invincibility). This was not a bad gamble: regardless of its final outcome, those who dared take it in Dayton should not be condemned. In the fall of 1995, even an unsatisfying reprieve from war was better than any of the alternatives available at the time. Without an agreement at Dayton, NATO would have been at risk. But after an agreement had been signed, NATO became instead more cohesive than it had been during most of the Cold War.

Yet, with more fighting to gain more territory and claim more sovereignty looming ahead, reconciliation was plainly going to take longer than initially assumed. By 1996 there were signs of more discord, therefore, among the main countries included in the intervention force – within NATO, as well as between NATO and Russia – over the final withdrawal, turning over war criminals to justice, rearming the Bosnian army, resolving remaining territorial issues between an ambitious Croatia and a vulnerable Bosnia, ending sanctions against Serbia, and debating the role of Iran and the post-IFOR role of Russia. On every such issue, Europeans and Americans have different perspectives, shaped by interests, nurtured by history, and conditioned by geography. Failure to discuss these issues, both with and without Russia, risked leaving Western countries with the same confusion they faced in 1993–1994, and with the same dilemmas they confronted in 1995 – but with little prospect of another Dayton-like rescue of the Alliance.

Early in 1996, these questions were all the more troubling as they were raised on the eve of a presidential election in Russia. This is not the place to review the implications of an election during which Russia debated its commitment to reform at home, and following which the West could expect to taste Moscow's commitment to restraint abroad. Suffice it to say that with or without Boris Yeltsin there will be no escape from new debates among and within Western countries over such issues as the pace of NATO enlargement, the need for Western aid, and legitimate Russian interests and aspirations in Europe and beyond. With Russia, too, the last few years have confirmed what was already known but had been somehow forgotten: that the Cold War was about more than communist ideology and its pervasive intrusiveness – it was also about Russia and its expansionist power. The former has collapsed, but the latter remains.

Issues of peace and war in Bosnia, and their duplication in the East, however central to our thinking and apprehensions, should not leave us indifferent to the many other facets of post-Cold War Europe. Irrespective of what ultimately happens in the Balkans, the nation-states of Western Europe have also entered a defining moment during which they will test the centrist consensus built during the previous generation, even while the states of Eastern Europe test the democratic resilience they must maintain during the coming generation. Already, the political overhaul that is characteristic of any postwar era is nearing completion. It began in 1990 and 1992, with the fall of Prime Minister Thatcher and President George Bush, two of the dominant architects of Western policy during the terminal phase of the Cold War. In October 1994, Chancellor Helmut Kohl barely escaped, but a few months later François Mitterrand left, after four-teen years in office – nearly as long as Felipe González, defeated in Spain in March 1996. John Major's government appeared in jeopardy well before it faced re-election in 1997. As new [or] fragile political majorities consider their next steps, the last phase of this postwar overhaul is about to get under way. In the fall of 1998, Germans will vote without fearing a war they lost, might be preparing, or could justifiably fear – or, as Finance Minister Theo Waigel put it in late 1995, when Germany will stand 'for the first time in this century, on the side of the winners'.[6] As shown in France in December 1995, the last has not been seen yet of social disorders in the major Western European capitals; as shown in Italy in April 1996, the last has not been heard from old political movements whose new labels are not sufficient to make them more appetizing, even though they have become admittedly more palatable than before.

While the states of Europe are fragile, the European Union, too, is in a fragile state. Indeed, the condition of one helps explain that of the other. In the end, the treaty signed in Maastricht in December 1991 was not a good idea. Concluded on the eve of the worst economic crisis in Europe since World War II, its timing was poor, its goals too ambitious, its timetable too rigid, and its intentions too explicit. Too much austerity justified by the discipline of the European Union – rather than by the indiscipline of its members – has caused public anger aimed at the European institutions which Maastricht was designed to strengthen. Accordingly, in each country in Europe, the EU is a central political issue that acts as a substitute for the ideological cleavages of the Cold War. In short, Europe today is astray.

HALF BEFORE EUROPE

The European Community was not conceived to end the nation-state but to save it.[7] It was launched by states that moulded its institutions according to national traditions and interests, as these traditions had evolved over time and as these interests stood at the time. Over the years, however, these institutions have refashioned the nation-states into member states – states, that is, whose sovereignty has been modified by the collective will of the Union they have formed.

This transformation is much deeper than anything that was envisaged initially. Started as a foreign policy initiative with fundamental domestic implications, the EU has become a central domestic issue that affects foreign policy. As a result, neither the governance of the nation-states nor the management of their Union is made easier. What the nation-state demands to fulfil its responsibilities to the people appears denied by the member state's obligation to satisfy its commitment to the Union, and vice versa. Within each of its members, 'Europe' challenges the ideals, if not the idea, of democracy – that is, the ability of elected representatives to represent their constituencies. Worse yet – for some member states, at least – 'Europe' may erode a national unity said to be an obstacle to remaining competitive within the broader single boundaries of the European Union.

Therefore, attitudes for or against Europe now move the political debate. These attitudes define the new ideological divide, and they are the new test of party loyalties. Harassed by the restrictive discipline imposed by Brussels, citizens view the EU as an obstacle to their welfare and well-being. Trust between the government and the governed determines a society's willingness to accept the need for and price of change. But what kind of trust can there be if the laws and regulations that define such changes originate with a political authority that lacks democratic legitimacy, and if they respond to the subculture of institutions about which their own members are in doubt? Feeling abandoned, electorates show unprecedented political volatility. Liberated from past party loyalties and ideological attachment, voters pick their representatives as they would purchase a small household appliance: with little interest in the brand, and with an extended return policy pending the first evidence of failure. Thus, established national leaders and their parties, as well as populist figures and their organizations, rise and fall in a political moment that used to take a lifetime.[8]

Some of this political volatility has to do with the end of the Cold War, which has denied Western Europe the passions that used to surround political battles then aimed at saving the nation, whether against an enemy abroad or the enemy within, or *changer la vie*, as the French socialists still pledged to do in May 1981. More of that volatility, though, has to do with the economic rigour of the 1990s. High levels of unemployment, much of it long-term and unknown in much of postwar Europe, have created a class of citizens who are economically disenfranchised – that is, removed from the nation's economy for reasons over which they have little or no control. But neither the end of the Cold War nor economic austerity are enough to explain the mood of Europe. Thus, even an improved economic performance in Britain did not end the growing public dissatisfaction with Prime Minister John Major's Conservative majority, nor could it prevent substantial numbers of East Germans from bemoaning the passing of the communist regime – as if there was now in most industrial countries a new nostalgia about a past that was less affluent and less dangerous, but more satisfying and more safe.

The message heard during the Cold War had more to do with the state of the world than with the state of the nation. Now that there is less to worry about in the world, no message about the nation is heard: 'We' won, to be sure, but who are We and what did We win? 'They' lost, admittedly, but who are They and what did They lose? Identities are all the more elusive as the gap between us and them, however defined, has become either too difficult to describe or, if it can be described, too embarrassing to acknowledge.

To make matters worse, severe budgetary constraints reduce the state's ability to fulfil citizens' expectations. As worried voters find it increasingly difficult to choose between the programs of candidates they viewed with growing scepticism, each feeble majority is reduced to awaiting the next election instead of attending to the tasks of governing. From one election to the next, a sort of electoral plagiarism therefore prevails: outgoing candidates compete with a perpetually reborn 'man of confidence' who pledges a 'new majority' that will be responsive to the 'heart and mind' of its constituents. Needless to add, no sooner has the 'new' majority been elected than the 'heart' of its voters feels betrayed and their 'mind' fooled – a condition quickly corrected at the next election.[9]

Changing from one issue to another, this flexible majority increases the number of citizens who feel left out. Their faith, their values, their education, and their very lives look disturbingly irrelevant, relative to the global and institutional forces that have assumed many of the sovereign responsibilities of the state – and, by implication, those of the people. Isolated and even besieged, these citizens make their identity exclusive rather than inclusive. Their passions return to imaginary communities – national, ethnic, or tribal – which are remembered wistfully as having been smaller, more homogeneous, and safer before they were invaded by foreigners and alien ideas that distort their love of God, of the flag, or of the market-place.[10] The point is that people who might agree to be something more than what they used to be will not easily agree to become something else, especially in the context of the group – familial, ethnic, or national – which they recognize most spontaneously. Yet this is what is now demanded from the people of Western Europe: to identify with something, 'Europe', that their reason fails to understand rather than with the something, the 'nation', that still arouses their emotions. Hostility to the EU as an institution disruptive of its members' identity may turn especially visible when that identity is threatened from within. In Spain, for example, reliance on 'Europe' as an alibi for more autonomy in Catalonia could cause an anti-EU backlash that would be especially significant, as the advantages of Spain's membership in an expanding EU erode with fewer agricultural subsidies, lower levels of structural funds, and a lesser voice in the institutions of the Union.

With Europe's past 'stealth' status gone, the open flight plan calling for more integration and less sovereignty is cause for criticism and even anger. To be sure, problems that feed such anger at Europe are not new. Mostly, they result from societal discontinuities that have been in the making for many years: the end of the peasantry in post-industrial societies, the erosion of sociocultural uniformity and the rise of ethnicity as a feature of post-imperial societies, the withering of national culture as a repository of a distinct historical experience in post-Cold War societies, the adulteration of language in a global community of mass audio-visual entertainment and communication.[11] In short, these are not problems which the EU or any of its related institutions have created – or even worsened. Yet, even when the public does not blame the EU for these problems, it still insists on knowing why and how the EU can fare better than its individual members in dealing with this agenda. Now as before, membership has privileges – that is, expectations of gains that must outweigh the obligations it entails; otherwise the agonizing decision to opt out of the Union may be less demanding than the agony of staying in it. Criteria for continued membership have to do, therefore, with questions of fairness, efficiency, and transparency: not only who gets what, but also who gives what compared to every other member state; not only whether doing less might be better, but also whether doing more may not be worse for the EU institutions; and not only which decisions are made by whom, but also how these decisions are made and how they affect the citizens of each nation-state.

Another lesson that did not need Bosnia has to do, therefore, with the unfinished condition of Europe as a union of states. Admittedly, what has been achieved over the past forty years has been impressive and must be taken seriously. But all too clearly, too, there is no union yet, and the will to go further, let alone faster, may be fading as issues on the EU agenda become ever more complex and increasingly intrusive. In short, what has been exposed since the end of the Cold War is that this is not Europe's time. Irrespective of whether European states act alone, a few at a time or as a union, they do not have the capabilities, the resources and the will needed to attend to their own security on the continent.

Americans should not applaud – and Europeans should not misconstrue – this lament over the sad shape of post-Cold War Europe. This is not another expression of America's exasperation with, or ambivalence about, Europe's future as a restored force for order in world politics.[12] The development of an ever more united and strong Europe was the most successful foreign policy launched by the United States after World War II, and the most far-sighted and courageous undertaking achieved by European states during the Cold War. The idea of Europe was a splendid European idea which became possible when Americans made it their own. To this extent, the idea of Europe was also an American idea. It is an idea that worked – an idea that satisfied not only the interests of its European members but also the interests of the United States. It is also an idea that remains all the more compelling as it continues to have no alternative – if not uniting in order to become stronger, what and why? If not with the United States in an Atlantic context, how and with whom?

Since Maastricht, however, Europeans have been promising too much and delivering too little. At a time when people on both sides of the Atlantic expect more from their allies and partners, and at a time when they may understand less about them because the simplicity of the Cold War is gone, what they are told by their leaders about the future of integration in Europe and about its benefits is so overstated as to reinforce the image of Europe as an institutional underachiever that cannot do what it says and does not say what it does. Thus the criteria of economic convergence devised at Maastricht for economic and monetary union (EMU) seem more intent on keeping countries out – mainly those in Southern Europe, including Italy – than on bringing countries in. Only a loose interpretation of each state's performance for the calendar year 1997 would permit a few EU members to qualify for EMU membership at the final selection in early 1998 – on the eve of significant national elections in France and Germany, and at a time when Britain will assume the presidency of the European Council.

Whatever economic risks there may be in stopping the clock to review these criteria and their calendar, the political risks of going ahead on the basis of Maastricht's existing criteria may prove to be even worse.[13] The conditions and even the logic that prevailed when these criteria were set in 1991 are now distant and not convincing. Why impose, for example, a ceiling on the debt level relative to the size of the economy: the monetary union formed by Belgium and Luxembourg after World War II did not need such a clause, and the enormous build-up in Belgium's debt level had no impact on Luxembourg or on price stability in either country. Moreover, EMU criteria on debt and budget deficits assumed a sustainable economic growth of three per cent, which seemed reasonable in 1991 but has become unrealistic in 1996.[14] EMU need not be transformed into a Greek tragedy. Too much Europe can kill it, and too much Europe too soon may kill it quite soon, which is the risk raised by a timetable that was also set too arbitrarily and too hastily.

The same scepticism applies to enlargement to the East: it will not be swift and comprehensive, but slow and gradual. Unlike the transatlantic debate over NATO's enlargement, the intra-European debate over EU enlargement is only about feasibility. For nearly all non-member countries in Europe, EU membership is a high-priority economic objective which they have explicitly endorsed; for nearly all member states, EU enlargement is a political imperative which they have broadly recognized. But for enlargement to proceed, there must be a common ability and a shared willingness to accept the cost it will entail. For incoming countries, that cost has to do with the capacity to endure the EU discipline imposed by a growing body of EU laws and agreements (*acquis communautaire*) that becomes ever more difficult to comprehend, let alone implement. Indeed, even the EU's current members are finding that discipline politically unbearable. Proceeding with enlargement too quickly could be worse than moving slowly, since it might endanger the stability which EU membership is designed to promote without permitting the prosperity it is expected to provide.

But enlargement will also come slowly, because EU countries themselves are not prepared to accept the institutional reforms needed to absorb many new members, to pay the enormous budgetary costs of enlargement, or to withstand the domestic cost of reforming (or even abandoning) programmes to which many EU states are most attached, including the EU's common agricultural policy (CAP) and the EU's structural programmes of development aid worth hundreds of millions of dollars for those countries that receive it. Thus, extending the benefits of the CAP to the estimated seventy million hectares of farm land spread in the six countries of central and southeastern Europe would be catastrophically expensive: CAP already consumes about half of the total EU budget. But reforming CAP to contain these costs would be politically disastrous in many current EU states; the Commission is ruling it out. To make matters worse, the new maths of EU budgeting at twenty or more member states will also be worsened by the many categories of EU regional (structural) aid for which most or all projected new members would qualify: the combined GNP of all ten prospective new members in the East barely amounts to that of Holland.[15]

Finally, the budgetary cost of enlargement is muddled further by the needs of other countries – especially in North Africa – that do not qualify for membership, but are of concern to several EU states, including the Mediterranean troika of France, Spain, and Italy (plus, admittedly, Greece and Portugal). In Barcelona in November 1995, these countries and their partners north and south of the Mediterranean reaffirmed the EU pledge made at a previous summit at Essen to provide nearly the same amount of aid to the South as to the East. A pledge difficult to enforce for one group of developing or underdeveloping states will be more than twice as difficult to enforce for two such groups. In short, even under the best possible circumstances, many years of negotiations and preparation will be needed before some of the states in Central Europe join the EU a few years into the twenty-first century. Even then, around the years 2003–2005, their membership may lack the full range of EU subsidies (especially in agriculture) and obligations (especially in monetary matters) for many more years.

In a sense, the worsening short-term prospects for EMU and enlargement may improve the prospects for a common foreign and security policy (CFSP). This is because the main EU states, and those among their leaders who have invested so much political prestige in Maastricht, especially Chancellor Kohl, could view CFSP as the most readily available conduit for the EU's relaunching should the IGC flounder, and the most dramatic alternative to EMU should monetary union stall. But here, too, the debate would be helped by a more realistic assessment of what is feasible. Henry Kissinger's celebrated plea for the telephone number of a mythical 'Mr Europe' did not stipulate that such a single contact be more than merely an answering service – now voice-mail – placing the caller on hold while delivering the messages. Similarly, the intention to organize a European policy-planning bureau makes for good theatre, but little more. In fact, in the short term, decisions of this type would worsen the institutional confusion between the new CFSP czar and the head of the Commission, or between think tanks, official or not.

'Europe' needs more than the recycling of a former head of state or government, and more than a new setting for more academic debates, to be able to claim a 'common' foreign and security policy. It needs, for example, more of a commitment to make WEU operational, a better understanding of the WEU's place within NATO and/or the EU, and a more specific comprehension of how political decisions will be made within the WEU and between WEU and NATO. Most of all, the development of a CFSP demands more unity between the leading EU countries in defining priorities, in assessing interests, and in committing capabilities and resources. When it comes to matters of war and peace, consultation does not create a consensus but presupposes it: whether at two (France and Germany) or at three (with Great Britain), a consensus on foreign and security policy among leading EU states does not exist yet, and it is not likely to emerge soon.

HALF PAST NATO

If this is not Europe's time, it follows that five years after the Cold War this remains America's time – a fact Europeans tried to forget and Americans hoped to ignore, though no more. Why the latter chose to do so reflects the mood of a nation that shows little taste for the cost of power – not only the cost of acquiring it but also, and above all, the cost of using it. Unlike the previous two wars, however, the Cold War has not given rise to an urge for withdrawal, for a return to the isolationist spirit that animated the nation during much of its history. Rather, post-Cold War America seems receptive to a continued and selective role in the world so long as it is shown why, with whom, and how that role will be played in the future.

In the end, it is such a willingness to discuss the reality of US interests as the catalyst for US commitments that has been missing since the end of the Cold War. Instead, the foreign policy debates of the past few years have been waged over single ad hoc issues wrapped in grand principles: whether to save lives in Somalia or to build democracy in Haiti, America's foreign policy has become geared to public service more than to the national interest.[16] Especially after President Clinton's election in 1992, the debate that erupted in the United States over the nation's policies in Bosnia was arguably the most passionate foreign policy debate of the past twenty years, including a debate over the Gulf War which ended as soon as the war actually began, and a sporadic debate over the war in Central America, which seemed more sensitive to political circumstances in Congress than to military conditions south of the border.[17] Abstract exaggerations about the global meaning of the war in the Balkans could not serve as the conceptual basis for such a debate, because these exaggerations lacked credibility as well as relevance. As was the case in other instances when President Clinton considered military or diplomatic action, there was little explicit discussion of the US interests at stake, the risks faced by these interests, and the capabilities required to face those risks. In Bosnia, it was a commitment made earlier by the President (to help extricate allied forces) that still defined the US interest in the summer of 1995, rather than the other way around. When the time for enforcement came, justification took mainly the form of an institutional interest, i.e. NATO, that failed to explain the national interests served by such an institution.

In short, the traditional postwar debate over future US foreign and defence policy has not even started yet. Instead of doomsday projections suggesting a return to prewar or interwar years as inducements for continued involvement, and even instead of repeated charges of neo-isolationism aimed at one's detractors, it would have been more effective for both political parties to debate

– whether US interests in Europe have become so significant as to make divorce no longer possible, as it was once or twice upon a time; and
– how a united Europe continues to serve the United States well, and which US policies can continue to serve it equally well.

What the crisis in the Balkans thus teaches, if anything, is the depth of what the Cold War has accomplished.[18] As shown at Dayton – after years of pretending otherwise – the United States can no longer hide behind a dividing line between Europe's problems and America's. While history moved on from one war to the next, geography, too, moved across Europe's national boundaries and across the Atlantic – creating a common Euro-Atlantic space between the nation-states of Europe and America within which the European civil space – previously developed as an exclusive European Economic Community – could prosper in peace. In short, over time the 'over there' of yesteryear has progressively come over here. To be sure, this Euro-Atlantic space can still be separated. If nothing else, Bosnia also confirmed the asymmetrical nature of security interests on the two sides of the Atlantic: there can still be war over there and peace over here. But such separation is more and more difficult to achieve, because it entails a cost that reflects the growth of US interests in – and therefore commitment to – Europe on the eve of the twenty-first century.

To an extent, that interest is still determined first by geopolitical circumstances – by the residues of the security threats raised by two successive hegemonial bids defeated by the United States and its allies on three previous occasions. No new case for America's involvement is needed here. These legacies point to a Germany that cannot be neutered without the EU, a Russia that cannot be balanced without NATO, and, consequently, both an EU and a NATO that cannot be sustained without US power.

But the US interest in attending to the common transatlantic space it occupies with the states of Europe and their Union has to do also with the political economy of their relations. With about $1.5 trillion a year in shared economic activities with and in Europe, including the output of US subsidiaries, the United States cannot afford to live without Europe, and vice versa. Nor can either hope to approximate that sort of relationship anywhere else for many years to come, if ever. Thus, Asia – the new focus of US interest, but also a growing interest of the EU – is an appealing target on economic grounds. But it remains a hope rather than a reality – a speculative investment for Americans and Europeans alike, unlike the actual earnings on an investment Americans made in Europe nearly half-a-century ago.

Admittedly, at the time Europe was a matter of speculation too. America might easily have gone home in 1945, as it did in 1919. But the point is that it can no longer do so in 1996. For now, when the reality of the American presence in Europe far exceeds the accounting of troop deployment, what would be the meaning of coming home? The Cold War has done what neither world war could do. America is a major power in Europe, in effect a non-European state within the

European Union, where its economic presence, political influence, and military weight are larger and more significant than those of most EU member states.

So presented, such a case may not always be applauded in Europe. However much America might be wanted there as an invited hegemon, it remains feared as an intrusive guest. But this is a case that must be heard in America before it is heard in Europe too. It is a case based on interests which, in turn, define the nature and scope of America's commitment to Europe. More specifically, because NATO is the most visible and easily recognizable institutional tie between America and Europe, it remains the primary tool available to the United States to:

– maintain a US presence that can deter an outburst of Russian geopolitical revisionism, unlikely though possible;
– guarantee the security of the former Warsaw Pact countries, not because they are explicitly threatened but because there are risks of instabilities, exported or manipulated by their neighbours;
– consolidate Germany's confidence (as well as that of other states in Europe) in a Western structure that is more reliable, and certainly less controversial, than any alternative;
– deter and possibly defend against small conflicts in and even out of Europe, where there is a compatibility of Western interests and where there can be a convergence of Western views; and
– prepare for, and respond to, the common concerns outlined in the Transatlantic Agenda of December 1995, including terrorism, the environment, and the proliferation of weapons of mass destruction.

This, however, is not only America's case for NATO and continued ties with Europe. It is also Europe's case for continued ties with the United States through NATO. For European states that thought – or hoped – otherwise during the Cold War, the past five years have taught differently. Today, there is still much debate about the future of NATO – the enlargement it seeks, the reforms it needs, the capabilities it demands, and the purpose it lacks. But, pointedly enough, the reality of NATO's future is no longer debated.

REVITALIZING WESTERN SECURITY

These considerations at last raise the fundamental question of the post-Cold War organization of Europe and its security. The structure that was built after World War II was based on the unstated assumptions that neither the disintegration of the Soviet empire nor the unification of Germany was likely to happen in the foreseeable future, if ever. Without a strong and hostile Soviet Union, fears of Germany would have lingered longer than they did. Probably these fears would have stood in the way of the unification of Europe along the lines that were started in Rome in 1957 after a revitalized but small Federal Republic was brought into an Atlantic framework guaranteed by American forces pointedly deployed on German territory.

Thus, the post-World War II security structure relied on two institutional blueprints that were not only compatible, but also complementary. One type of institution – European by name but often American by design – attended to the reconstruction of Western Europe and, hence, to reconciliation among those states in a community that helped gain economic affluence and, in turn, political stability. Eventually, that community grew into a collective security organization. The other type of institution, Atlantic by name but European by design, attended more explicitly to the security of its members: first with a loose pact signed in Washington in April 1949, then through an integrated military organization developed mainly after the outbreak of the war in Korea, and enlarged twice (in 1952 with Greece and Turkey, and 1955 with the Federal Republic of Germany). This was a collective defence institution – that is, one aimed at threats raised by states outside the group.[19] In both cases, the catalyst was the United States, however different the threat perceptions that prevailed at the time in America and Europe, or among the states of Europe.

After the Cold War, both Russia and Germany remain at the centre of the ongoing quest for a new security structure. But unlike previous postwar settings – when the quest for security had to be launched in an institutional vacuum and without much of a road map – the new security structure can rely on the institutions inherited from the past. Thus, after the terrible wars waged in and over Europe in the twentieth century and before, the United States and the countries of Western Europe face a dual challenge: a challenge of change and enlargement, designed to widen their institutions to former adversaries in the East, but also a challenge of continuity and consolidation, designed to deepen these institutions in the West.

These two challenges will be met most effectively if the dual processes they demand are kept in unison and if unrealistic timetables are avoided – whether for reconciliation in Bosnia and monetary union in Western Europe, stability in Russia and reform in Eastern Europe, or

NATO and EU reform and enlargement. The dangers of having either process hijacked by a single issue or concept are shown by EMU, whose criteria have been made the centre of public concerns about Europe's future, and by NATO enlargement, which has become the centre of allied debates about the future of the Western Alliance. Multilateral institutions change, but ever so reluctantly, as they remain the captives of member states who respond to the vagaries of their own national agendas. The institutions expand, but ever so slowly, as they follow the meanderings of history, itself known as a slow mover. In short, the quest for Western security and the reorganization of Europe, however defined, is a process – not an end game – that will take time, time to reconcile differences among NATO and EU members, time to accommodate objections from non-members, and time to prepare each institution for the consequences that initiatives adopted by one will have on the other.

The Cold War has permitted the establishment of a common Euro-Atlantic space. After the Cold War, this space ought to be extended as far east and south as these institutions can bear, that is, short of Russia and on the European side of the Mediterranean, but including Turkey. That much should be beyond discussion. It is absurd to claim that the end of the Cold War leaves America without any interest in Europe, and either NATO or the EU without any mission and purpose. Admittedly, a vision of how to proceed next appears blurred. Yet, the decisions ahead suggest a pattern of converging parallelism, whereby what is planned separately by the EU among fifteen members and NATO among sixteen, can be implemented as one. Only together can these institutions satisfy all the needs of their current members and future partners.

In late 1995, the institutional distance between NATO and the EU was reduced significantly by France's reconciliation with the organization it left in 1966. Most usefully because of the deadlines faced by the Implementation Force (IFOR) in Bosnia, France's return to NATO's military command structure made it possible to implement the concept of a Combined Joint Task Force (CJTF) in a NATO context that includes WEU operations, rather than in a more restrictive WEU context that is independent of NATO operations. A NATO-led CJTF will make sure that allies are not separated – since the vitally important Article 5 guarantee of the Washington Treaty would keep them together – even if they use their forces separately.[20] Reliance on CJTF will also make room for occasional participation of non-NATO countries, including Russia, with arrangements similar to those negotiated for the deployment of an intervention force in Bosnia.

Such an approach would be immediately relevant to many issues that require the use of military force – which Americans have but are not willing to use, and which Europeans are willing to use but do not have. In Bosnia, for example, additional European forces placed in a NATO-led CJTF could 'represent' the Western commitment to security in the area, with fewer US ground forces deployed there or redeployed as insurance in a nearby country (including Italy or Hungary). Later, in the future, NATO-led CJTFs could also emerge as the force of choice for missions such as the extraction of Western nationals from an unstable area – Algeria, for example – should such action ever become necessary.[21] Issues of command would remain. But a European deputy Supreme Allied Commander Europe (SACEUR) – most probably French or British – would provide European command for a force without Americans but with large numbers of French and British troops (relative to the contributions of other NATO states such as Germany, for the time being) without compromising control of the US nuclear capabilities, which would remain under SACEUR command.[22] With uses of European forces assigned to NATO thus possible without US forces, and in or out of the original NATO area – just as US forces designated for NATO can be used for non-NATO purposes – WEU and NATO would be made separable without fear of separating the allies either in the planning or the enforcement stage.

Similarly, a NATO–EU co-operative action group could address existing regional conflicts that involve EU and NATO member states, from Northern Ireland to the Aegean Seas. Such a contact group would bear some resemblance to the *directoire à trois* – America, Britain, and France – proposed by the French government as early as September 1958. The idea was wrong at the time because of the state of Europe and the nature of the US–Soviet balance. But conditions have changed on both accounts: the idea can be adjusted to make room for the reality *communautaire* in Europe and the devolution of American power within NATO. Now, US leadership enforced unilaterally satisfies neither America's nor Europe's interests: the issue is not over the availability of US power, which remains abundant, but over the will to use it, which has become ever more uncertain.

A NATO–EU co-operative group would also be more effective than the EU troika, which does not make room for the United States and whose effectiveness is often a matter of schedule (the EU troika is limited to the three presidents of the European Council – previous, current, and future). As EU membership continues to expand, the days of such a troika are likely to be numbered, anyway, because the larger EU states will no longer be willing to await their turn for a brief six-month presidency of the Council. A NATO–EU co-operative group co-chaired for one- to two-year assignments by the US Secretary of State, the EU Commissioner for External Affairs, and the Foreign Minister of one of the three largest EU countries would regroup the power and the influence of the leading states of both Western institutions, either directly or after consultation. Such a group could be organized all the more quickly as it would remain informal and gain its legitimacy from existing consultative mechanisms developed within NATO and the EU during the years of crisis in Bosnia. Indeed, such a co-operative group would permit a process of transatlantic policy co-operation that might resemble the earlier process of European Political Co-operation (EPC) started nearly three decades ago. Such co-operation might produce the first draft of allied policies for impending crises, including an early allocation of responsibilities in a given crisis. Depending on the issue at hand, such a contact group could rely on other EU and NATO members, thus showing an adaptability compatible with the variety of the issues at hand, without being encumbered by the idea that all members of every institution must participate fully in all decisions in all instances.

The tension between Greece and Turkey could be defused by such a joint NATO–EU approach to conflict resolution. In early 1996, the war that nearly erupted between these two NATO countries served as a reminder of the explosiveness of a conflict that neither Europe nor the United States can afford. Turkey and Greece are too important to leave the region at the mercy of *agents provocateurs* who can rely on their countries' passions to escalate a minor crisis into a major war from which there would be no recovery for years to come. But the conflict in the Aegean is also much too deep for either country to take the proverbial first step toward peace convincing enough for its neighbour to reciprocate. While an external catalyst is therefore needed, no state, not even the United States nor any institution, whether NATO or the EU, can play that role alone.

To seek normalization between Greece and Turkey, a NATO–EU co-operative group would require two preliminary EU decisions. Admittedly, neither would be easy: first, a quick negotiation for Cyprus's membership in the EU shortly after completion of the IGC; and second, an unequivocal EU commitment to negotiate Turkey's membership on the basis of criteria over which Greece would voluntarily abandon its right of veto. Even as these two preliminary decisions are considered, the NATO–EU group could begin consultation aimed at facilitating an early treaty of non-aggression between Greece and Turkey. Normalizing relations between these two countries is an issue important enough to place on the broad Transatlantic Agenda. In turn, this would mean that the NATO–EU co-operative group would report to the transatlantic troika every six months, beginning at the earliest acceptable time.

In an ideal world, it would have been preferable to wait for EU enlargement to proceed with NATO enlargement. But what was done in September 1995 – about the whether and why of NATO enlargement – cannot be undone. The decision for enlargement was made with the approval of all sixteen members: its postponement, or even a prolonged delay prior to ratification after the decision has been made, would be more damaging than its prompt enforcement. The issue compares with the debate waged in the Alliance over the deployment of intermediate nuclear forces (INF) after the NATO decision of December 1979. During the following four years, implementation of that decision proved to be the cause for much tension within the Alliance. But it is not difficult to imagine how different the course of subsequent events would have been if the outcome of the INF debate had itself been different.

Waiting for EU enlargement to occur first is an alibi for delaying action on NATO enlargement. Although the EU committed itself to starting negotiations with new members six months after completion of the 1996 IGC (but before ratification), it is apparent that even after resolving the cases of Malta and (with more difficulty) the Republic of Cyprus, these negotiations will prove tedious. Notwithstanding occasional suggestions that Poland might enter the EU as early as the year 2000, it is extremely doubtful that enlargement to the East will begin so soon: as argued, even under the best possible political and economic conditions, there is just not enough time for such a deadline. Yet an unequivocal EU commitment to accept new members within a reliable time-frame would represent a de facto expansion sufficient to enforce the pre-enlargement and pre-accession reforms needed by the EU and its prospective members. In other words, how long the transition period will last is less significant than how long it will take before the formal beginning of transition period toward full membership.

While the EU moves on with de facto enlargement, de jure NATO enlargement will proceed on a faster track – meaning that the Alliance should complete a first wave before the end of the century. The year

1999 will mark the fiftieth anniversary of the Washington Treaty: this is an appropriate target date for completion of an initial enlargement, likely to include Poland and more than one of its neighbours in Central Europe (at least Hungary and the Czech Republic). Irrespective of the pace of EU enlargement, the enlargement of NATO from sixteen to nineteen members should be co-ordinated with any WEU enlargement: for WEU to do otherwise would cause a backdoor escalation of US commitments without US approval. Indeed, ultimately, both NATO and WEU should have overlapping European membership.

Even as NATO enlargement proceeds in spite of Russia's predictable objections, some attention to legitimate Russian concerns will continue to be needed and recognition of these concerns will have to be demonstrated. These reassurances should be extended after the new members have been named and a timetable set. Doing otherwise could be misunderstood as a Russian right of interference over NATO decisions. Beyond the steps already agreed upon at the Russian–American Summit at Helsinki in March 1997, when the time comes, reassurances to Russia could include a declaration by the governments of the projected new NATO members – including Poland – that they seek no deployment of Alliance forces on their territory because they fear no immediate threat to their security. These reassurances might also include an informal understanding that the next wave of enlargement will take longer than the first, and that a NATO at nineteen members will be satisfied with strengthening the Partnership for Peace formula for many years to come.

To fit the United States and Russia more directly into the two processes of NATO and EU enlargement to the East, a bi-multilateral approach would make room for one-to-many formal relationships: across the Atlantic between the EU and the United States, but also across the continent between Russia and both the EU and NATO. Preferably, these bi-multilateral agreements would be negotiated quickly enough to be completed and signed before, or at the same time as, either NATO or EU enlargement gets under way.

A treaty between the EU and the United States could be signed at the earliest possible time, asserting a special partnership usually sought on a state-to-state basis, and as a renewed confirmation of the US commitment to the organization of an ever stronger European Union. This commitment, however, does not suggest that any sort of united Europe fits US interests and qualifies for US endorsement equally well. This was not the case during the Cold War, and it need not become the case after. But here, too, progress has been made over the past five years. Thus, the Transatlantic Agenda signed in Madrid in December 1995 represents a solid base for the development of a multi-dimensional relationship between the United States and a European Union that is:

– open, flexible, and competitive in economic structure and practice;
– democratic and compatible with the social values and policies that prevail in the United States;
– resistant to protectionist pressures exerted by EU institutions or advocated by some of its members for selected growth sectors;
– open to economic and political ties with its neighbours in the East, beginning with Central Europe; and
– able to assume a larger share of the defence burden with a Western European Union responsive to the need for a special relationship with the United States within NATO.

Finally, a treaty between the United States and the EU would also anticipate the negotiation of a free trade area within ten years – say, by the year 2007, symbolically picked as the fiftieth anniversary of the signing of the Rome Treaties that started the fusion of economic space in Europe.[23] Similarly, a treaty between NATO and Russia, signed at the earliest possible time, would confirm NATO's commitment to a co-operative partnership with Russia, and might associate Russia to NATO guarantees for such non-NATO members as the Ukraine. Going beyond current NATO partnership arrangements, such a treaty could adapt the early structure of the Franco-German Treaty of Friendship of January 1963 – a treaty that framed the historic recon-ciliation between these two countries. A treaty between Russia and the EU would also need to go beyond the banalities of associate status, while remaining short of the specifics of actual membership. Together, these two treaties with Russia would provide additional assurances that the enlargement of NATO and the EU to the East is not designed to reorganize Europe either against or without Russia.

The post-Cold War quest for Western security suggested here will take time: past the end of the century and when the first decade of the next century nears its end. This multi-year process of continuity and change began neither with the fall of the Berlin Wall in 1989 nor with the end of the Soviet Union in 1991, but in 1995 when common Western action was finally taken in Bosnia. The quest, too, will end neither with NATO enlargement in or around 1999, nor with EU enlargement in or around 2003, but in subsequent years as these two organizations form the pivots of an increasingly common Euro-Atlantic space. Given the length of this process, the need to deal with change with renewed patience and determination should come, therefore, as no surprise. As shown after each of the last wars, history recognizes its defining moments slowly, and it allows them to unfold only erratically. But even as the need for time is thus acknowledged, the clock continues to tick – faster than has ever been the case. As NATO passes its fiftieth birthday and prepares to turn sixty, the time is half before Europe, half past NATO, and a quarter before Russia – because after the Cold War, Europe, NATO, and Russia need to complete what was started fifty, forty, and five years ago.

NOTES

1.   Jacques Poos was the Foreign Minister of Luxembourg when he made that claim (*Financial Times*, 1 July 1991). The boast was not his alone. The day before, Chancellor Helmut Kohl used the past tense to claim that 'Europe has shown that it can use its combined weight to find solutions for conflicts like the one in Yugoslavia.' *Washington Post*, 30 June 1991.

2.   John Keegan, 'After Wars', *Swiss Review of World Affairs* (July 1995), 8. A shorter version of this paper is 'America and Europe Beyond Bosnia', *The Washington Quarterly*, 19 (Summer 1996).

3.   John L. Harper, *American Visions of Europe: Franklin D. Roosevelt, George P. Kennan, and Dean G. Acheson* (Cambridge: Cambridge University Press, 1995).

4.   'Terrible events', complained Thatcher in mid–1992, 'are happening in Bosnia; worse ones are threatening....The matter is urgent' cited in 'Stop the Excuses: Help Bosnia', *New York Times*, 6 August 1992. In 1996, German warnings about a resurgence of nationalism proved especially contentious. 'The question of war and peace in the twenty-first century', Kohl reflected in Munich on 2 February 1996, 'really hinges on the progress of European integration'.

5.   Simon Serfaty, 'History, Hysteria and Hyperboles', in Jeffrey Simon (ed.), *NATO: The Challenge of Change* (Washington DC: National Defense University Press, 1993); and 'Fragile Peace', in Charles L. Berry (ed.), *The Search for Peace in Europe* (Washington, DC: National Defense University Press, 1993).

6.   Speech held at a meeting of experts of the Hanns Seidel Foundation, pointedly entitled '40 Years of the Bundeswehr: Vigilance Remains the Price of Freedom', *Foreign Broadcast Information Service-Western Europe*, 16 November 1995, p. 8.

7.   Alan Milward, *The European Rescue of the Nation-State* (Berkeley: University of California Press, 1992). Also, Simon Serfaty, *Decisions for Europe*, GPIS Working Papers, Old Dominion University (October

1995) and 'European Perspective', in Michael Brenner (ed.), *Multilateralism and Western Strategy* (New York: St Martin's Press, 1994).

8. See George Ross, 'A Community Adrift: The Crisis of Confidence in Western Europe', *Harvard International Review*, 16 (Summer 1994) 14; Franco Ferrarotti, 'The Italian Enigma', *Géopolitique*, 38 (Summer 1992) 20ff; Simon Serfaty, 'All in the Family', *Current History*, 93 (November 1994) 353–57.

9. Portugal's national elections in 1991 and 1995 relied on a political rhetoric that proved to be interchangeable. David White, 'Where the roads lead to Europe', *Financial Times*, 30 September and 'Portugal hopes for socialist stability', *Financial Times*, 3 October 1995.

10. Eugene Weber, 'Nationalism and the Politics of Resentment', *American Scholar*, 63 (Summer 1994) 421–28.

11. Ezra Suleiman, 'Change and Stability in French Elites', in Gregory Flynn (ed.), *Remaking the Hexagon* (Boulder, Colorado: Westview Press, 1995) 165, and Richard Kuysel, ibid., 'The France We Have Lost', pp. 37–8.

12. Especially coming from this author. See, for example, 'An Ascendant Europe', *Harvard International Review*, (1983) and *Taking Europe Seriously* (New York: St Martin's Press, 1992); also, 'Refashioning Space and Security in Europe', in Daniel N. Nelson (ed.), *After Authoritarianism* (Westport, Connecticut: Greenwood Press, 1995).

13. The political risks are faced not only before the go- ahead decision but also after, when there will have to be a quick demonstration of the advantages of monetary union. Yet, there is little specific knowledge as to the extent to which unemployment in France is structural and to what extent it results from the *franc fort*. The risks, however, are not only political but also economic: for instance, a bad choice for the final conversion rate – from one national currency to the other within EMU, and from the single currency to the dollar and to other European currencies – could spell disaster for large layers of the EMU's economy. Samuel Brittan, 'Fear of something worse', *Financial Times*, 18 January 1996.

14. Paul de Grauwe, 'Why the link should be cut', *Financial Times*, 2 November 1995. Philippe Plassard, 'Les enfants infernaux de Maastricht', *Le Nouvel Economiste*, 8 December 1995.

15. Hendrick Jan Brouwer, et al., *Do We Need a New EU Budget Deal?* (Philip Morris Institute, June 1995); Desmond Dinan, 'The Commission, Enlargement, and the IGC', and Fraser Cameron, 'The 1996 IGC – A Challenge to Europe', *The ECSA Newsletter* (Spring-Summer 1995).

16. Michael Mandelbaum, 'Foreign Policy as Social Work', *Foreign Affairs*, 75 (January-February 1996), 16.

17. Robert W. Tucker and David C. Hendrickson, 'America and Bosnia', *The National Interest* (Fall 1993) 14–27.

18. Simon Serfaty, 'Half Before Europe, Half Past NATO', *The Washington Quarterly*, 18 (March-April 1995) 49–58.

19. Stephen Cambone, 'Organizing for Security in Europe: What Missions, What Forces? Who Leads, Who Pays?', GPIS Working Papers, Old Dominion University (January 1996).

20. Calls for making the Article 5 of the Washington Treaty 'looser and less automatic' are hardly a solid foundation for the 'Atlantic Union' that accompanies some of these calls. Charles A. Kupchan, 'Reviving the West', *Foreign Affairs*, 75 (May-June 1996), 100.

21. In the spring of 1995, bilateral talks between the United States and France reportedly led to contingency plans for flying in troops (mostly French and none American) to secure oil and gas installations and, most importantly, bring out expatriate staff (including about 80,000 French nationals and 500 US nationals). Such co-operation had been seen before in a few countries in Africa (although on a smaller scale than that contemplated for Algeria). Michael Sheridan, 'US and France prepare for Algerian evacuation', *The Independent*, 22 March 1995, p. 12.

22. Stanley R. Sloan, *NATO's Future: Beyond Collective Defense*, (Washington, DC: Congressional Research Service, 1995), pp. 30–32.

23. More on TAFTA in my contribution to 'Policy Forum: Transatlantic Free Trade', *Washington Quarterly*, 19 (Spring 1996) 105–133.

2 NATO and the Evolution of a European Security Identity

Gale A. Mattox

Fundamental structures and concepts of European security have undergone dramatic transformation since the decade began. Numerous states have turned democratic and established free- market economies, while military threats have decreased in intensity and changed in character, or vanished altogether.[1] These developments have naturally challenged Europe's security system to reflect the realities of a new era. Buffeted about in seas of change, the system has emerged with some damage, some need of repair, and even the prospect of some stormy times yet to come. But it has come out intact, with a more experienced crew and clearer vision of the way ahead; as a result, it should be better able to deal with the potential – even inevitable – challenges of a very different international environment.

Drawing on this naval analogy just a little, despite rough waters and obvious battle scars, the flagship NATO has shown particularly admirable resilience. But the European security system today is necessarily broader than just NATO; while anchored by the Alliance, it can truly succeed only as a fleet that includes supporting and auxiliary ships. Given the discussion of NATO elsewhere in this volume, the focus here will be on these other critical ships of the fleet, some in NATO's tow, such as the North Atlantic Co-operation Council (NACC), Partnership for Peace (PfP), and Combined Joint Task Forces (CJTF), others organizationally separate from the Alliance, but with partially overlapping crews such as the Organization for Security and Co-operation in Europe (OSCE) and Western European Union/European Union (WEU/EU).

BACKGROUND

Looking back over the years since the fall of the Berlin Wall in 1989, one is struck by how many very fundamental decisions have actually been taken with regard to an appropriate European security system for the post-Cold War era. Amid discussions over redesign of the existing system and proposed innovations, there has been disagreement at times on what direction to take, or on which organizations should continue, but also important consensus in a number of areas. As we look to the new century and attempt to finalize the blueprints for European security, that consensus will be important to an overall design for the future.

First and foremost, the US has made a clear commitment to remain in Europe for the foreseeable future – albeit not necessarily at the same level as during the Cold War. European security, defined as an alliance of vital interests between North America and Western Europe, has been reaffirmed. Furthermore, there is essentially a consensus that the system must be more broadly defined than in the past to include Eastern Europe, in principle, and potentially other former Eastern bloc states as well. As of 1996, consensus had not yet emerged on the 'who' and 'when' of enlargement, particularly with respect to the extension of security guarantees.[2] But any question about the US perception of its interests in Europe and NATO, or about American resolve to remain a presence, was answered with the 1995 US- negotiated Dayton Agreements, and particularly with the commitment of forces to Bosnia in 1995–96. The US is and remains committed to Europe. That the manifestation of that commitment is fewer troops – reduced on the continent from over 300,000 in 1989 to approximately 100,000 today – or other changes shaped by post-Cold War realities does not change the bottom-line commitment, illustrated by America's role in the Balkans.

Second, after ponderous academic debates and serious considera-tion of alternative structures by such personalities as German Foreign Minister Hans-Dietrich Genscher and others, NATO has clearly estab-lished itself as the anchor and framework for European security – pre-eminently as a military alliance, but also with political and even economic foundations.[3] While perhaps self-evident today, this was far from a foregone conclusion immediately after 1989, and NATO is only now emerging from an identity crisis – if, in fact, institutions can be said to have identity crises.[4] While the decision on Bosnia in 1995 challenged its position, and elements of its organization remain in need of redesign, NATO has clearly reasserted itself as the flagship of European security. Leaving aside the membership question, confer-ences debating the death of NATO – its last gasps, its last will and testament – have been replaced by those considering 'the quest for post-Cold War security' – as the title of this volume attests – by Alliance members, as well as by states of the former East bloc.

A third point, a corollary of the first two, is that Europe's geopolitical parameters have changed in a number of ways. NATO's Partnership for Peace (PfP) expanded the Alliance's geographical reach, and enlargement of membership will do so even further. The artificial border defined by the advance of Soviet troops in 1945 has been replaced by a concept of a truly continental Europe. This is true not only for NATO, as manifested in NACC, PfP and CJTFs, but also for the North Atlantic Assembly, the Council of Europe, and other organizations with new members or plans to include them. And the business community is even further out ahead, with multinational conglomerates now making inroads into all the markets of the broader Europe–often having to wait for the political leaders to catch up with enabling legislation.

Fourth and finally, NATO cannot stand alone as the sole guarantor of European security. European security is and must be much more broadly-based. That is, while in the days before the dramatic changes in Europe, there was lip service to the need for broader definitions of security, the dictates of the formidable Soviet threat meant that security almost by necessity was equated with the structure, positioning and fire-power of the stationed armed forces in Europe. Security was – and had to be – defined in narrowly-gauged military terms. While such forces continue to underpin security, there is no question that today it must be measured as well by political and economic standards. Security is no longer simply the absence of active East-West conflict; it is stability across the continent which permits a free flow of goods, services, people, and ideas. States of the former Western bloc expect a lack of tension and conflict that will sustain a high standard of living, while the former Eastern bloc nations expect eventual attainment of such conditions, also possible only under stable conditions. The flagship NATO must be accompanied and reinforced by other vessels – in particular, by the OSCE and the economic-political bodies of the European Union, as well as the WEU – broadening the scope of security beyond just armed force.

These organizations, in concert with others, are part of the necessarily broader concept of security for Europe. They do not and should not be seen as replacements for NATO, as some proposed in the early 1990s discussions, but are vital facets of the larger picture. Although conceived during the Cold War, to different degrees these institutions have all also suffered identity crises, or are still in the throes of one that has not yet been resolved, and all are learning to adapt and change to the post-Cold War realities.

North Americans and Europeans have travelled quite a distance since the fall of the Wall. But there is also quite a distance to go. While the elements of the European security framework are there, a lot of work remains to be done before stability on the continent is assured; one need only witness the Bosnian bloodshed of the recent past. Just as military enforcement of peace in the Balkans at best offered to mark the beginning of the end of the conflict, the viability of political and economic structures is vital to long-term stability. Unfortunately, the appeal of security on the cheap for the US and European publics has meant that insufficient attention has been given to the importance (particularly) of organizations such as OSCE. And yet it is exactly the functions performed by these organizations which could assure the longer-term stability of the continent. As in a fleet, the flagship needs the support of other assets. This is why a comprehensive concept for security must address not just military, or political, or economic concerns, but all facets of security critical to long-term peace on the continent.

Given the changes in Europe's strategic, political and economic environment, as well as in the transatlantic relationship, the only sensible approach today is within a broad framework of interlocking and complementary organizations. In the heady days following the collapse of the Berlin Wall, many in the West imagined that the task of European security had become easier when, in fact, it was simply becoming more complex. With this complexity comes a need for structures appropriate to the tasks. While the Soviet military threat to NATO members has receded, there has been an increase in the external threats of ethnic conflict, terrorism, extra-territorial conflicts with the potential for spill-over and intra-state conflicts grounded in nationalistic sentiments and resource scarcity, even environmental challenges. NATO must and has begun to address these threats, but its structure is not always appropriate and certainly the instruments at its command are often not adequate to the tasks.

Beginning with its London summit agreement for a strategic review, and continuing with France's decision to rejoin the Military and the Defence Planning Committees, the Alliance has undertaken organizational changes, while addressing conceptual changes in strategy, readiness and many other aspects of operations.[5] A logical and actually cost-effective approach to addressing these challenges is an interlocking system of responsibilities, in which NATO provides the foundation of military security structured to respond to conflict situations; the European Union both addresses economic stability on the continent and, through the WEU, provides any necessary forces for meeting extra-territorial threats to Europe (including those the US does not perceive as endangering its interests); and the OSCE expands its competencies in conflict prevention, issues involving arms control, and other areas such as cross-border and/or intra- state human and minority rights.

THE NATO SECURITY FRAMEWORK

Bosnia focused NATO to an extent not seen since the end of the Cold War. Confronted with the bloodiest European conflict since World War II, and the only real disruption to the continental peace since its establishment, NATO can be said to have risen admirably to the Bosnia challenge once it committed itself in late 1995. It became engaged militarily in a way that has only really occurred during manœuvres in the past; its military capabilities and ability to use them in concert with the allies are being tested as never before. Far different than in the Persian Gulf, in which many of the allies participated but which was not an alliance undertaking, the Bosnian situation proved to be a real test of the Alliance. The fact that NATO troops went there to enforce the peace calls on the Alliance to be able to do all the military tasks for which it long practised *and*, at the same time, to do much more given the uneasy situation on the ground.

In addition, many PfP partners and potential future members are engaged alongside NATO members. The Russian role, however modest, was critical from both a practical standpoint – could Russian troops co-operate and contribute, etc. – and from the longer-term potential for true peace in the region between Serbs, Croats and Muslims. Russian participation offered encouragement for Serb adherence to the accord's terms. Likewise, other PfP involvement – Hungarian, Ukrainian, and Czech, for example – has proven valuable for longer-term co-operation. And a survey of Europe's geography indicates many other arenas in which such co-operation with non-members, particularly the PfP partners, might be necessary and desirable in the future. A secure Europe remains essential for the United States, and if Bosnia has taught no other lesson, it is that America must remain engaged on the continent to assure its security. This is most logically done through NATO. However, that does not mean that the US should always be directly involved in the resolution of every conflict that arises.

In fact, it is in the US and European interest that America be able to choose, as necessary, to play a supporting rather than direct role in continental conflicts, for a number of reasons. First, the nature of a potential conflict is much different today than in the past. Whereas the anticipated threat in the first forty years of the Alliance came from the Soviet Union, and clearly required a superpower response, future conflicts will more likely be intra-state, or arise from nationality crises and other disputes. Second, given the dispersion of the perceived threat, it is likely that US and European priorities will differ with respect to perceptions of vital interest. Finally, and not to be under-estimated, there is the level of public support for engagement within each member state. What the traffic will bear, and even what the public might demand, may differ significantly from country to country. From the US perspective particularly, the continued presence of troops in Europe will require careful consideration of any decision to put them in harm's way. What may pass an acid test for vital interests in Britain, for example, may not be acceptable to Americans.

The logical conclusion: NATO must be NATO and more – that is to say, it must have the flexibility to respond to a range of military threats and diverse circumstances itself, or provide the framework for other structures to address perceived threats. This could be done through existing Alliance structures – NACC, PfP and CJTF – or through complementary structures such as EU/WEU, comprising European members, and the OSCE with its inclusive membership.

One of the most important developments within NATO as the Cold War ended was creation of the North Atlantic Co-operation Council (NACC), the first step toward enlarging the Alliance to include non-member states. The NACC has provided a vehicle by which a range of countries can meet and discuss problems confronting Europe, matters on which NATO action in some manner might be appropriate. Most importantly, it has demystified NATO for countries that previously blamed the Alliance for all of Europe's problems. It is an excellent vehicle for anticipating and avoiding potentially explosive issues out-side the traditional realm of NATO responsibilities.

A natural and critical next step in the evolution to a broader con-cept of European security was the Partnership for Peace (PfP).[6] With its co-ordination cell and staff officers in Mons and ambitious sched-ule of joint activities, PfP has developed co-operative programs among NATO member and non-member states virtually inconceivable in the past. It has been at once a mechanism whereby states not comfortable with membership may work with members to enhance continental stability, *and* an important means to bring countries interested in membership into the NATO system without the commitment of - Article 5.[7] Through joint manœuvres and activities, interested countries can improve their interoperability and generally reduce or remove obstacles to membership, if that is the course they have chosen to take. While there is little debate over the need for still more structural adaptations to the Alliance, NACC and, particularly, PfP have been vital in its post-Cold War evolution.

The ministerial meeting of the North Atlantic Council in Berlin, in June 1996, agreed in principle to the concept of Combined Joint Task Forces (CJTF) as a mechanism within NATO to address potential out-of-area conflicts or situations which only selected countries feel need addressing.[8] Such a CJTF would permit more 'flexible and mobile deployment of forces, including for new missions'. Furthermore, it would permit a diversification of responsibility, whereby 'coalitions of the willing' could determine that action is necessary in some situations, even if other members might not. While final approval by the North Atlantic Council would be necessary, and NATO resources could be used, all members would not necessarily be expected to participate in a given CJTF's task. The concept has added flexibility through the ability to include even states that are not members of the Alliance: for instance, PfP countries would be able to participate in CJTFs, in concert with some NATO members, to address an issue others might not perceive as affecting their outside interests. In one respect, this may involve NATO in more potentially conflictual situations; however, it also gives the Alliance an ability to respond in a flexible and less confrontational manner, heightening the potential for success.

Still another conceptual change in the Alliance with operational ramifications is the European pillar. For those who have long worked these issues, this is often the place for an open yawn and nod. But such a reaction would be a mistake and would reflect a failure to appreciate the steady, albeit slow, improvements in European co-ordination. It will be important for the United States to confront the inevitability of greater European cohesion on security issues. The Clinton administration has gone a long way in this respect, and mutual accommodation that recognizes the needs of both sides of the Atlantic will remain critical.

The Maastricht Treaty lays out the objective of a Common Foreign and Security Policy (CFSP) to be addressed in the 1996–97

Intergovernmental Conference (IGC) discussions. As is usually the case – and, by the way, an approach that works quite well for the European Union – the IGC's end effect will be less than it could be, but the momentum of the process itself, if nothing else, will result in progress toward a European CFSP, probably more on foreign policy issues but also, at least symbolically, on security issues. The US should and will accommodate movement toward a CFSP. There have been and continue to be questions about the degree to which a European defence component will operate within or outside NATO, equal or subordinate to the Alliance, and with overlapping or different memberships.

The Combined Joint Task Forces (CJTF) are exactly the type of effort which can provide the necessary link to NATO while also supporting European efforts. As presently envisaged, CJTF would be available for three types of missions – NATO only, NATO plus, and WEU-led CJTF.[9] While all the details have not been finalized at the time of writing, the latter could comprise WEU members, associates and associate partners, with or without US participation, but under the purview of the North Atlantic Council and with NATO assets (though note that, as presently structured, it would be difficult not to involve US assets, possibly including personnel). Whatever the IGC's results, there is no way around the fact that practical and very positive European foreign and security policy co-ordination is in fact already occurring – at NATO, at the UN and in other fora. Inevitably and in each instance, the organizations have institutionally adapted to these concerted efforts.

But that does not mean that other states, including the United States, are and will always be comfortable with EU decisions. To the contrary, differences of opinion over potentially important, even vital, interests are virtually unavoidable. In fact, the design of CJTF inherently could lead to sharp differences among allies on its appropriate use, official American reassurances notwithstanding.[10] European efforts need to be understood from the broader context of a security framework that embraces not only NATO, but other components outside and separate from it.

EUROPEAN UNION/WESTERN EUROPEAN UNION (WEU)[11]

A comprehensive, broadly-based security structure must include at its base a strong economic component, without which stability on the continent is not possible. The EU provides this framework for Europe, and is essential to the economic viability of its individual members as well as other countries. Although the United States is not a member of the EU, the Union's success has meant a lesser burden for America and will continue to be an effective stabilizing factor in the future. Not only does it provide a high standard of living for member countries, but it also acts as a reinforcement for democratic structures that in the long term have also been essential to the security of the continent. Finally, the European Union has established criteria for members-in-waiting, who – in almost all cases – aspire to join NATO as well. EU requirements spell out clearly the free market criteria, as well as the democratic standards, that will be expected for participation in the European security architecture. In this sense, enlargement of the two organizations is mutually reinforcing.

This does not necessarily mean that decisions over membership will be easy in either organization. Some states, including the US, will continue to insist there be no 'back door' entry into NATO. But the debate over which should admit new members first, and which countries should receive priority, is less important than the fact that the overlapping requirements are a clear incentive to prospective members to meet a prescribed set of standards. At the very least, countries admitted to NATO should also have sufficiently strong credentials for EU membership as well. Security today can indeed be said to constitute more even than its parts: without a strong economic base, the democratic viability of a state and its military security could be undermined, while the absence of an effective military security structure would in turn undermine economic and political security.

In this context, then, is a European military pillar distinct from NATO desirable? Not necessarily, but its impact is and could translate into greater security in the future for several important reasons all too often overlooked by the United States. First, closer co-ordination in foreign and security policy by the Union would reinforce general integration of members, with positive consequences for all. Second, with ever scarcer resources, it would permit a pooling of resources among Europeans and a decrease in redundancy of arsenals, capabilities, etc. Finally, it could permit more flexibility by members to respond to crises by reducing the need for the United States – or even all Europeans, for that matter – to commit forces in all instances. It is thus quite clear that, even if the Europeans were to choose a separate organization, there must be a high degree of co-ordination between a 'European Pillar' and NATO in such a way that security is enhanced for all members.

But despite any perceived potential advantages of a *separate* European security organization, its likelihood is remote. All indications are that the Europeans will instead co-operate within NATO rather than outside or even in competition. While there has been an American tendency in the past to exaggerate the consequences of a second defence pillar, recent decisions by the Alliance – on CJTF, for example – encourage 'Europeanization' within NATO, rather than as a challenge to it, which is thus more palatable to, even comfortable for, the United States.[12]

This does not necessarily mean that the trend toward independent activity by the Europeans will cease, but that it will instead be exercised within the NATO organization – a situation that could work to the advantage of both sides if properly pursued. With the French decision to play a greater role in Brussels, even if not as a formal part of the Integrated Command, many of the critics of a separate European identity have fallen silent.[13] There is apparent agreement now for the Western European Union to remain an arm of the EU and as a support for NATO, not in competition or as a counterweight.[14] Such a construction promises to strengthen NATO rather than to undermine its efforts. This is not to say that there will be no disagreements and/or debates between the United States and Europe, particularly as the latter more explicitly defines its interests. But it could mean that both developing flexibility, such as through CJTF, and better co-ordination of immediate and longer-term goals will be necessary. From the US side, this will require greater consideration of European interests, but it also encourage greater responsibility on the part of the Europeans.[15]

EURO-CORPS

Less clear and almost running on a separate track is the Franco-German-Belgian-Spanish-Dutch Corps, essentially outside NATO but under 'dual-hatting'. It will be important to co-ordinate both this unit and any Mediterranean force with NATO assets so that they remain strictly complementary and non-competitive. There is strength and weakness in overlapping competencies in European structures. On the one hand, until the structures have adjusted to often dramatic changes in the strategic, political and economic environment, overlapping functions have been reassuring and promoted stability. On the other hand, as new responsibilities are assumed and adjustments made to the sharing of burdens, the interrelated organizations will need more clearly delineated responsibilities that reinforce the overall objectives of stability, without undermining confidence in the new outlines of European security.

ORGANIZATION FOR SECURITY AND COOPERATION IN EUROPE (OSCE)[16]

While NATO employed its forces for the first time since 1949 in Bosnia, a comprehensive definition of European security dictates that other organizations – the auxiliary ships of the fleet – be focused on preventing such conflicts from occurring in the first place. The Organization for Security and Cooperation in Europe is vital to that picture, and – with fifty-four members – is the most inclusive organization in the 'fleet'. A product of the Helsinki agreement of 1975, the OSCE is a daughter of the Cold War, but was even at that time an attempt to rise above it. The OSCE, known until January 1995 as the Conference on Security and Cooperation in Europe (CSCE), has been the political and diplomatic wing of the continent's 'security architecture'. The only body within Europe's political and security structure with a comprehensive membership, its members signed the Final Act in Helsinki in 1975, establishing politically binding norms and principles on key issues of both their internal and external affairs at the height of a period of détente in East-West relations. Since then, the OSCE has pursued a broad concept of security based on the promotion of human rights, democratic and free market precepts, and non-use of force, the rule of law, and arms control. Its work on all of these issues contributes substantially to European security.

The organization's record on human rights goes back over twenty years, when the CSCE in the East facilitated holding governments accountable to compliance with agreed norms, thereby sparking the formation of Helsinki Monitoring Groups in the USSR and the Baltic States, Charter '77 in Czechoslovakia and the Committee for the Defence of Workers (KOR) in Poland, among others. At its 1980 Madrid and 1986 Vienna follow-up conferences, as well as other meetings, the CSCE provided an ongoing international forum where Western countries could voice human rights concerns about victims of Communist repression. Its standards provided a framework within which Baltic independence, German unification, and the emergence of the newly independent states of the former USSR peacefully occurred. The OSCE continues to regard itself as a protector of human rights and freedoms for 'all individuals, regardless of race, colour, sex, language, religion, social origin or of belonging to a minority...'[17]

It has also brought about measures reducing tensions in Europe. At the 1984–86 Stockholm Conference (CDE) and other meetings, the CSCE pursued a number of confidence- and security-building measures (CSBMs) designed to reduce the danger of miscalculation and surprise attack. Those steps laid the foundation for the Vienna Document of expanded CSBMs and the Conventional Armed Forces in Europe (CFE) agreement dealing with force levels and structures from the Atlantic to the Urals.

But its mandate has been wide-reaching in more recent years as well, and this type of activity must be a part of the European security framework. Concluded in 1990 as a response to the end of the Cold War, the Charter of Paris for a New Europe underscored CSCE members' desire to overcome the ideological divide and unify Europe within a framework of common values and democracy based on human rights and fundamental freedoms, the rule of law and minority rights (added at Copenhagen in 1990), equal security, and market economies. It is this dimension of OSCE that at once supports the efforts of NATO and reinforces those efforts through programmes the Alliance is not equipped for and should not undertake. In recent years, OSCE has enhanced the security, human, and economic dimensions of its activities, including increased conflict prevention and conflict management; establishment of a comprehensive framework for conventional arms control, as well as confidence- and security-building; initiation of a comprehensive security model study; increased attention to human rights and humanitarian issues; and improvement of economic co-operation through the Economic Forum.

The OSCE has established a Permanent Council to assure ongoing consultation and a structure for decision making, a Chair-in-Office for executive action, and a Senior Council. In addition, summits are held every two years, ministerials at least annually. An important reflection of the potential increase in OSCE responsibility is the establishment of the office of High Commissioner on National Minorities, a Conflict Prevention Centre, and the Office for Democratic Institutions and Human Rights, along with ongoing missions to areas of conflict or potential conflict, such as Chechnya and Bosnia, as well as other election-monitoring and conflict-prevention activities. There is, however, a need to match the organization's efforts with funding and more concrete results, something few states have the resources or political will to do.

A further convincing argument for a broadly-based European security concept is the need to recognize and include those countries not now, and possibly with no near-future prospect of becoming, full NATO members. An important factor in this security equation is Russia. The Partnership programme is important in this respect, and potentially CJTF as well. The need for a NATO–Russia, as well as possibly a NATO–Ukraine, agreement, along with mechanisms for involving Moscow and Kiev, is fairly well recognized, despite differences on the details. But beyond this, the OSCE is a forum in which many early stages of conflict can be addressed and defused. For this reason, it can facilitate co-operative measures in arms control and other areas, helping to lower tensions and creating the type of security vital for long- term stability on the continent.

While the primary institutions in such a broad security framework are NATO, EU/WEU and OSCE, certainly support from other organizations also contributes to the objective of stability on the continent. These include the Council of Europe, the Nordic Council, or other fora for regional economic and political collaboration to solve potential challenges on a smaller scale.

In sum, there is a need for overlapping and mutually reinforcing structures for tasks beyond the traditional NATO activities, both as a result of the broader geographical understanding and definition of Europe today and because the parameters of security as understood in the Cold War have widened. Over the next few years, these institutions will need to adapt to the radically different demand of the post-Cold War era; any overlap in responsibilities can be clarified as the adjustment to new challenges takes place. There is a truism often cited – that we are always fighting the last war – and, in a sense, some institutions today are indeed still largely structured to fight the Cold War. But it is also true that the stability we seek on the continent requires a comprehensive approach, adapting traditional approaches to new circumstances, and thus assuring military security, as well as the economic and political stability necessary to that objective.

To conclude on the analogy with which this chapter began, the formation of European security is like a maritime task force, with NATO as the flagship – heavily-armed, yet also vulnerable – reinforced by numerous other vessels, each with distinct but essential responsibilities, and without which the entire fleet would be ineffective. Europe needs such a broadly-based, interdependent armada undertaking the diverse tasks necessary to assure stability and security. This is not to say that smooth sailing is assured; on the contrary, shoals – anticipated or unforeseen – likely lie ahead. The aim should thus be greater readiness and ability to navigate those waters successfully.

NOTES

1. The views presented here are those of the author and do not represent the views of the US Naval Academy or any other government agency or organization.
2. NATO planned a special summit for Spring 1997 to agree on which countries would initially be offered membership and the timetable for their potential admission. It is important to note that enlargement will require a change to the NATO treaty and ratification by the sixteen member state parliaments. In the case of the United States, the Senate is expected to consider each potential member individually.
3. One of the criteria for enlargement is a free-market economy.
4. After 1989 and before retirement, German Foreign Minister Hans-Dietrich Genscher clearly flirted with the idea of a more prominent OSCE role for common European security.
5. The result of the decision was the November 1991 Strategic Concept agreed in Rome. NATO, *NATO Handbook*, 1995, 235–248.
6. 'Partnership for Peace Invitation', and 'Declaration of the Heads of State and Government Participating in the Meeting of the North Atlantic Council', Brussels, 10–11 January 1994. NATO, *NATO Handbook*, 1995, 265–275.
7. Article 5: 'The Parties agree that an armed attack against one or more of them in Europe or North America shall be considered an attack against them all; and consequently they agree that, if such an armed attack occurs, each of them ... will assist the Party or Parties so attacked by taking forthwith, individually and in concert with the other Parties, such action as it deems necessary, including the use of armed force, to restore and maintain the security of the North Atlantic area.' The North Atlantic Treaty, Washington, DC, 4 April 1949. Cited in Lawrence S. Kaplan, *NATO and the United States: The Enduring Alliance* (Boston: Twayne, 1988) pp. 219–21.
8. NATO, 'Final communiqué of the Ministerial Meeting of the North Atlantic Council, Berlin', 3 June 1996, *NATO Review*, 44, no. 4 (July 1996).
9. The CJTF concept would permit 'a more flexible and mobile deployment of forces, including for new missions ... facilitate the mounting of NATO contingency operations, the use of separable but not separate military capabilities in operations led by the WEU, and the participation of nations outside the alliance in operations such as IFOR'. Ibid.

10. Based on official comments made in discussion of CJTF, IISS-Institute for National Security and Strategy meeting, National War College, 6 June 1996.
11. For an official review of the role of the WEU in European defence, see West European Union, Press and Information Service, 'WEU: History, Structures, and Prospects', March 1995.
12. In fact, some have argued that the recent steps toward the 'Europeanization' of NATO is nothing short of myth. Phillip Gordon, National War College/International Institute for Strategic Studies meeting, Washington, DC, 4 June 1996.
13. See Robert P. Grant, 'France's New Relationship with NATO', *Survival*, 38, no. 1 (Spring 1996) 58–80. Grant urges France's partners to take advantage of its current pragmatism. Unofficially, there have even been suggestions of significantly closer French relations with NATO in the near future, even reintegration.
14. The Kirchberg declaration left open the option of the relationship of the WEU to NATO, commenting that an EU common defence policy could lead to a 'common defence, compatible with that of the Atlantic Alliance'. West European Union, Council of Ministers, 'Kirchberg Declaration', Luxembourg, 9 May 1994.
15. The ability of the Europeans to assume those responsibilities is questionable as states rush to meet the European Monetary Union (EMU) criteria and cut defence budgets. All NATO states (including the United States) have cut their percentage of defence expenditure as percentage of GDP. *The Military Balance 1995/96* (London: International Institute for Strategic Studies, 1995) p. 264.
16. For original documents and other materials on the OSCE, see Arie Bloed, *The Conference on Security and Co-operation in Europe: Analysis and Basic Documents, 1972–1993* (Boston: Martinus Nijhoff, 1994). John Fry, *The Helsinki Process: Negotiating Security and Co-operation in Europe* (Washington DC: National Defense University Press, 1993) also contains basic documents as well as discussion of the major CSCE review and other conferences, including the Charter of Paris.
17. Organization for Security and Cooperation in Europe, 'Budapest Summit Declaration', 1994.

3 The Alliance and New European Security Challenges

Stephen F. Szabo

To the surprise of many who believed it had no future after the Cold War, NATO has emerged as the central security institution of post-Cold War Europe. Rather than losing its mission and sense of relevance after the fall of the Berlin Wall and the collapse of the Soviet Union, the North Atlantic Treaty Organization has seen both the partial re-entry of France into its military decision-making structures and a rush of new applicants for membership. It seems to have re-established the credibility which was damaged in Bosnia, while the United States has made a renewed commitment to remain in Europe through both its efforts to restructure NATO and its engagement in Bosnia, culminating in the Dayton accords.

While this record of adaptation to a changing milieu is encouraging for those who hope that the positive legacies of the Cold War will not be lost, NATO faces the challenge of shaping a continental concept of Europe to replace the bipolar one which characterized the Cold War. It will also have to define its new roles in relation to other institutions that will also be essential to the preservation of European security.

THE WANING OF COLLECTIVE DEFENCE AND THE RISE OF CRISIS MANAGEMENT

A number of key dilemmas face the new Europe in the post- Cold War era. The first and most important is what has been called the dispersion of the threat. The end of a single hegemonic threat to European security has already had and will continue to have major implications for NATO, the West European Union (WEU) and other institutions as they grope for new roles in the face of new missions. As Christoph Bertram has cogently observed, the disappearance of a single hegemonic threat means that each member of the NATO alliance is affected in different ways by different threats. Threats are now divisive rather than unifying; they are coalition-breaking rather than coalition-forming in nature.[1] There are few better ways to illustrate this change than by recalling General De Gaulle's immediate support of President Kennedy during the Cuban Missile Crisis, despite his differences with Kennedy over the Atlantic Alliance: such a scenario today is highly improbable.

The end of the hegemonic threat to Europe means that the role of the United States will become more uncertain and less central. The key element of continuity in American security policy in Europe during the twentieth century has been that the US only became seriously engaged when one power threatened to dominate Eurasia. While the United States is not returning to isolationism, it is becoming more preoccupied with its own problems and no longer has a clear beacon guiding its policies toward Europe.

Generational change in the American leadership, especially among new Republicans elected to the House of Representatives in 1994 – many of whom were in high school during the Vietnam War – is also reinforcing strong trends toward domestic priorities and away from international entanglements. Even NATO has been called into question by some of these House Republicans, who see it as an outmoded and costly artefact of the Cold War.[2]

Geostrategic interests are also drawing American attention towards Asia. While Europe has developed an extensive network of interlocking institutions and has moved toward the integration of national economies and even defence and foreign policies, Asia remains an area lacking such institutions and patterns of behaviour. Balance of power politics and national rivalries and insecurities are much more prevalent; and the need for the United States as the key balancer of the rising power of China, and guarantor of security for the states which fear this power, means that more attention will have to be paid to creating a security structure in Asia.

In Europe, the need for collective defence, for which the United States has been indispensable since it entered World War I, is declining, while that of crisis management is gaining importance. In NATO language, Article 5 contingencies – collective defence of Alliance territory – are becoming more remote, while non-Article 5 missions – those more indirectly affecting common security interests – are gaining in salience, yet it is these latter contingencies which are problematic for both NATO and the United States. For decades, NATO has worked as a credible system of deterrence against the very real threat posed by the Soviet Union. It has also served well as a network of reassurance, providing a framework for German security in a manner which did not threaten Germany's neighbours. It has been ineffectual in dealing with crisis management either out-of-area or when two NATO allies have engaged in armed conflict, as have Greece and Turkey. Prior to Bosnia it never deployed forces outside the NATO treaty area. The US guarantee has been rock solid when it faced Soviet threat contingencies, but it has been less certain in non-Soviet scenarios.

The case of Bosnia is not reassuring in this regard. Both the Bush and Clinton Administrations were indecisive during the crucial stages of the crisis. The Clinton administration finally acted with some decisiveness only when the situation on the ground stabilized following the achievement of most Serbian and Croatian objectives. The Dayton accords were, in the words of one keen observer, 'partition disguised by lawyerly fictions'.[3] NATO did act effectively, but its actions merely helped to stabilize and ratify ethnic cleansing at a horrible cost in human life. Perhaps this is all that can be realistically expected in a war that seemed far away for a long time from central Western concerns, although Richard Holbrooke has characterized the Western response as the greatest failure in collective security since the 1930s.

In any event, Bosnia is hardly a justification for NATO triumphalism – not only because of what it has ratified there, but also because of the uncertain nature of the Western response both during the early-mid-1990s and in regard to the near future as well. While the EU and the WEU did not perform any better in Bosnia than did NATO, serious questions about the American role remain nonetheless. The serious differences in threat assessment and strategy which developed between the United States and its key European allies remain unsettling, as does the example of the leader of the Alliance openly disregarding the NATO arms embargo policy in the Adriatic while not allowing the Europeans to use NATO assets. The ultimate decision on withdrawing American forces from Bosnia also seemed potentially fraught with danger for Alliance cohesion.

DILEMMAS OF ENLARGEMENT

In addition to crisis management demands, there are the dilemmas presented to the Alliance by Eastern extension. NATO is now committed to enlarging in East Central Europe. Although the academic debate on the wisdom of this policy will continue, the policy debate has moved on from one over whether to enlarge to one over when, how and with whom. For NATO to back down from its declared policy now would be disastrous to Alliance credibility and would only strengthen the worst nationalist tendencies within Russia.

However, even if NATO enlargement is a fact, the Alliance will be faced with finding a way to do so without either provoking Russian hostility or destroying through concessions the force and credibility of its collective defence, including nuclear deterrence.[4] It seems likely that ways will be found to extend NATO membership in a 'non-provocative' manner, that is without deploying American or German forces in the Visegrad states as well as by avoiding nuclear deployments. This is likely to result in a further erosion of Article 5 commitments on collective defence.

A EUROPEAN PILLAR IN AN ATLANTIC STRUCTURE

All of these factors have led to an even looser alliance in which the unravelling of military integration is taking place.[5] The creation of Combined Joint Task Forces (CJTF), the recognition by the Alliance in January 1994 that WEU will be its European pillar, and talk of 'coalitions of the willing' and separable (but not separate) forces, are all indicators of this trend. Yet peacekeeping operations in Bosnia have shown that heavy and large forces with effective lift and reconnaissance are required, and that these operations may not be all that different than those required for coalition defense under Article 5.

The rationale for a more cohesive and independent European defence identity, either within the EU, the WEU or NATO, rests on the realization that crisis management cannot rely upon consistent American leadership and involvement. In those cases where the US does not want to get involved, the rationale of CJTF is that coalitions of the willing among the Europeans can use NATO assets under the WEU umbrella to intervene. But as Ian Davidson asked in the *Financial Times*, 'The unresolved problem is how to secure US acquiescence in a European operation using NATO facilities which are partly American, without giving the US a veto over it.'[6] As he argues, 'it is hard to believe that conflicts of interest affecting questions of peace and war can be comfortably resolved by a process of subcontracting'.[7]

Another dilemma is raised, this one for the US–European relationship – namely, how to organize a European pillar without undermining the American commitment, on the one hand, or transforming European troops into 'little more than foot soldiers under the control of the Supreme Allied Commander, Europe (SACEUR)' on the other.[8] Under which conditions of abstention will the US provide NATO assets? If the US opposes intervention, how can European autonomy be insured?

UNITING A DIVIDED EUROPE

It is for these reasons that the need for a European security identity will grow rather than diminish in the post-Cold War period. Yet while the need is growing, internal divisions pose serious questions about the capability of Europe to not only develop a common foreign and security policy (CFSP) but to move towards a common defence policy and finally a common defence. The answers will be found in the context of the European Movement, namely within the EU and WEU, as well as within NATO.

Fundamentally, questions of European foreign and defence policy remain in the intergovernmental rather than the supranational domain, and are likely to remain so for at least the medium term. Thus any significant movement will have to take place as a result of an agreement between the key European states, especially France, Britain and Germany. The announced, partial reintegration of France back into NATO was an important step towards the creation of a European consensus on a security identity. While this means that European defence efforts will now come in support of NATO rather than in competition to it, French re-entry is predicated upon the belief that NATO is now the best path toward a European security identity. This requires a fundamental reassessment of the structure of post-Cold War NATO rather than a reaffirmation of the old NATO.

Yet important divergences emerged between the three in the run-up to the 1996 Turin Intergovernmental Conference and these differences largely remain. The British remain committed to a minimalist vision for the WEU and reject any link between the WEU and the EU, while the Germans and French are looking for ways to link them. The French and German foreign ministers have jointly proposed the establishment of a senior representative for CFSP who could speak for the Union on foreign and security policy issues. They also favor giving the

Council a greater role in this area and for allowing the Council to task coalitions of the willing to undertake joint crisis-management missions based on the following principles:

– the right to abstain or opting out – no state should be obliged to participate in military operations against its will;
– coalitions of the willing – a majority of states should not be prevented from acting by the veto of one or two states;
– variable unity or hard cores – those states which wish to move further towards military integration should not be prevented by those which are reluctant, thus producing a hard WEU core which may be similar to a hard monetary core of states in the European Monetary Union (EMU).

This process faces many hurdles, not the least of which is the trend of declining defence spending throughout the WEU states, a decline which must be halted if Europe is to be more than a civilian power. The rationalization of armament procurement and production is also a necessary condition. Yet while the barriers seem quite high, the need for Europe to organize itself in the strategic realm will be unavoidable in the new era.

If NATO is to remain a central and vibrant institution in the new European milieu, it will have to do what its Secretary- General, Javier Solana, said it must do at his first press conference, namely, 'reflect growing European responsibilities for defence and security'. It is this task, more than the enlargement of NATO to the east or even the shaping of a new NATO relationship with Russia, which is at the core of NATO's future. If NATO gets this right, everything else can follow. If it does not, enlargement will resemble a hollow Potemkin village.

Senior American military and civilian leaders have resisted changing anything which they fear could undermine the integrated command structure and the principle of American leadership. In 1995–96, Americans and Europeans quarrelled over who would be the Secretary-General of NATO, and over European objections to a US deputy to the EU official in charge of the civilian and economic elements of the Dayton accords. However, if American policy makers do not seize the opportunity afforded by the new French policy, the Alliance will risk losing its chance to make the necessary changes.

Alliance restructuring is a large topic – too large for this chapter. However, serious proposals for reform have already been discussed to move NATO in the right direction. The Alliance has reached a compromise on CJTF which will make it easier to allow the European members to use NATO assets without American participation. There also is a broad transatlantic consensus that SACEUR should continue to remain an American general officer. Yet change below this top level is both feasible and desirable as well. One of the more interesting proposals for such adaptation comes from Stanley Sloan of the Congressional Research Service, who has urged that both the Deputy SACEUR and Deputy Supreme Allied Commander, Atlantic (SACLANT) be Europeans, nominated by the WEU or the EU, and who could direct operations from which the US decided to abstain, either with or without NATO assets.[9] The French government has picked up on these ideas and placed them on the NATO table.

The end of the initial mandate for the Implementation Force (IFOR) in Bosnia allowed the Alliance to test the will and the capability of the Europeans to use NATO to continue a presence with a reduced American role. IFOR II or SFOR could become in effect a NATO CJTF operated under the NATO command structure, but downsized, with few or no American ground forces. Overall command of ground operations would remain, as during the first year of IFOR, under command of a British officer with a largely European contingent. Lift, air support, reconnaissance and intelligence would continue to rely heavily upon American capabilities. While not optimal, this option would be preferable to a complete termination of IFOR, and could provide the beginnings of a real shift toward a more European NATO.[10]

Reformalizing and restructuring the Atlantic relationship through new institutions, even new treaties, is needed to give new life to what remains both the pillar of European stability, and a key pillar of a stable and open global order.

NOTES

1. Christoph Bertram, *Europe in the Balance: Securing the Peace Won in the Cold War* (Washington: Carnegie Endowment for International Peace, 1995) p. 19.
2. Helan Dewar, 'World of Difference: GOP Generations Vie on Global Affairs', *Washington Post*, 9 April 1996, p. A1,A5. One of this group, Representative John Linder of Georgia is quoted as stating during the Bosnian debate, 'I'm not the least bit interested in the prestige of NATO'.
3. Michael Ignatieff, 'The Missed Chance in Bosnia', *The New York Review of Books*, 29 February 1996, p. 8.

4. See Nicole Gnesotto, 'Common European Defense and Transatlantic Relations', *Survival*, 38, no. 1 (Spring 1996), 24.
5. Bertram, *Europe in the Balance*, p. 24.
6. Ian Davidson, 'Close to the crossroads', *Financial Times*, 3 April 1996, p. 14.
7. Ibid.
8. Gnesotto, 'Common European Defense', p. 26.
9. Stanley R. Sloan, 'Negotiating a New Transatlantic Bargain', *NATO Review*, 44, no. 2 (March 1996), 19–23.
10. For some options see Stanley R. Sloan, *Bosnia After IFOR*, (Washington: Congressional Research Service, 1996).

II
Considering New Responsibilities: The Case for Enlargement

4 NATO's Double Enlargement: New Tasks, New Members

Ronald D. Asmus

The North Atlantic Treaty Organization is perhaps the most successful alliance in history, but it faces a growing paradox. On the one hand, hardly a week passes without senior officials in the US and Europe lauding its importance. The Alliance has become involved in peace implementation in Bosnia and is preparing to embrace the new democracies in East-Central Europe. Even Paris, Washington's old nemesis in the struggle for leadership in Europe, has abandoned its traditional Gaullist aspirations of an independent European defence and shifted gears to become more deeply engaged.

A survey of the European security debate in the 1990 reveals that NATO is the only show in town. In today's Europe there are no signs of anti-Americanism. No political forces of any significance question the US presence, or call for Europe to develop a security identity entirely independent of Washington.[1] Support for American engagement and presence is even stronger in the continent's eastern half, where the new democracies are eager to join US-led institutions such as NATO. All of Europe, it seems, has truly accepted the United States as a permanent European power, not just a temporary protector during the Cold War.

On the other hand, looking beyond the proclamations of unity and success presented by transatlantic officialdom, one finds far less certainty, let alone agreement, about the future purpose or function of the transatlantic partnership. Nagging doubts persist about its long-term viability. Perhaps nowhere is this more clear than in the United States itself, where creeping doubts about the Alliance's future importance or usefulness for US interests seem to vindicate European uncertainty about American commitment. At a time when elite and public support for the Atlantic Alliance in Europe appears stronger than ever, a growing number of voices in the United States are asking how Europe and NATO fit into America's evolving strategy and priorities. Bosnia revealed fault lines in the US body politic and strong political reservations about NATO's relevance. In the end, the United States committed its power and prestige to a peace settlement, but Bill Clinton in effect had to wager his Presidency – for a mission by an Alliance in which America is supposed to be the leading power!

But the issue is not just Bosnia, burden-sharing or any other single contentious matter. The United States faces a global security agenda in the post-Cold War world. No longer consumed by concern over Soviet military power, Americans are correspondingly less worried about Europe. Events there, while important, are no longer as central to their concerns. This has much less to do with ostensible US isolationism than with the fact that America faces a new and much broader set of security concerns. Its European allies, on the other hand, remain focused on stabilizing their own continent – in strategic terms, insular, if not isolationist.

This structural problem lies at the heart of the paradox sketched out in this chapter.[2] There is a basic mismatch between emerging US strategic priorities and what the Alliance currently does. Similarly, there is a parallel disconnect between what the Europeans want their larger ally to do in Europe and America's own priorities. How this mismatch and paradox have come about will be discussed in the next section, which briefly examines the impact of the end of the Cold War in Europe and the United States, respectively. Another section describes how this mismatch can be resolved by what I refer to as NATO's 'double enlargement'. A final section examines the challenges the Alliance must face if it is to realize such a vision.

THE END OF THE COLD WAR IN EUROPE AND THE UNITED STATES

For Europe, the collapse of Communism in 1989 and the subsequent dissolution of Soviet power marked twin revolutions that ended the Cold War. At the same time, these events overturned the peace orders established at Versailles and Yalta, following the two world wars in this century. Initially, Europe appeared to be on the threshold of a new era. Its eastern half was liberated, Germany was unified, and the troops of the former Soviet Union were being withdrawn some one thousand kilometres eastward. History may not have ended, but a generation of European leaders who emerged from World War II, determined to end internecine conflict once and for all by building a new Europe based on integration and co-operative security, could see their dream within reach.

This initial euphoria has since faded, however. While no longer divided, Europe also seems less stable than it initially did with the Cold War waning. The greatest instability and most dramatic scenes on this new political stage are taking place in the Balkans, as well as in Russia and the newly independent states of the former USSR. The great fear, of course, is that the kind of destructive nationalism unleashed in the former Yugoslavia could spread elsewhere.[3]

There are also signs of growing instability to Europe's south. If one assumes a broad definition of the Greater Mediterranean region as ranging from the Maghreb to the Middle East, even into the Black Sea and the Caucasus, then this strategic space could be considered one of the least stable and most likely to produce conflict. The combination of radical Islam, trends toward arms proliferation, and the apparent fragility of traditional pro-Western pillars such as Turkey have combined to produce enormous uncertainty. Often considered Europe's strategic backwater during the Cold War, the Mediterranean has in many ways emerged as its new front line as the West awakens to emerging strategic challenges there.[4]

To be sure, the collapse of communism, the unravelling of the Soviet Union and the withdrawal of the former-USSR's troops some one thousand kilometres eastward removed any direct military threat to Alliance territory. These events also seemed to eliminate the most direct, immediate rationale for the US military presence and, indeed, for the very existence of NATO – namely, the need to deter a direct Soviet military threat against Western Europe. Europeans thus confronted questions fiercely debated for years by academics in theoretical terms, and carefully avoided by politicians. Was the US presence destined to function as a temporary protectorate, or was it to become a permanent feature of the European landscape? Did the Americans stay in Europe solely to balance Soviet power, or did the rationale for their presence transcend this threat? What would happen if the Americans went home? Would Europe coalesce in new ways or fragment? In short, had the time come to test a theory advanced in the 1980s by Joseph Joffe, who termed the US military presence Europe's 'pacifier'?[5] So long as the Americans remained, he argued, Europeans would succumb to the comfort of this protection and never undertake a serious effort at their own defence. Only when that pacifier was removed, Joffe contended, would Europe start to mature, developing the wherewithal to handle its own security.

Some on the continent did initially feel that the Cold War's passing gave Europe an historic opportunity to assert its own independent role and destiny separate from the United States. But such sentiments quickly dissipated. Faced with the unsettled future of Russia, the emergence of a newly unified Germany, fears of renationalization, other new uncertainties on the post-Cold War landscape, and their own doubts about managing European security alone, Washington's allies decided that testing the 'pacifier thesis' could prove too risky. Moreover, at the time, not even Moscow objected to the continuation of the Atlantic Alliance and the US presence, as became evident in the German unification process of 1989–90.[6]

More importantly, Europeans have increasingly rejected the basic premise underlying Joffe's 'pacifier theory' – that an American presence actually hindered Europe's own integration and efforts to assume greater responsibility. Nowhere is this new attitude more dramatic than in France, which had long taken a lead in warning against undue dependence on the US By the mid-1990s, President Jacques Chirac was quietly burying much of the Gaullist heritage by initiating a strategic shift back towards closer co-operation with the Alliance, even with Washington.[7] In short, European leaders have now accepted that, far from hindering their continent's integration, the Alliance and the US presence actually provide the necessary basis for sustaining and, indeed, expanding that process, especially to new democracies in the East. The US role is thus still considered vital, yet as a 'unifier' rather than a 'pacifier', for the Atlantic Alliance and especially America's presence offer a framework that would best allow Europe to knit itself back together.[8]

Initial reactions in the United States to the end of the Cold War were similar in some respects, yet radically different in others. As in Europe, the initial response was defensive. Confronting the same uncertainties as their allies, US officials feared being shut out of Europe in both security and economic terms. What could Washington do to remain engaged there? Would the Europeans want the United States to remain engaged, or would they seek to build an independent identity?

As policy evolved, American officials came to embrace a new rationale of the US as a European power with the same commitment, presence and voice in the continent's security affairs as the Europeans themselves. Initially embraced under the Bush administration, this line was also adopted by President Bill Clinton's foreign policy team. The US was no longer Europe's protector, they argued, but a permanent participant in European affairs – in short, a 'European power'.[9] This new rationale rested on a reading of twentieth-century history that assumed an active American role was essential if Europe was to avoid falling back into old nationalisms, geopolitical rivalries and internecine conflict. A US presence in Europe was required not only as strategic insurance against a residual Russian threat, but also as a means of keeping Europe – above all, Germany – integrated, and avoiding the renationalization of European politics. Indeed, it was argued, only with America playing the role of political broker and facilitator could a formerly divided Europe successfully grow together.

At the same time that Washington officialdom was struggling to come up with a politically viable rationale for keeping the US engaged in Europe, the end of the Cold War also undeniably downgraded the continent's importance in American strategy. Despite the rush of initiatives to secure peace there, reunify Germany within NATO and negotiate a peaceful withdrawal of Soviet power back beyond the borders of a now truncated Russia, American strategic attention had begun shifting elsewhere.

To a large degree, of course, this change in emphasis was good news, as it underscored the fact that Europe no longer faced a direct threat. During the Cold War, that region had been at the centre of the American international strategic calculus: the US saw itself as confronted with a global challenge from the USSR, with Europe in many ways the prime arena for competition and influence. The continent's priority was clearly reflected in America's national military strategy, and in the role that theatre played in Washington's planning. Europe was the place to be: it was where the action took place, where US presidents had to prove their mettle, where diplomatic and military careers were made.

After the Cold War, however, Europe no longer occupies centre-stage. It plays a reduced role in US diplomacy and strategy. Long-range American defence planning has become increasingly reoriented away from Europe – with the exception of a very remote possibility of danger from a resurgent Russia – toward other regional contingencies. The Clinton administration's 'Bottom-Up Review' (BUR), for example, left Europe entirely out of the defence planning process, although the United States has remained committed to stationing some 100,000 troops there, mainly in Germany.[10]

Equally, if not more important, a new debate about Europe's relevance has started to percolate through the US strategic community and beyond. It centres on the following question: just how relevant is

Europe and the Atlantic Alliance today in light of America's new post-Cold War needs and priorities? What role should Washington want traditional Cold War alliances such as NATO to play in this new era? How could these alliances be better harnessed to meet the new challenges of the post-Cold War era? Jim Thomson framed the problem by proposing a *Gedankenexperiment* imagining two worlds, one in which the Atlantic Alliance exists and one in which it does not. If there were no NATO today, he asked, would we want to recreate it?[11]

There are clearly some powerful reasons why the United States might want a close transatlantic relationship. Having fought two world wars this century and spent nearly one trillion dollars in insuring European security during the Cold War, the last thing the US can afford today is instability across the Atlantic. Moreover, if one compiles a list of major problems facing the United States today and for the foreseeable future, one quickly realizes that this is essentially a catalogue of common challenges facing both Americans and Europeans. Indeed, the length and scope of such an agenda would underscore the need for policy-makers on both sides of the Atlantic to work together.

These shared concerns would include completing Europe's unity; managing the very uncertain futures of Russia, Ukraine and the rest of the former Soviet Union; and preventing the spread of the kind of aggressive nationalism seen in the Balkans. The Middle Eastern peace process also remains uncertain and fragile. Rogue states such as Iran and Iraq continue to threaten the security of the Persian Gulf and world oil supplies. As noted earlier, the Greater Mediterranean has begun to emerge as a new area of potential instability. The proliferation of weapons of mass destruction and delivery technologies alike poses new threats that could endanger Western societies in ways as yet only too poorly understood.

One need hardly be a strategic genius to point out that the US would be much better off facing these challenges alongside a strong, powerful European partner with a shared global agenda, co-ordinated policies and joint capabilities for action. More than ever before, the political imperative for the United States lies in acquiring partners and shaping alliances to successfully address such common challenges. By building effective coalitions with like-minded countries, the United States could maximize Western influence and save its own resources.

Even listing these goals, however, already underscores how the American agenda is no longer as Euro-centric as during the Cold War. It suggests that Washington is seeking a relationship not only to manage or ensure European stability, but also to work together with allies and partners beyond that region in areas and on issues where they have common interests. If America had to renegotiate the transatlantic security bargain today, it would certainly still want a close strategic partnership with Europe, but it would have less interest in replicating today's Alliance than in shaping a more global, more equal partnership.

Europeans often misinterpret this trend, equating past US Eurocentrism with internationalism. If America is not preoccupied with their continent's affairs or prepared to intervene immediately in messy conflicts such as Bosnia, they conclude that it is 'going isolationist'. To be sure, the US faces considerable pressure to address domestic concerns and is also experiencing its own, at times confused, post-Cold War foreign policy debate. And while isolationist voices undoubtedly can be heard, there is little evidence that they will dominate US policy. While Europeans worry about the instincts of a new generation of post-Cold War American politicians, even such adversaries as Bill Clinton and Newt Gingrich are both essentially globalist, not isolationist, in outlook. Indeed, the United States is more inextricably involved in global security affairs than at any time in its history.

The real problem lies elsewhere. The end of the Cold War left the United States and Europe strategically out-of-synch, their respective debates evolving in different directions. Simply put, NATO's basic problem today lies in a mismatch between what it is best geared to do and the most pressing strategic challenges facing the Western world. A comparison of NATO's current planning priorities with a list of possible conflicts affecting both US and European vital interests suggests that the Alliance is best equipped and most firmly committed to meet what may be the least plausible threat – one to the territorial integrity of current or even future members – yet least prepared with weak, ad hoc or no obligations vis-à-vis the most likely dangers to common interests beyond their borders.

NATO'S DOUBLE ENLARGEMENT

The question, therefore, is whether NATO can be reformed to address and harmonize the strategic priorities of Washington and its allies. From a US perspective, can Europe become the kind of partner it is looking for, and is NATO the right place to forge such a partnership?

And, for Europeans, does this new American agenda make sense, and is it compatible with their own aspirations?

If a strategic planner were to lay out a blueprint for such a new NATO, what would it look like? To borrow a phrase from the American political vernacular, what might be the Alliance's 'vision thing'? The ideal for such a new transatlantic strategic partnership would be a unified and integrated Europe – 'whole and free' – in permanent alliance with the United States. It would envisage a partnership of equals, a tandem devoted to the dual tasks of managing Europe's security while pursuing common interests beyond.

This vision differs markedly from the rationale that guided Alliance efforts during the Cold War. It is not based on the premise that the US is the protector and the Europeans the protected, but rather on an assumption that both share vital interests in Europe, as well as beyond. It transcends the old Cold War rationale, namely to deter – and, if needed, defend Western Europe against – a Soviet attack. It also envisage an Alliance no longer focused exclusively on or limited to Europe as such, but one in which all members see themselves as a force for promoting Western values and interests in a global context.

A simple philosophy would undergird this new bargain: it is more effective to address challenges collectively that cannot be addressed alone. Europeans have long realized and accepted that their common interests require a common, co-ordinated foreign and defence policy. In NATO, that principle was accepted only for defending Western Europe from the USSR during the Cold War. It now needs to be expanded to include the continent's eastern half, as well as the new security challenges beyond the borders of an enlarged NATO. In short, the US and Europe need the functional equivalent of a common foreign and security policy.

'Double enlargement' captures the essence of this vision. The first enlargement would extend the transatlantic partnership's structures and institutions to those new democracies in Europe's eastern half who qualify for NATO membership and whose security Alliance members can and will guarantee. Specifically, it means extending both the European Union (EU) and NATO eastward to project stability to the region. Yet Alliance reform should not be viewed solely in geographic terms. A second enlargement would broaden the horizon, agenda and functions of transatlantic partnership beyond the confines of Alliance borders to areas and issues where new threats may emerge that affect shared US-European interests. NATO must enlarge its functional scope beyond collective defence and expand its capabilities to deal with challenges or crises beyond that threaten vital interests of members beyond their immediate borders.

While there are debates over enlarging NATO geographically and functionally, the two processes are mutually reinforcing, even synergistic, and must be pursued in tandem if they are to be pursued at all. Before turning to this interrelationship, however, it might be useful to step back and briefly survey the arguments for each component of double enlargement.

NATO's eastward enlargement has in many ways become the defining issue of post-Cold War security in Europe.[12] When a full history of this issue is eventually written, it will show that nearly all early proponents of the idea were motivated by a desire to integrate and stabilize Europe's eastern half – a positive vision, one inspired by the way Western Europe benefited from Alliance policy in the 1950s. Just as NATO had been essential to a secure framework for democracy in the West, they hoped a new Alliance could now perform a similar function for Eastern Europe's emerging democracies. In this view, NATO enlargement would be the core component in a new peace order.[13]

Much of the subsequent debate over the pros and cons of NATO enlargement has obfuscated these motives. As Moscow's stance hardened and its opposition grew vocal, many commentators began suggesting that enlargement was either overtly or covertly aimed against Russia. Critics singled out Kremlin resistance as the reason why NATO should not move forward. This overlooked four mutually reinforcing imperatives that produced the original consensus in favour of enlargement, most of which had little to do with Russia and any real or imagined Kremlin threat.

Opening NATO to the new democracies of East-Central Europe is, first and foremost, a *moral* imperative. After all, it was German aims in World War II, along with the vagaries of post- war allied diplomacy, that combined to leave these countries beyond the Iron Curtain during the Cold War. Countries such as Poland or Czechoslovakia were no less Western or European than Italy or Germany. Thanks largely to quirks of history and the crimes of dictators like Hitler and Stalin, many of these countries ended up as part of the Warsaw Pact, not NATO. While some critics worry that enlargement could create new lines, they fail to grasp the importance of erasing the old and arbitrary lines imposed by the actions and decisions of past tyrants.

Thus NATO enlargement reflects the desire of these countries to 'return to Europe' and to enjoy the same kind of security long taken for granted by their Western neighbours. In this vision, the reunification of Germany was just a first step toward reintegrating a continent artificially divided for over forty years. Warsaw, Prague and Budapest have every right to the same level of prosperity and security enjoyed by Bonn, Paris and London. After all, with what justification can the West pledge to guarantee the defence of, say, Copenhagen, but not Prague?

This moral imperative does not stand alone. The *political* case for NATO enlargement is rooted in a conviction that the Alliance was crucial in providing an overall security framework, helping to stabilize democracy in Western Europe in the early postwar period, and in the belief that extending such a security framework eastward will be equally valuable in consolidating post-communist democracies as well.

This view is especially strong in Germany, where a broad consensus holds that membership in NATO and the European Community were essential in Westernizing the country's political culture.[14] Konrad Adenauer's determination to anchor his state in the West reflected a belief that it needed to break free from the trap of the *Mittellage*, as well as from old patterns of geopolitical jockeying and nationalism, in order for democracy to establish firm roots. Based on this successful experience, German leaders are thus especially sensitive to the link between a country's foreign policy orientation and its internal order.[15]

It is thus hardly surprising that, when Polish leaders invoke the Adenauer legacy and the need to stabilize fragile democracies as a primary reason for seeking EU and NATO membership, such arguments resonate well among the German political elite.[16] Bonn's Defence Minister Volker Rühe has been an especially outspoken proponent of this view. In numerous speeches, he has repeatedly argued that postwar West German democracy was so successful precisely because the country became rapidly integrated into Western institutions.[17]

The *economic* imperative for enlargement flows from a similar set of calculations. Although almost impossible to quantify, simple common sense suggests that ongoing uncertainty over where Eastern Europe belongs is hardly a positive incentive for foreign investment. These countries are more likely to reform faster and with greater Western investment if they are clearly inside the Western club rather than outside. Similarly, they themselves would be more willing to expand mutually beneficial trade with countries like Russia. During his tenure as Foreign Minister, Wladyslaw Bartoszewski used to point out that, so long as Poland was not in the Alliance, it would be reluctant to become more deeply involved in trade with Russia that could create deeper dependence on Moscow in key strategic areas. Conversely, a Poland in NATO, able to deal with Russia based on Alliance support, would not hesitate to expand such bilateral eastern trade.

Perhaps most important of all, however, is the *strategic* imperative – or rather imperatives – for NATO enlargement: a need to fill the vacuum created by the collapse of the Yalta and Versailles peace orders. Leaving Eastern Europe in this strategic no-man's-land could not only tempt Russia to try to restore its hegemony in the region, but would also create a major dilemma for Germany. This concern is one reason Bonn has led calls for NATO enlargement. Its dilemma can be summed up in a nutshell: the borders of both the EU and NATO are contiguous with Germany's vital interests in the South, but not in the East. Bonn's objective must thus be to extend the EU and NATO to cover its newly discovered interests in Eastern Europe. Although just how far those interests extend may be controversial, there is little doubt that Poland's basic security, for example, is now clearly seen as a vital interest of the Federal Republic.

Germany's preference is to extend those institutions that solved its own security dilemmas. For this generation of leaders in Bonn, the answer is to tie the countries of Eastern Europe into the West just as Germany itself has been integrated. They realize that any attempt to fill this vacuum alone would exceed Germany's economic resources and be politically counterproductive. Extending *multilateral* institutions like the EU and NATO would pre-empt the danger of Bonn having to deal with instability in the East on its own. In this sense, enlarging both the EU and NATO to Eastern Europe, in the words of Karsten Voigt of the opposition Social Democrats, is the final step in resolving 'the German question'. Speaking in the Bundestag debate following the January 1994 NATO summit, Defence Minister Rühe articulated a consensus view among the mainstream political parties in Germany when he stated:

The opening of the Alliance to the East is in our vital interests. One does not have to be a strategic genius to understand this. I have often been surprised how little our debate on this issue has been guided by a clear analysis of German interests. A border of stability and security – unstable east of us but stable here, prosperity this side of the border, poverty on the other – such a situation is not sustainable in the long run. It is for this reason that Germany's eastern border cannot be the eastern border of NATO and the European Union. Either we will export stability or we will end up importing instability.[18]

A desire to avoid so-called 'back door' commitments that might arise from EU enlargement not matched by NATO enlargement is a final strategic concern. As the new democracies of Eastern Europe join the European Union, they will have the theoretical option of membership in the Western European Union (WEU) as well, acquiring a fully fledged security guarantee on paper, but one without teeth. And while Washington's closest NATO allies would be extending guarantees to their eastern neighbours without a US say, in a crisis, America would almost inevitably become involved, especially if escalation led traditional Alliance members to invoke Washington's security commitment. In other words, a country like Germany, already under the US guarantee, would be pledging to protect Poland through the WEU without American involvement, yet ultimately relying on Washington's assistance. Such a situation, in which the entangling commitments of a country under a US guarantee could be seen as drawing America into a conflict over which Washington initially had little direct control, could destroy the Alliance. It would clearly be better to have any such arrangements spelled out within a new NATO, where they would be credible, and where the US could better influence them.

How NATO should enlarge has been an issue of considerable debate. The Alliance has essentially embraced a strategy based on using enlargement as a vehicle for projecting stability to the east.[19] It has also agreed to treat candidate countries individually. Without listing explicit criteria, the Alliance made its overall preferences clear leading up to the 1997 summit in Madrid. In the final analysis, everything depends on the votes. As US Secretary of State Warren Christopher noted in a speech at Prague in early 1996, NATO enlargement must begin with the strongest candidates, because if the Alliance does not start there it will never start at all. At the same time, NATO will also have to develop strategies to help stabilize countries excluded from the first – or perhaps any – round of enlargement. In this context, how to deal with the Baltic states, as well as Ukraine, poses the most acute political and strategic dilemmas for the Alliance.[20]

The cost of enlargement has also been a central topic of debate. Much will depend on how many countries join and how NATO decides to implement guarantees of collective defense against armed attack under Article 5, that is, what kind of posture and strategy are employed. What it costs will also depend on what the 'it' is, something the Alliance had yet to decide by 1997. However, given a low threat environment, a consensus has emerged that NATO can rely on a posture combining key elements of force modernization among new members in Eastern Europe and other allies' improved capabilities for reinforcement in a crisis through a strategy of power projection.

RAND estimates that the cost of such a posture for the Visegrad countries, for example, would run to about $42 billion.[21] The entire Alliance, including both new and old members, would pay this price, spread out over a ten to fifteen-year period. It would amount to less than two per cent of planned defense spending among new and old members. The individual share of that cost would, of course, depend upon the country, as well as the role that its forces play in carrying out NATO strategy. To put these outlays in perspective, however, one might note that the costs for maintaining and operating one American armoured division over a ten-year period are estimated at $60 billion. In short, the estimated price tag for enlargement to East Central Europe is about two-thirds of what it would cost to build and maintain a single US Army tank division.

It is also important to realize that enlargement was never conceived as merely extending the old NATO eastward. Early proponents of the idea also viewed it as but one step in an overall transformation of the Alliance beyond a traditional focus on collective defence. Although the phrase was only coined later, the philosophy underlying 'double enlargement' was present from the beginning. For example, Volker Rühe's speech at London's International Institute of Strategic Studies, which in many ways started the official debate on enlargement, spoke of transcending the traditional Cold War conception of deterrence in Europe going beyond old categories of balance-of-power politics to embrace new missions – enlargement, peacekeeping and crisis management.

Similarly, the early RAND proposals favouring NATO enlargement viewed it as but one of seven key steps in the overall transformation of the Alliance. Other key stages in this process were to include US–French strategic rapprochement and a reorganization of NATO structures, better enabling it to project power and stability beyond Alliance borders to those areas where member states' interests would most likely be threatened. Similarly, Senator Richard Lugar's early calls for eastward expansion also came coupled with the warning that NATO had to go 'out-of-area' lest it go 'out of business'.

From the outset, however, the key issue has been how far NATO's double enlargement should go in embracing missions beyond collective defence. One can envisage four alternatives. The first, essentially the status quo, might be termed 'Border Defence Plus'. In this model, NATO's main mission would remain the collective defence of current members, complemented by a willingness to perform peace-support missions in Europe. A second model, 'Stability in Europe', envisages NATO as the security manager in an enlarged Europe. Under this rubric, the Alliance would open itself to eastern members as planned, and its new missions would thus include both new Article 5 and new non- Article 5 missions, again primarily in the form of peace-support operations on Europe's periphery. A third model might be entitled 'Stability *of* Europe'. The key distinction here is that NATO would become the security manager in and around Europe, assuming respons-ibility for managing stability on the continent, as well as in those geographically contiguous areas that could affect it. Under this rubric, NATO would not only become more active in Eastern Europe, but its defence planning horizon might include the greater Mediterranean region, including North Africa, as well as perhaps even the Persian Gulf. Such a scheme would require a significant increase in current Alliance power projection and crisis management capabilities.

A fourth and final model, which might be labelled 'Defend Com-mon Interests', conceives of a NATO with its scope limited not by geography, but by how the US and Europe define their common vital interests. Such a NATO would, in principle, be willing and able to act wherever and whenever a consensus existed among its members. Its mission profile would clearly include the Persian Gulf and the Greater Middle East, as well as the other missions outlined under each other model. Indeed, should the consensus exist, this NATO would also be willing to assume broader global missions, such as playing a more active role in containing the threat of weapons of mass destruction.[22]

These models underscore the importance of viewing NATO's geo-graphical and functional enlargement as two sides of the same coin. Geographical enlargement is needed to stabilize Europe's eastern half and the continent as a whole. It is a moral and geopolitical corner-stone in constructing a stable, post-Cold War European political and strategic order. Enlargement would serve as a stepping-stone for this new transatlantic bargain. A Europe successfully on its way to greater political, economic and strategic coherence would be far more capable of becoming the new partner the United States wants and needs. Thus double enlargement is an indispensable means for helping to keep the US deeply involved in the region's security affairs and for facilitating a more stable, strategically outward-looking Europe.

Finally, there are political and structural reasons to view NATO's double enlargement as a single package. Politically, the Alliance must manage the very different agendas and priorities of its different members. For some, especially Germany, eastward enlargement is the top strategic priority. For others, especially in the south, enlarging NATO's functional missions in their region may take higher priority. In the United States, it may well prove easier to obtain political support for Alliance reform based on double enlargement, especially if the strategic horizon of this new NATO extends to areas such as the Persian Gulf, where the US would clearly welcome a greater allied contribution. In other words, Senate ratification of NATO's eastward enlargement would be much easier if the Alliance is simultaneously broadening its scope beyond collective defence.

Similarly, in structural terms there is also a natural synergy between each part of NATO's double enlargement. The Alliance is discussing how both its political–military nexus and its military command structures can be adapted for new missions. It makes little strategic sense to view the demands of new Article 5 missions in isolation from the demands of new non-Article 5 missions. This is especially true if reform in Russia continues and new non-Article 5 missions prove the more salient, challenging future missions. In some ways, Alliance planning requirements and the capabilities needed may be growing more similar.

RUSSIA

Where does Russia fit into this vision of a new transatlantic partnership? The US and Europe have an enormous stake in the success of that country's reform process. A stable, reformed Russia can be an active partner in maintaining security in Europe, in resolving regional conflicts, and in fighting the spread of weapons of mass destruction. The West would clearly benefit from the establishment of a strategic partnership with Moscow if sufficient common ground existed for such teamwork.

Russia's place in this vision is nevertheless quite clear: it is not a candidate for Alliance membership. Russia is simply too big and too different to be part of NATO. No member of the Alliance today or in the foreseeable future would be willing to extend an Article 5 guarantee to its border with China. And Russians – unlike the East Europeans – have no real interest in assuming the obligations and responsibilities membership entails.

At the same time, the rationale for double enlargement would not depend on the existence or re-emergence of a Russian threat. As noted above, this new partnership would consciously seek to go beyond old Cold War understandings of America as the protector of an endangered Europe. Its purpose would be to defend shared Western interests wherever threatened, and where there is a consensus to act. This new venture's existence would thus not hinge on the failure of reform in Russia. On the contrary: a successfully reformed, democratic Russia could be a future partner, not a foe, of this enlarged Alliance. In other words, the rationale for this new NATO is completely independent of Russia. To be sure, if Moscow does re-emerge as an aggressive power threatening Western interests in Europe or elsewhere, deterring and containing its power would again become an important Alliance objective. But Russia is unlikely to again become the kind of global threat that dominated US global defence planning during the Cold War, placing Europe front and centre in US strategic thinking. Today, even an aggressive Kremlin would likely constitute at most a regional threat.

Indeed, at least in principle, an enlarged Alliance is very much in Russia's interest. It would be both willing and able to co-operate with Moscow. In conceptual terms, there are even strong reasons why both components of NATO's double enlargement could be beneficial to the Kremlin. Early proponents of extending NATO eastward actually saw it as a step toward, not against, Russia. For no government, least of all in Moscow, wanted instability in East Central Europe. The same logic that makes it beneficial for Russia to have Germany firmly anchored in NATO applies to its view of other countries. A secure Poland integrated into the West is likely to be far less anti-Russian and more interested in co-operation and bridge-building than an insecure Poland caught in the age-old geopolitical no-man's-land between Berlin and Moscow.

NATO's functional enlargement could also potentially serve Russian interests by making the Alliance both capable and willing to act in areas where Moscow and the West might have similar interests. Joint action in Bosnia is just one example of such co-operation. Ideally, the day will come when the Kremlin enjoys close, friendly relations with NATO, and where the Alliance's border with Russia is just as stable and secure as any in Europe.

But it takes two to tango, and Moscow clearly does not view either component of NATO's double enlargement in such benign or positive terms. On the contrary, Russians almost unanimously oppose the Alliance's eastward enlargement. Moscow is plainly concerned about being marginalized. Moreover, democrats there fear that enlargement will play into the hands of nationalists. The military worries about an ostensible new NATO threat. More generally, there is an instinctual feeling that enlargement will lead to a European security system that neither leaves room for nor recognizes Russia's ostensible great power status.

Many Russians are sceptical as well of NATO's functional enlargement. A handful of commentators do acknowledge that, in principle, a strong, organized Atlantic Alliance capable, for example, of effectively deterring rogue states might also serve Moscow's interests, but most react with alarm to the prospect of NATO contingency planning or military intervention beyond Europe.

Thus, the Alliance must be willing to face the likelihood that Moscow may oppose both components of double enlargement. Even though the approach outlined above explicitly decouples NATO's future from a real or imagined Russian military threat, suspicions about Western motivations and power still run deep. Nevertheless, the Alliance should accelerate its efforts to build co-operative ties with Moscow in parallel with this new transatlantic arrangement, efforts advanced at the 1997 Clinton-Yeltsin summit at Helsinki. Russia must not have a *droit de regard* over NATO actions, including prospective new missions outside Europe. But it should engage in regular and frequent exchanges with the Alliance on all security issues of mutual concern – from Eastern Europe to the Commonwealth of Independent States, the Middle East, the Persian Gulf, Northeast Asia, proliferation, defence planning, and arms control. A NATO–Russian agreement or charter will codify this new consultative mechanism. Even if Moscow hardliners reject such an offer, the Alliance will have done all it reasonably could to establish a new relationship, short of allowing itself to gradually become a hollow shell because of Russian concerns.

THE HURDLES AHEAD

Can such a new transatlantic relationship based on this concept of double enlargement be forged? What are the major questions to be answered; what hurdles would have to be overcome?

First and perhaps most important, Europe must decide whether it really wants the kind of partnership implied by NATO's geographical and functional enlargement. Do Europeans believe that they and the US not only face common problems, but also share common interests in and beyond their continent, along the lines laid out in this chapter? Only Europeans themselves can answer this question.

At a minimum, double enlargement would require Europe to abandon once and for all the myth that its unity and integration can only be built in opposition to the United States. This new transatlantic partnership will prove impossible if Europeans see close partnership with America as harmful to the continent's integration, and so long as the motivation for building Europe is a perceived need for independence from the US. Many proponents of integration in the past have sought to promote that cause as a contrast or even an alternative to transatlantic co-operation and alleged American 'hegemony'. The result has been an insular, protective perspective, a suspicion of co-operation with the US on anything beyond a narrow scale. This mindset ignores the influence of shared values and the imperative of responding to shared risks; it will always be a recipe for an inward-looking Europe, not the kind of partner Washington seeks.

Second, double enlargement requires a broader understanding in Europe of what Alliance reform is all about. Statesmen there repeatedly talk about the need for a new transatlantic bargain, but often understand it only within the confines of an older strategic understanding. Their concept of a new arrangement is often limited to redistributing the burdens and responsibilities for managing ongoing or residual security problems within Europe. At most they seek to deepen ties that bind while lightening the security burden on Washington, hoping this will foster new transatlantic links and lower the 'price' of the US security engagement in Europe to a level America's elite and public opinion find acceptable. Europeans thus fail to grasp that the relationship's underlying problem is structural. Even few senior officials are willing to acknowledge publicly that the key issue in the transatlantic relationship may also lie in the lack of a common US–European approach to problems *beyond* Europe affecting vital common interests. Thus the need is for a broader vision in which both the United States and Europe become co-equals in shaping a new international agenda.

A third, closely related question is whether Europe can broaden its strategic horizon in the manner that double enlargement will require. Today it remains self-absorbed. Leaders are consumed by knitting together and reconciling a continent divided for nearly four decades by Communism. Ghosts of the past and fear of a return of nationalism and old inter-European geopolitical rivalries lurk just below the surface. Fixing Europe remains their top priority; reconciliation within the continent takes precedence over asserting its interests beyond. Some Americans may dismiss post-Cold War Europe as a largely stable region more or less on track, but a stable and durable post-Cold War order there is still very much a work in progress, one with an uncertain outcome. Europe will likely remain inward-looking until its two halves are fully reconciled, and until its leaders and publics believe stability on the continent is secure. Against this backdrop, any prospect of US engagement in the old world declining only reinforces Europe's trend toward an inward-looking strategic perspective.

While globalization of markets and competition in key areas, especially high technology, have expanded Europe's economic and commercial horizon, its strategic outlook remains regional. In one of history's ironies, its mindset is more narrow and insular at the end of the twentieth century than it was at the beginning – a result of two world wars, and more than forty years of Cold War. To be sure, the continent's future outlook will depend in no small part on internal developments. Only when it is well on the way toward greater political, economic and strategic unity will it be able to make the transition into this new transatlantic bargain.

Thus, Europe needs NATO enlargement for its own stability and as a stepping-stone toward this broader bargain. But such stability may be only the necessary, not the sufficient, precondition for change. What is needed, above all, is a recognition of Europe's own interests – and the threats to those interests – beyond the Alliance's immediate borders. To be sure, Europeans have started to broaden the narrow mindset that dominated their strategic thinking throughout the Cold War: it now extends beyond the confines of the continent's western half, and accepts the need to stabilize Eastern Europe as well as the Mediterranean littoral. But there Europe's strategic attention essentially stops, and for this new transatlantic bargain to work, its horizon must extend still further.

Fourth, is America also willing to make the changes double enlargement requires? Is Washington prepared to play its full role in unifying Europe and extending new security guarantees to the continent's eastern half? And is the US ready to try forging a truly common approach to problems beyond Europe's borders? Genuine coalitions, of course, require sharing influence and responsibility with allies, something America will have to be ready for in places like the Middle East and the Persian Gulf if it is to become a real partner, in spirit as well as in name.

Of course, some Americans remain ambivalent about encouraging Europe to become a major strategic partner actively engaged in managing new international security challenges elsewhere. They fear that allied priorities will not be the same, or that such a partnership would unduly constrain US policy, and that Washington would inevitably lose influence as the result of a more active Europe. Even among Americans who favour such a European role, there are serious doubts that it is feasible. They fear the United States runs the risk of giving up its freedom for unilateral action, while getting little in return.

In fact, while Americans often complain about Europe's strategic myopia, Washington has not yet made a serious effort to engage it on these issues, make NATO's double enlargement a top priority, or propose – let alone build – a new transatlantic relationship that would strike a new balance between 'keeping Europe stable' and managing shared security concerns elsewhere. Indeed, a quick look at US defence planning suggests that Washington currently does not expect its NATO allies to play a major role in future contingencies beyond Europe.

But political and fiscal pressures to do so in the future may be building. To be sure, Washington will always be reluctant to limit its freedom of action, traditionally used to protect America's own interests and take the lead in rallying coalitions around common causes. Many will continue to argue that the US must simply pay the premium of leadership and be willing to act alone if the natural coalition of Western powers does not come together. But America has also long since accepted the constraints and obligations of coalitions and alliances. There is no reason for assuming a priori that it would fail to do so in dealing with future crises – so long as the real benefits are present and visible. To be sure, leaders in Washington will have to build the case and explain any benefits of such new arrangements to their voters. It will help if they can show that our European allies are willing and able to participate in a broader partnership that produces better outcomes at lower cost than the US could achieve by itself.

A fifth important precondition for forging this new US–European strategic partnership is a shared strategic culture on both sides of the Atlantic when it comes to perceiving and addressing potential threats, such as was effectively forged during the Cold War, when NATO deterred Soviet pressure. Whether and how such a culture might be replicated or expanded to include the new challenges of double enlargement seems less clear.

Following two world wars, the US came to realize that its interests needed protecting not only at American borders or shores, but often at some distance. This strategic culture rests on the recognized need for military intervention, the forward deployment of (at times) substantial numbers of troops in foreign countries, and a willingness to assume the costs of leadership. A different set of factors and historical experiences has moulded Europe's strategic culture. The Cold War turned the mindset of its key powers inward. Their colonial legacy left some of these countries ambivalent about using force overseas. For many Europeans, moreover, history taught the futility of striving for geopolitical gain and employing armed power. Except for France and Britain, which retain small but potent expeditionary capabilities to protect national interests beyond their shores, the military establishments of most European countries are geared exclusively toward territorial defence.

Moreover, prejudices exist on both sides of the Atlantic. Europeans today see the United States as prone to over-rely on military force, as opposed to political and economic instruments. Many fear being pulled into a US-led coalition in which they will have little influence over the conduct of actual strategy, their role reduced to that of cannon fodder. Americans, in turn, see Europeans as fixated on commercial gain and either blind or oblivious to the important strategic ramifications of their actions. Bridging this gap would be an important step towards broadening a shared strategic culture, where allies define problems and policy solutions within a common framework.

Many Europeans have also come to assume a division of labour whereby they take on a leading role in terms of 'soft power', leaving the lion's share of 'hard power' burdens in international security to the superpower. They are comfortable with the notion of Europe as a 'civilian power'.[23] While criticizing how the US acts, they show little inclination to assume greater responsibility, let alone a more active effort to supplant American power. Many Europeans have managed to convince themselves of the merits of such a division of labour, neglecting or overlooking the fact that the US has never agreed to it and that most Americans – if asked – would find such an arrangement offensive and unacceptable in moral, political and economic terms.

Germany, a classic 'civilian power' throughout the postwar era, illustrates this problem. For Europe to emerge as a more cohesive, powerful, strategic partner for America requires that the Federal Republic change in important ways. To some extent, this is already happening. Germany has moved further and faster in assuming greater responsibilities, including those in the military realm, than many observers expected. Yet there is an ongoing debate between advocates of 'normalization', who insist the country assume the same obligations as other states in the international community, and others who already accuse the Bonn government of 'remilitarizing' its foreign policy and instead propose restricting its role to that of a civilian power.[24]

Finally, these diverse strategic cultures have left the US and Europe with very different military establishments that would also need to be harmonized. Though intimate partners for nearly half a century, their forces are badly matched for addressing the challenges of double enlargement. The American defence budget is not built around the principle of territorial defence. It totals some $260 billion, the tiniest fraction of which is spent on territorial defence. Most outlays go for power projection capabilities to defend values and interests overseas.

Most European military establishments face almost the reverse situation. The vast majority of their budgets focused on territorial defences during the Cold War.[25] They remain poorly equipped to carry out any mission requiring projection of significant power – be it, say, interregional reinforcement for Poland in an enlarged NATO, or a mission beyond, to the Persian Gulf, for example. To be sure, defence establishments in countries like France and Britain do have a broader outlook and some capabilities, while Germany has embarked on a major conceptual overhaul of its armed forces to create a modest but potent capability for deploying rapid reaction forces overseas with its allies.[26] Yet what is really needed – and still lacking – is a much more systematic, programmatic effort to boost European capabilities along these lines.

CONCLUSION

In some ways, the Atlantic Alliance is already inching, or being driven, toward the concept of 'double enlargement' laid out earlier in this chapter. The EU and NATO have embraced the goal of opening to new democracies in Europe's eastern half, while developing initiatives for reaching out beyond the current membership's southern borders to stabilize contiguous areas. NATO has expanded its functions – not only in paper communiqués, but on the ground in a conflict-torn region. For the first time in Alliance history, its forces have entered combat – not to defend Central Europe against a massive Soviet attack, but rather in an 'out-of-area' mission aimed at implementing a Balkan peace plan, quelling nationalism and preventing the spread of instability.

As important and impressive as these steps have appeared, however, they amount at best to a truncated version of 'double enlargement'.

Despite the need for a new, expanded transatlantic dialogue on strategic challenges to common interests on the continent and beyond, this discussion has remained focused primarily on managing security in Europe. Such a limited approach ignores the fact that the key to keeping America engaged even in familiar roles may lie in Washington having allies willing and able to form a broader, more equitable partnership that addresses the full spectrum of shared interests, not only in Europe but also beyond. In short, the best way to help secure US international engagement is not through an endless string of communiqués reiterating that desire, but rather by Europeans taking on more responsibility, joining America in addressing risks or threats to shared interests wherever they may arise.

Does this ask too much? Is it too hard? People often inquire what would be done differently under such a bargain, how specifically the US and Europe would benefit. The answer is simple and straight forward: there is no single scenario where America and its allies would not be better off with such a new bargain. Had such an arrangement been in place in the early 1990s, for example, NATO would have been able to act earlier and more decisively in ending the war in the former Yugoslavia. Looking ahead, the Alliance would also be better prepared politically, especially in a ratification debate in the US Senate, to manage what is likely to be a difficult process of eastward enlargement. It would also be in better shape to deal with other possible contingencies, ranging from some new crisis in the Persian Gulf to proliferation issues. Common sense tells us that we would be in better shape facing real threats to the shared vital interests of the United States and Europe in this post-Cold War period.

Building a new partnership will require leadership – on both sides of the Atlantic – of the kind and quality that produced NATO early in the Cold War. As daunting as this challenge might appear, perhaps the greatest cause for optimism is a simple realization that forging any such bargain is clearly in the shared interests of both the United States and Europe.

NOTES

1.   In Germany, for example, support for NATO is once again at levels as high if not higher than during the Cold War. Some 92 per cent of the German elite believe NATO to be essential for German security. See Ronald D. Asmus, 'Kein Kult der Zurückhaltung mehr', *Frankfurter*

Allgemeine Zeitung, 11 April 1996; and Germany's Geopolitical Matura-
tion: Public Opinion and Security Policy in 1994 (Santa Monica, CA:
RAND, MR-608-FNF/OSD/A/AF 1995).

2. For further details on this argument see Ronald D. Asmus, Robert D.
    Blackwill and F. Stephen Larrabee, 'Can NATO Survive?' Washington
    Quarterly, 19, no. 2 (Spring 1996) 79–101.

3. As Lawrence Freedman wrote in 1993: 'The underlying assumption of
    the early designs for the European order was that the benefits of the
    Western political system and economic system would gradually be
    extended eastwards as the new states adopted liberal constitutions and
    market reforms.... However, the faltering of the integrative push in the
    West and the strength of the disintegrative tendencies in the East have
    suggested a contrary possibility. Crudely extrapolated, this produces an
    almost apocalyptic image of inexorable fragmentation disrupting what
    had been assumed to be some of the world's most ordered and advanced
    societies.' See Lawrence Freedman, Strategic Studies and the New Eur-
    ope, in European Security after the Cold War, Part I, Conference Papers,
    Adelphi Papers, no. 284 (London: International Institute for Strategic
    Studies, January 1994), 15–27.

4. For further details see Ronald D. Asmus, F. Stephen Larrabee and Ian
    O. Lesser, 'Mediterranean Security: New Challenges, New Tasks',
    NATO Review, 44, no. 3 (May 1996), 25–31.

5. See Josef Joffe, 'Europe's American Pacifier', Foreign Policy, 54 (Spring
    1984), 64–82.

6. For further details, see Philip Zelikow and Condoleeza Rice, Germany
    Unified and Europe Transformed: A Study in Statecraft (Cambridge,
    Mass.: Harvard University Press, 1995).

7. For further details on French motivations see Robert P. Grant, 'Fran-
    ce's New Relationship with NATO', Survival, 38, no. 1 (Spring 1996),
    58–80.

8. One of the most vocal and eloquent spokesmen for this point of view
    has been German Defence Minister Volker Rühe. For Rühe's thinking
    see Volker Rühe, Deutschlands Verantwortung. Perspektiven für das neue
    Europa (Berlin: Ullstein Verlag, 1994).

9. See Richard C. Holbrooke, 'America, a European Power', Foreign
    Affairs, 74 (March-April 1995), 38–51.

10. See Les Aspin's The Bottom-Up Review: Forces for a New Era (Washing-
    ton DC: Department of Defense, 1 September 1993).

11. See James T. Thomson, 'Back to Square 1 with Einstein', Los Angeles
    Times, 21 March 1995.

12. Jeremy D. Rosner, 'NATO Enlargement's American Hurdle', Foreign
    Affairs, 75 (July-August 1996), 9–15.

13. See Volker Rühe, 'Shaping Euro-Atlantic Policies: A Grand Strategy for
    a New Era', Survival, 35, no. 2 (Summer 1993), 135–6. See also Ronald
    D. Asmus, Richard L. Kugler and F. Stephen Larrabee, 'Building a
    New NATO', Foreign Affairs, 72 (September-October 1993), 28–40.
    Senator Richard Lugar, 'American Leadership in the Post Cold-War
    World' (speech presented at a meeting of the Overseas Writers' Club,
    Washington, DC, 24 June 1993).

14. A survey conducted by Infratest Burke Berlin for the Friedrich Nau-
mann Foundation in late 1995, for example, found that 76 per cent of
the German elite supported NATO enlargement. For further details, see
Asmus, 'Kein Kult der Zurückhaltung'.

15. It was Adenauer's determination to put the stabilization of German
democracy along these lines ahead of the goal of national unity that
was, of course, at the heart of his dispute not only with Kurt Schuma-
cher but with rivals within his own party such as Jacob Kaiser. See
Hans-Peter Schwarz, *Adenauer, Der Aufstieg: 1876–1952* (Stuttgart:
Deutsche Verlags- Anstalt, 1986); and *Adenauer, Der Staatsmann:
1952–1967* (Stuttgart: Deutsche Verlags-Anstalt, 1991).

16. Janusz Reiter, Warsaw's Ambassador in Bonn, has drawn the parallel
with the postwar experience of the Federal Republic and emphasized the
need to 'tie' Poland to the West just like post-war West Germany was
firmly embedded in Western structures to guarantee that it remained on
a pro-Western course. Such a move, according to Reiter, was not
directed against Russia, but rather was designed to stabilize German
democracy against instability and nationalism. In the words of Reiter:
'Poland has a bad track record in terms of dealing with its geopolitical
situation. Just like Germany drew the conclusion from its own history
after the Second World War, namely that it had to be firmly integrated
into reliable structures, Poland today has drawn the same conclusion
from its history.' See Reiter's interview in the *Rheinischer Merkur*, 26
November 1993.

17. In the Bundestag debate following the January 1994 NATO summit,
German Defence Minister Volker Rühe remarked: 'What has bothered
me in the debate that we have been having for the last year are those
who have behaved like the judges handing out scores at a figure
skating contest. Let's wait a few years, they insist, to see if the
new democracies really qualify for membership and whether their
democracies are really stable after all. This or the other election,
after all, didn't turn out so well, and we don't know yet how economic
reform in Poland will turn out. I have to say that this is an incredible
attitude to take. We should think about our own postwar history. I
am convinced that the successful stabilization of our democracy
and economy in postwar Germany was at best half due to our own
efforts. The rest was the result of our early integration as full members
of the European Union and NATO. We Germans should never forget
that.' See Rühe's Bundestag speech reprinted in *Das Parlament*, no. 3
(21 January 1994).

18. Ibid.

19. For further details on the debate over the rationale and how this affects
the modalities of NATO enlargement, see Ronald D. Asmus, Richard L.
Kugler and F. Stephen Larrabee, 'NATO Enlargement: The Next
Steps', *Survival*, 37, no. 1 (Spring 1995), 7–33.

20. For some thoughts on how to deal with the Baltic states, see Ronald D.
Asmus and Robert Nurick, 'NATO Enlargement and the Baltic States',
Survival, 38, no. 2 (Summer 1996), 121–42; and F. Stephen Larrabee,
'Ukraine's Balancing Act', *Survival*, 38, no. 2 (Summer 1996), 143–65.

21.   See Ronald D. Asmus, Richard Kugler and F. Stephen Larrabee, 'What Will NATO Enlargement Cost?' *Survival*, 38, no. 3 (Autumn 1996), 6–26.

22.   For further details see Asmus, Blackwill, Larrabee, 'Can NATO Survive?'

23.   See Hanns W. Maull, 'Zivilmacht Bundesrepublik Deutschland. Vierzehn Thesen für eine neue deutsche Aussenpolitik', *Europa Archiv*, 10 (1992), 269–78.

24.   Some critics on the left go so far as to claim that 'normalization' will end up a slippery slope toward the remilitarization and renationalization of German society and a political shift toward the right. While such concerns are, in the view of at least this author, wildly exaggerated, they underscore the maze of problems which still need to be addressed. See, for example, Peter Glotz, *Die falsche Normalisierung, Essays* (Frankfurt a.M.: Suhrkamp Verlag, 1994). Former Foreign Minister Hans-Dietrich Genscher, who initially opposed an expanded role for the Bundeswehr at the end of the Cold War, is also reported to have harboured private concerns that a greater military role for Germany could lead to a shift to the right in German politics. In his memoirs, Genscher talks repeatedly about the dangers of a revival of destructive nationalism in European politics. See Hans-Dietrich Genscher, *Erinnerungen* (Berlin: Siedler Verlag, 1995).

25.   See Richard L. Kugler, *US-West European Co-operation in Out-of-Area Military Operations: Problems and Prospects* (Santa Monica, CA: RAND, MR-349–USDP 1994); and John E. Peters and Howard Deshong, *Out of Area or Out of Reach?* (Santa Monica, CA: RAND, MR-629–OSD 1995).

26.   For further details on the restructuring of the Bundeswehr see Ronald D. Asmus, *Germany's Contribution to Peacekeeping: Issues and Outlook* (Santa Monica: RAND, MR-602-OSD 1995).

5 East Central Europe: Problems, Prospects and Policy Dilemmas

F. Stephen Larrabee

Since the collapse of communism, the countries of East Central Europe have made substantial progress towards the establishment of stable democratic systems and the creation of market economics.[1] There are growing signs that the region – especially the three 'fast track' countries of Hungary, Poland and the Czech Republic – has begun to emerge from the recession that followed initial efforts to move toward market reform in 1990–1991.[2] Growth rates have increased, while inflation has dropped significantly; privatization has also taken root. As of 1996, sixty to seventy per cent of the region's economy was in private hands. Trade has been reoriented toward the industrial countries of the West. States in the region now conduct over half their trade with the European Union (EU). Foreign direct investment has also risen steadily, with Hungary leading the way.

THE POST-COMMUNIST RESURGENCE

The transitions in East Central Europe, however, are far from complete or irreversible. Indeed, Eastern Europe – and East Central Europe in particular – has witnessed a certain sense of 'reform fatigue'. Post-communist parties have made a comeback throughout the region, regaining power in Lithuania, Poland, Hungary and Bulgaria. This trend has caused concern in some Western capitals. This shift to the left in East Central Europe, however, needs to be seen in perspective. It does not reflect a longing for a return to Communism as much as it does disenchantment with the economic and social impact of reform. Many East Europeans had got used to what Wojciech Gebicki and Anna Marta Gebicka have aptly termed 'the nanny state' in which the individual could, to a large extent, dispense with personal responsibility and leave everything to 'the system'.[3] Free education and health care, as well as lifelong security, were taken for granted. This 'culture of entitlement' was reinforced by exaggerated expectations of a rapid transition to economic prosperity, associated in the minds of public in Eastern Europe with Western-style democracy and a flourishing market economy. Thus, many East Europeans were psychologically ill-prepared for the harsh dislocations that accompanied the collapse of Communism and the transition to a market economy.

Post-Communist parties were able to capitalize on this disenchantment and turn it to their political advantage, especially in Poland and Hungary. This does not mean, however, that East Central Europe is heading back toward communism. Far from it. The post-Communist parties in Poland and Hungary are strongly committed to the development of a market economy and ties to Western institutions. Indeed, in some cases, they have pushed these policies faster than their predecessors. In Hungary, for example, there was considerable concern when Prime Minister Gyula Horn fired the liberal Minister of Finance Laszlo Bekasi and replaced him with Lajos Bokros. Many Western observers also saw Bekasi's ouster as an indication that the Horn government was backtracking on reform. But Bokros implemented an austerity programme that went further than Bekasi's.

Similarly, in Poland, Finance Minister Gregorz Kolodko's economic programme was essentially a continuation of the reform programme carried out by the centre-left government of Hanna Suchocka. The main opposition came from Solidarity, which objected to many of the tough austerity measures. These cases underscore the way in which old categories and ways of thinking no longer fit the new realities in East Central Europe.

Nor should observers simply dismiss leaders of the post-Communist parties as 'Communist retreads'. Many, like Horn, had already begun to undergo a political evolution in the late 1970s and 1980s, well before the Berlin Wall fell. As Foreign Minister in the last Communist government, he played a key role in precipitating the Wall's eventual collapse: it was his decision in the fall of 1989 to allow the transit of East German citizens to West Germany that set in motion a mass exodus, eventually precipitating the disintegration of the GDR and ultimately the unification of Germany.

Generational factors have also played a role in the post-Communist resurgence. Many of its younger leaders were too young to be closely associated with the policies of the pre-1989 regimes. They have successfully shed their Communist backgrounds and projected themselves as young, forward-thinking technocrats more concerned about the future, while their democratic opponents have often appeared to be still fighting the ghosts and battles of the past. Poland represents a case in point. In the Presidential election of November 1995, Alexander Kwasniewski, leader of the Democratic Left Coalition (SDL) and a former minister in the Jaruzelski government, consciously sought to portray himself as a modern social democrat concerned with the future, whereas Lech Wałęsa often seemed to have little to offer except his anti-Communist credentials.

In short, the success of post-Communist parties in East Central Europe has more to do with a desire to preserve certain aspects of the 'nanny state' and cushion the shock of reform than with a desire to see the return of Communism. This trend should be seen as a natural part of the evolution towards democracy. The 'reform fatigue' currently evident in East Central Europe is not unique. Other countries undergoing transitions from authoritarian to democratic rule have witnessed similar problems. Spain, for instance, faced such a period of public disillusionment and disenchantment (*desencanto*) in the late 1970s as it sought to consolidate the transformation made possible by Franco's death.[4] Nevertheless, the post-Communist resurgence provides an important reminder of the fragility of the social consensus in East Central Europe, and how far these transitions must still progress before they too become fully consolidated.

ECONOMIC REFORM AND POLITICAL CONSOLIDATION: A BALANCE SHEET

The three East Central European countries have made important steps toward creating the foundations of stable democratic systems and market economies. The pace and modalities of reform, however, have varied from country to country – as has the degree of success.

The Czech Republic has led the pack. Under the leadership of Prime Minister Vaclav Klaus, head of the right-centre Civic Democratic Party (ODS), it has made steady progress towards market reform and political stability. In 1995 the Czech economy witnessed a four per cent growth rate, which many expected to keep rising. Inflation dropped to under ten per cent and unemployment to about three per cent – the lowest in Eastern Europe. At nearly eighty per cent, the private sector share of the Czech Republic's GDP is the highest in East Central Europe. Prague has also introduced the most extensive large-scale privatization programme in the region, and in November 1995 became the first post-Communist state in Eastern

Europe to join the Organization for Economic Cooperation and Development (OECD).

The success of Klaus's reform programme has prevented the emergence of the type of popular dissatisfaction that propelled post-Communist parties back to power elsewhere in East Central Europe. However, many of the hardest tests for the Czech economy still lie in the future. Unemployment remains low, for instance, partly because of the government's reluctance to implement a tough bankruptcy law, perpetuating hidden joblessness. A tougher policy toward bankruptcies could increase unemployment. Similarly, the privatization programme has been less successful than it appeared at first glance. Big banks, many of them state-owned, still hold a large portion of the privatized equity. Czech industry also remains highly inefficient. Thus, the Czech 'economic miracle' may lose some of its lustre once the full impact of the reforms begins to hit and as the country becomes more integrated into the world market.

After a difficult start, Poland's policy of shock therapy is beginning to show results. In 1994 and 1995 the economy witnessed a five per cent growth rate – the highest in Eastern Europe. This boom was led by an impressive increase in investment and exports rather than domestic consumption. Privatization has also expanded significantly. More than sixty per cent of the Polish work force is now employed in the private sector, which produces more than 65 per cent of the country's GDP. This turnaround has begun to attract increased foreign investment. Indeed, some economists believe that Poland, not the Czech Republic, will emerge as the real economic tiger in the region over the long run.

Poland's political transition, however, has been less smooth. The ruling coalition between the Peasant Party and the Democratic Left Coalition (SDL) has been racked by infighting, hindering the development of a coherent economic and social policy. Former President Walęsa's continued attempts to systematically weaken the ruling coalition and increase his own political stature and electoral prospects only compounded these problems. These tactics resulted in a continuous battle with the government and parliament, inhibiting the implementation of a coherent reform programme. Moreover, Walęsa's efforts while in office to weaken the Minister of Defence and bring the armed forces under the direct control of the President undercut previous efforts to establish civilian control of the military, damaging Poland's image in the West. Indeed, by the end of his tenure, many Poles – including many former colleagues in Solidarity – had come to view him more as a threat to democracy than as its protector. These developments led to a significant drop in Wałęsa's popularity and his eventual loss of the presidential election to SLD leader Kwasniewski. However, as noted earlier, Kwasniewski's election did not signal Poland's return to Soviet-style Communism. He campaigned as a Western-style Social Democrat and as the man most capable of leading his country into a new, modern era. During the campaign, he pledged to continue to press for Poland's integration into NATO and the EU. His election has thus not resulted in any pronounced shift in Poland's basic foreign policy orientation. Indeed, Kwasniewski has pushed closer ties to NATO and the EU as firmly as his predecessors in order to dispel any doubts about his pro-Western credentials.

On the domestic side, Kwasniewski's election has had important positive effects. First, and most important, it has ended the divisive power struggle between the President and government that marked Wałęsa's tenure, and also facilitated a smoother working relationship between the head of state and the Parliament. Unlike Wałęsa, Kwasniewski has not engaged in a constant effort to block legislation and destabilize the government. Aware of widespread concerns that all three branches of government – parliament, executive and presidency – are in the hands of former Communists, Kwasniewski has sought to transcend partisan politics rather than merely exploit the Presidency to help his own SLD.

Civil–military relations have also improved. Unlike Wałęsa, Kwasniewski supports the subordination of the General Staff to the Minister of Defence rather than the President. In addition, he has shown a readiness to replace some of the top officers on the General Staff who favoured greater autonomy for the military. These moves should end the destructive infighting over who controls the military that poisoned civil–military relations under Wałęsa. Such developments would also be welcomed in the West and enhance Poland's chances of obtaining NATO membership.

Finally, Kwasniewski's election has facilitated the passage of a new constitution – a long-delayed reform that will contribute to greater domestic stability over the long run. The task of drawing up the budget and pressing ahead with planned reform of the health and social-security systems – two top government priorities – has also proven easier.

Hungary's transition has proven somewhat uneven. On the political side, it has occurred relatively smoothly. The foundations of a stable democracy have been established and the extreme right – which a few years ago seemed likely to pose a political threat – has been marginalized. A broad consensus on foreign policy exists, especially on Hungary's membership in the EU and NATO. Relations with Hungary's immediate neighbours have also improved.

Hungary's economic transition, however, has proven more problematic. The Hungarian Democratic Forum (MFD), led by former Prime Minister Joszef Antall, adopted a more gradual approach to reform than the governments in Poland or the Czech Republic. Nevertheless, the reform programme created severe dislocations: Hungary witnessed a sharp drop in living standards, growing inequality of incomes and a sharp rise in public dissatisfaction with reform.[5] This growing disenchantment with reform eroded support for the MDF and enabled the Hungarian Socialist Party (HSP) under Horn to win an overwhelming victory in the May 1994 elections. The return of the Socialists prompted concern that the government might slow down economic reform. However, after some initial hesitation, it launched a tough austerity programme in March 1995. These austerity measures have contributed to a revival of the Hungarian economy.[6] The budget and current-account deficits have fallen and inflation has dropped slightly. However, Hungary's high indebtedness still remains a problem, as does the high percentage of GDP spent on welfare.

Continuity has marked Hungarian foreign policy as well. Like its predecessors, the Horn government has given top priority to Western integration, especially membership in the EU and NATO. The one real change has occurred in its approach to the issue Hungarian minorities in neighbouring states. In contrast to the MDF, Horn's government has downplayed the controversy, giving higher priority to reduced tensions with Slovakia and Romania. A bilateral treaty was signed with Slovakia in March 1995, though differences over treatment of the Hungarian minority continue to affect relations.[7] Relations with Romania have also gradually improved. The two countries concluded a long-delayed bilateral treaty in August 1996.

Of all the four East Central European countries, Slovakia has made the least progress toward creating a stable democratic system and market economy. In fact, the pace of economic and political reform has slowed since Prime Minister Vladimir Meciar's return to power in September, 1994.[8] His government has cut back the mass privatization program initiated earlier and increased the role of the state in the economy. Meciar has also sought to curb the independence of the media and engaged in an open effort to oust President Michal

Kovac. These developments have damaged Slovakia's chances for early membership in the EU and NATO.[9]

MILITARY REFORM AND DEFENCE POLICY

Since the collapse of Communism, governments in East Central Europe have carried out an extensive process of military reform, the extent and depth of which have varied from country to country.[10] The Czech Republic's has been the most extensive, whereas Slovakia's is still in its embryonic stage. All the countries of the region, however, face severe budgetary constraints that inhibit their ability to carry out reforms.

Civilian control of the military also remains a problem.[11] Here again the pace and extent of reform has varied. It has gone the furthest in the Czech Republic, which carried out an extensive purge of the top officer corps, and has put civilians in many of the major policy-making posts at the Ministry of Defence. Reform has been most problematic in Poland, largely due to former President Wałęsa's effort to weaken the position of the Minister of Defence and subordinate the military directly to the head of state. Hungary made some early progress, but initially showed some signs of backsliding after the Socialist Party's return to power in May 1994. In Slovakia, civilian control barely exists. Moreover, Mecier's Minister of Defence belonged to the ultra-nationalist Slovak Nationalist Party. In all the countries, however, civilian control of the military remains superficial and often does not extend much below the deputy minister or state secretary level. Most civilian appointees do not have deep or detailed knowledge of defence issues, and they remain dependent on the military for advice and analysis. There is no 'counter-elite' or cadre of civilian specialists who can challenge the military's views and provide an alternative viewpoint, such as exists in the United States and many countries of Western Europe. This vacuum has inhibited the establishment of effective civilian control over the military.

All the East Central European countries have reduced and restructured their militaries. The Czech Republic has probably made the most progress. Personnel and equipment from the former Czechoslovak army were divided on a two-to-one basis when the federation became two separate states in January, 1993. The new Czech army has been radically reduced and restructured, from a force of 106,477 men at the time of the split to about 65,000 by 1995 – a forty per cent reduction. About half of these were professionals. Czech ground troops, which numbered about 43,000 in June 1993, were cut by one-third to about 28,000 men by 1995. The old system based on divisions was to be replaced by a brigade-based system. The new structure will consist of the following:

– A Territorial Defense Force of fifteen brigades, with each brigade operated in peacetime by only a skeletal garrison;
– An Expeditionary Force, composed of seven mechanized brigades, four in Bohemia and three in Moravia;
– A Rapid Deployment Force, made up of one brigade of 3,000 men, which will be compatible with NATO units.

Military restructuring, however, has had to come in an atmosphere of economic austerity, putting severe constraints on resources that could be devoted to defence. Financial limits, for instance, initially led the Czech Ministry of Defense to decide to modernize its fleet of MiG-21s, rather than buy used F-16s, as Poland is considering. However, many Czech parliamentarians and experts strongly criticized this decision, and the Ministry later suspended it. Financial concerns also appear to be inducing the Czechs to take a more positive attitude toward defence co-operation with their Visegrad neighbours, particularly regarding the co-production of fighter aircraft.[12]

Poland's military has also undergone a significant restructuring. A new draft doctrine was announced in July 1992. It calls for creating a relatively small military force – about 200,000 regular troops, or 0.5 per cent of the population – and National Guard units. The doctrine also reiterates Poland's determination to seek membership in NATO and the West European Union (WEU).[13] In connection with this reoriented defence doctrine, Poland has expanded the number of its military districts from three to four (two in the east and two in the west), and has begun to redeploy forces, stationing more troops in the east.[14] However, this process requires building a costly new infrastructure, and the country faces a severe budgetary crunch. Thus, Poland can only implement these changes gradually. In addition, the new doctrine emphasizes developing lighter, more mobile forces that can react quickly to local conflicts, especially with immediate neighbours.

In carrying out its military reform programme, Poland has placed a high priority on upgrading equipment and making it compatible with NATO's, as well as preparing for joint peacekeeping missions with the Alliance. A first peacekeeping battalion was ready by the end of 1995. According to Polish officials, it will be fully compatible with NATO command-and- control, operational and equipment standards.[15]

Upgrading its air defence system and modernizing its air force are also top priorities for Poland. As part of a five-year modernization plan, it is currently shopping around for replacements for two hundred MiG-21s, which have to be scrapped because they are obsolete and can be neither updated nor modified. Like the Czech Republic, Poland has also considered buying used F-16s. However, because of their high cost, Warsaw is investigating possible ways of sharing production costs with other Visegrad countries, particularly the Czech Republic.

Strong economic constraints have inhibited the military reform and modernization process in Poland. Defence spending has declined by 38 per cent in real terms since 1986. As a share of gross domestic product (GDP), it fell from 3.2 per cent in 1986 to 1.9 per cent in 1993.[16] As a result, little money has been allocated for procuring new weapons: only eleven per cent of the defence budget went for procurement in 1993.

Perhaps the biggest obstacle to reform, however, was the constant infighting between President Wałęsa and a series of defence ministers over control of the armed forces in the early 1990s.[17] This bickering not only weakened effective control over the military, but also inhibited implementation of a coherent reform programme. However, as noted above, these problems have significantly diminished with Wałęsa out of office.

In March 1993, Hungary adopted a new defence doctrine, which attempts to bring the country's military force structure and tasks into harmony with its post-Cold War national interests. The doctrine emphasizes that Hungary has no 'main enemy', and that the task of its military forces is solely defensive. Small- scale incursions, provocations, and violations of national airspace are identified as the most likely threats. In case of general war or large-scale aggression, these principles leave open the possibility of outside assistance by friendly states. To handle possible small-scale incursions by neighbouring states, Hungary is developing a rapid-reaction force. Border guards, under the Ministry of the Interior, are also being augmented, and a special centre for training peacekeeping forces has been established. The army has also been reorganized into three regional commands. Hungarian forces, deployed primarily in the west under the old Warsaw Pact system, will be distributed more or less equally over the country, with highest-readiness forces in areas most likely to face attack, such as the south. The army has also been reduced from a high of 150,000 troops in 1989 to about 90,000 by the end of 1995. It is expected to be down to 60,000 by 1998 and 50,000 by the year 2005.[18]

Hungary has also launched an ambitious ten-year program to revamp its antiquated air defence network. The first phase began in 1995 and will be completed in the year 2000. The second phase, beginning in 2000, will be completed by 2005. The programme is designed to reinforce early-warning radar capabilities along Hungary's southern border and prepare the country for a contributing role in NATO.

Slovakia has just begun to develop its own armed forces and military concept. The new Slovak army is expected to comprise about 35,000 men – less than half the size of its current Hungarian counterpart. As a part of the division of military assets when Czechoslovakia split, Slovakia received ten MiG-29s. It acquired five more from Russia at the end of 1993 as an offset against Moscow's debt. However, Slovak airfields are incapable of handling these and other combat aircraft. The country also lacks a viable air defence system.

REGIONAL CO-OPERATION

The initial period after the collapse of Communism saw a marked growth of and more interest in regional co-operation within East Central Europe. The most prominent example was the Visegrad group, formally established in February 1991. Originally composed of Hungary, Poland and Czechoslovakia, the group came to include the Czech Republic and Slovakia after the two became independent states on January 1, 1993. Co-operation was largely ad hoc and informal, initially designed to co-ordinate an approach to Western institutions, especially the European Community.

By the mid-1990s, however, co-operation within the Visegrad group had stagnated, largely due to resistance and opposition on the part of the Czech Republic. Prime Minister Vaclav Klaus has consistently expressed doubts about the utility and efficacy of such co-operation, which he fears will inhibit his country's integration into the European Union. As a result of the Czech 'go-it-alone' strategy, Visegrad has become little more than a free trade zone. Nevertheless, the group plays a useful role in co-ordinating trade policies and promoting closer economic co-operation.

In October 1995, Slovenia became a full member of the Central European Free Trade Zone (CEFTA). Its inclusion could offer a new impetus to co-operation within the group, especially in the economic area. At the same time, this move reflected Slovenia's effort to distance itself from its Balkan neighbours and develop stronger ties with Europe. Slovenia has made significant progress toward the creation of a strong market economy and a stable democratic system since its departure from the former Yugoslav federation in June 1991. Moreover, it has more in common culturally, economically, and politically with the Visegrad countries than with other members of the former Yugoslavia or countries in the Balkans. For example, Slovenia has the highest per capita income in all of Eastern or Central Europe. Thus, its inclusion in CEFTA makes political and economic sense. This step also enhances its chances of obtaining membership in the EU and NATO down the line.

Co-operation within the Central European Initiative (CEI), another important regional organization, has also languished. Originally formed in 1978 to co-ordinate co-operation between the border regions of Yugoslavia, Italy, Germany (Bavaria), Austria and later Hungary, the CEI – initially called the Alpen-Adria Co-operation – was expanded in May 1990 to include Czechoslovakia. A year later Poland joined. In July 1992 Croatia, Slovenia and Bosnia-Herzegovina signed on, while in July 1993 Macedonia became a member. Conflict in the former Yugoslavia, however, has seriously retarded co-operation. In addition, an ongoing political crisis in Italy – one of the group's original promoters – has reduced Rome's interest in actively participating. Finally, co-operation has been hindered by differences over minority issues, especially between Hungary and Slovakia. As a result, the CEI has lost considerable momentum.

To be sure, efforts have been made to give it new life. At Warsaw in October 1995, leaders of the CEI decided to formally invite Ukraine, Belarus, Romania, Bulgaria and Albania to join the group at an upcoming meeting, and pledged to assist in the reconstruction of Bosnia and Croatia.[19] They also agreed to set up a new information and documentation centre in Trieste, financed by Italy. The CEI thus provides a useful means for linking countries like Ukraine, Romania, Bulgaria and Albania more closely to European and regional structures. But its influence is likely to remain modest. The group has little money of its own and depends almost entirely on funding by outside sources such as the World Bank and the European Bank for Reconstruction and Development (EBRD). Moreover, the Czech Republic has remained reluctant to 'institutionalize' co-operation, an attitude likely to inhibit any significant deepening of co-operation.

THE RUSSIAN FACTOR

Russian policy toward East Central Europe has stagnated visibly since 1991. In the initial period after the break-up of the former Soviet Union, Moscow was preoccupied with the problems of internal consolidation and essentially adopted a policy of 'benign neglect' toward the region. Indeed, Russia initially seemed to have no coherent policy toward East Central Europe at all. President Boris Yeltsin's policy largely consisted of ad hoc initiatives designed to settle outstanding issues left over from the Soviet period, particularly resolution of debt questions. His government made little effort to develop an overarching policy toward the region as a whole.[20]

Since then, however, Russia has begun to define its interests toward Eastern Europe more clearly. This has manifested itself above all in an effort to block NATO enlargement. During his visit to Warsaw in August 1993, President Yeltsin implied that Russia would be willing to accept Polish membership in the Alliance, but a few weeks later – apparently under strong domestic pressure – reversed this view. Since then, Moscow has consistently opposed East European membership in NATO. In effect, Russia appears to want to keep East Central Europe as a neutral buffer zone, or at least deny its political–military potential to the West as long as possible.

This resistance is seen by many East Central Europeans, especially the Poles, as proof that Moscow has not entirely given up its desire to retain some residual influence over their security options. Moreover, elites in the region have grown worried by Russia's more assertive policy toward the Baltic countries and 'near abroad'. While they recognize that Russia is too weak at the moment to pose a real security threat to their security, they fear that Western hesitation and vacillation over NATO enlargement could encourage Moscow to exert greater political pressure. At the same time, they see membership of NATO as an important 'insurance policy' against the emergence of a resurgent Russia.

This concern is particularly evident in Warsaw. Polish leaders see Russia's main goal as the creation of a belt of economically and politically weak states in the region, until such time as it is strong enough to redraw spheres of influence there.[21] They worry that further Western vacillation and equivocation regarding NATO enlargement will reinforce instability in the region and encourage Moscow to step up its efforts to block enlargement. Alternatively, these moves could stimulate a strong anti-Russian backlash in Poland and throughout the region. Either scenario would spark instability and tension, with negative repercussions for Poland's security and that of other countries.

For Poland, moreover, Kaliningrad – formerly Königsberg – poses a specific problem. After World War II, the Soviets turned this enclave into a huge military base closed to all foreigners, and the area remains highly militarized. Polish officials regard the large concentration of Russian troops, many in a high state of readiness, as a political security problem. They would like to see the Kaliningrad district demilitarized or, failing that, a significant reduction in the number and combat-readiness of Russian forces.

However, this seems unlikely in the near future. Many of the troops in Kaliningrad were withdrawn from Eastern Europe, Germany and the Baltic areas. Given Russia's own acute housing shortage, it has nowhere to put them. Moreover, the loss of air and naval facilities in the Baltic states has increased Kaliningrad's military significance to Moscow. Hence, the Russian military is likely to insist on maintaining a sizable military presence in the area. Russian officials have even threatened to increase the level of troops and armaments there as a response to any NATO enlargement, a move that would clearly heighten tensions with Poland.

Since Yeltsin's re-election in June, 1996, Russia has appeared to grudgingly accommodate itself to NATO's enlargement, provided the Alliance does not station foreign combat troops or nuclear weapons on the soil of new members and limits enlargement to Poland, Hungary and the Czech Republic. However, as NATO moves closer to 'naming names', Russia is likely to concentrate more heavily on the military modalities of enlargement and preventing a second stage.

UKRAINE: THE CRITICAL SWING FACTOR

The future of Ukraine – an important geopolitical buffer between Russia and East Central Europe – will also bear heavily on the region's security: the country's reintegration into Russia or a Russian-dominated Commonwealth of Independent States (CIS) would remove that buffer, bringing Moscow's power back to East Central Europe's doorstep. Hence the region has a strong stake in the continued survival of an independent, stable, democratic Ukraine.

If Ukrainian independence became curtailed and it were reincorporated into a 'Russian geographic space', Poland and, to a lesser extent,

Hungary and the Czech Republic would find their political room for manœuvre constrained. Hence, both have made the improvement of relations with Kiev a key element of their foreign policy, and, both have sought to encourage Ukraine's integration into European institutions to the maximum extent possible. Warsaw thus has made a rapprochement with Ukraine the cornerstone of its Eastern policy. Poland was the first country to recognize its neighbour's independence in December, 1991, and bilateral relations between the two countries have developed rapidly since then. In May 1992, they signed a comprehensive Treaty of Friendship and Co-operation, in which each side affirmed the inviolability of frontiers and renounced all territorial claims against the other. Military co-operation has also strengthened. In particular, the two countries have discussed the formation of joint peace-keeping battalion.[22]

However, Poland's ability to affect developments in Ukraine is limited. Given economic constraints, Warsaw does not have the resources or capital to help stabilize its neighbour's economy in any major way. Moreover, Poland must to be careful to avoid giving the impression that it is seeking to build an anti-Russian alliance or axis with Kiev. Both these factors place objective limits on the degree of bilateral collaboration likely to develop, especially in the security field.

So far, Ukraine has refused to join any CIS collective defence arrangements, but pressure on it to do so could increase. Moscow has pushed hard for closer economic and military co- operation within the CIS. In January 1995, Russia signed important agreements with Belarus and Kazakhstan that call for increased economic and security co-operation, including the creation of a Customs Union. And at the CIS summit in Almaty in February 1996, the members discussed setting up a joint air defence system. Ukraine's possible military integration into such a CIS collective security or defence system would have geopolitical significance, depriving East-Central Europe of an important geostrategic buffer and again putting Russian troops on Poland's border. This development, in turn, would intensify pressures to enlarge NATO sooner rather than later.

One other country's future orientation will also have an important impact on the security environment in East Central Europe. Belarus has traditionally served as an invasion corridor to Poland. Hence, Warsaw has strongly supported its eastern neighbour's independence, while also encouraging Minsk's ties to Western political and economic structures. Bilateral co-operation has been strengthened as well. In June 1992, the two countries signed a Treaty of Friendship and

Co-operation, obliging each to respect existing borders and renounce any territorial claims on the other. Military co-operation has also been expanded.

Yet Polish officials have also watched the growing rapprochement between Belarus and Russia since early 1993 with considerable concern. Closer defence co-operation between Moscow and Minsk – especially the possible integration of Belarus into a serious CIS collective defence arrangement – would have a negative impact on Poland's security. It would not only open up another prospect for having Russian troops stationed on Poland's border, but could also increase pressure on Ukraine to join such an arrangement. However, Polish and East Central European leaders have little influence over Belarus's policy; there is little they can do to prevent its closer economic and political reintegration with Russia.

TIES TO THE EUROPEAN UNION

Membership of the European Union is a top priority for all the countries of East Central Europe. All see EU membership as an indispensable part of their broader effort to 'rejoin Europe' and integrate themselves into Western institutions. The EU has also made Eastern enlargement an important priority. In December 1991 the Community (as it was then known) signed association agreements with Hungary, Poland and the former Czechoslovakia.[23] These accords provided for liberalization of trade and political consultations. Similar, though slightly more restrictive, association agreements were signed with Bulgaria and Romania at the end of 1992, as well as with the Baltic states and Slovenia in 1996. At its meeting in Copenhagen in June 1993, the European Community went a step further, inviting the East European countries, including Bulgaria and Romania, to join the Community as soon as they have met the economic and political requirements for membership. It also endorsed a package of trade concessions designed to speed up the reduction of tariffs and quotas blocking Eastern Europe's most competitive exports. At its summit in Essen in December, 1994, the EU laid down a 'pre-accession strategy' based on modest trade liberalization and expanded political contacts. And, in June 1994 the European Commission followed up this step with a White Paper defining the *acquis communautaire* (the EU's body of laws and regulations) that the East European countries must adopt in order to create a single market in labour, goods and capital.

However, since that point, doubts about the speed of enlargement to the East have become more pronounced in Brussels. One reason is the magnitude of the adjustment countries of the region will have to make, which dwarfs those needed for earlier accessions, such as with the admission of Spain and Portugal in 1986, or Greece in 1981. While a sizable gap in the standard of living separated these earlier entrants from those of the Community members, that gap is much bigger in the case of the East Central European countries. This problem has raised serious doubts in Brussels about whether the latter could cope with the competitive pressures and high standards imposed by the EU's internal market.

The costs to the EU of adjustment are another factor. The Commission calculates that extending regional aid policies to the five applicant countries (Hungary, Poland, Slovakia, Latvia and Romania) and the five likely to apply (the Czech Republic, Slovenia, Bulgaria, Estonia and Lithuania) would cost an additional $50 billion a year, a sum exceeding previous estimates. Extending the Common Agricultural Policy (CAP) eastward could prove even more expensive. These considerations have caused some EU members to favour slowing down the process of enlargement.[24]

Moreover, little progress on enlargement is likely until the EU sorts out its own institutional problems, the focus of discussion at the Intergovernmental Conference (IGC) that began in March 1996. Until the EU makes key decisions about issues such as Economic and Monetary Union (EMU), a new budget and institutional changes such as qualified majority voting, members are unlikely to give enlargement much attention. Without such reforms, many EU members think managing a twenty-five-member Union would be impossible. Thus, the turn of the century may arrive before the EU begins to confront decisions about enlargement in earnest. Taking into consideration that accession negotiations will take one to two years, and that the final agreement must be ratified by all fifteen members of the European Parliament, it could be well into the first decade of the twenty- first century before the initial East Central European states join. For Poland, with a larger economy and more heavily dependent on agriculture, it could take even longer given the complexities of CAP.

This has led some European officials to suggest new forms of transitional membership. However, such arrangements would challenge the traditional EU approach of insisting that new members adopt the *acquis communautaire* prior to membership. It would also encourage other member states to adopt a policy of 'selective co-operation' favored by Britain, weakening the solidarity and cohesion of the Union – although with twenty-five members, such an approach may be inevitable anyway.

Ultimately, however, EU heads of government, not the Commission, will decide the issue of enlargement – and inclusion in the first tranche. At this level, broader political interests, not the Commission's narrower concerns, will dominate. Moreover, as in the past, the process could well involve a considerable degree of old-fashioned political horse-trading. Germany's voice will be critical. The Federal Republic regards enlargement as a top national priority: Bonn does not want to be the easternmost boundary of the EU. Moreover, Chancellor Helmut Kohl has promised several East Central European leaders he will make sure their countries are in the EU by the year 2000 or thereabouts. Thus, he is unlikely to sign up to the EMU unless it sets the stage for enlargement.

In the end, such political considerations and imperatives are likely to drive the EU debate, and they will count more than some of the Commission's narrower, technical concerns. Moreover, some compromises may be found. New members, for instance, might not gain access to the CAP and regional aid at the outset, thus reducing the immediate financial burdens on the EU and providing it with more time to restructure both programmes. This approach would disappoint some applicants, since EU cash is one reason for seeking admission – although what the East Central European countries need most is not subsidies, but open markets.

NATO ENLARGEMENT

The uncertainties surrounding EU enlargement have lent even greater importance to the issue of NATO membership for the countries of East Central Europe. They are motivated by more than a simple fear of a potentially resurgent Russia, although this is clearly an important factor, particularly in Poland. The desire for NATO membership reflects a more fundamental and deep-seated historical desire to be part of 'the West'. Membership in the European Union and WEU are an important, but not sufficient, means of achieving this goal because the US is not a member of these institutions. One of the prime advantages of NATO in the eyes of these countries is that the Alliance binds the United States to Europe and provides a means of maintaining a strong transatlantic connection. The leaders of the Visegrad countries, for example, are strong Atlanticists. They regard a strong US political and military presence in Europe as an important stabilizing factor. As Czech President Vaclav Havel has noted:

> I am convinced that the American presence in Europe is still necessary. In the twentieth century, it was not just Europe that paid the price for American isolationism; America itself paid a price. The less it committed itself at the beginning of European conflagrations, the greater sacrifices it had to make at the end of the conflicts.[25]

For the countries of East Central Europe, membership in the EU and WEU alone is not enough because it does not provide *a strong transatlantic connection*, which they regard as a sine qua non for ensuring their security over the long run. This view helps to explain the initial scepticism and disappointment that greeted the Clinton Administration's proposal for Partnership for Peace (PfP) in much of East Central Europe. Most of the countries, especially Poland, were initially cool to the idea because they saw it as a substitute for or an alternative to NATO membership. East Central European perceptions of PFP, however, have changed considerably since the Brussels summit. President Clinton stated at the summit, and again during his trip to Warsaw in July 1994, that the issue is 'no longer whether but when and how NATO will expand', which reduced East European concerns about membership and created a much more positive attitude toward PFP on the part of the Visegrad countries. In contrast to the pre-summit period, they now see it as a *means to NATO membership, not a substitute for it*. As a result, these countries have begun to use partnership programmes as a vehicle for reshaping their defence policies in ways that will make it easier to achieve eventual membership.

Nevertheless, there is still a considerable way to go before Alliance enlargement becomes a reality. An internal NATO study, released in September 1995, lays out the general principles and modalities according to which enlargement should proceed. But the Alliance put off 'naming names' until after the Russian presidential elections in June 1996, pledging to do so at its Madrid summit in 1997. The most likely initial candidates are Poland, the Czech Republic and Hungary. Slovakia's chances have receded owing to a slowdown in the pace of its economic and political reform.

PROSPECTS FOR THE FUTURE

NATO enlargement is likely to emerge as *the* key European security issue facing the US and its allies in the late 1990s. How well it is managed will have a critical impact not only on stability in East Central Europe, but on the evolution of the continent's security order and the future of transatlantic relations more generally.

Several factors will influence the enlargement debate. The first is Russia's attitude and policy. Opposition in Moscow will complicate the process, but is unlikely to stop it. A clear consensus within the Alliance opposes giving Russia a veto over decisions about NATO's future. At the same time, the Alliance will need to continue developing a co-operation package with Moscow and defuse its sense of isolation by integrating Russia more closely into all-European security structures.

A second factor in this debate will be the price of enlargement. Yet the price need not be as large as many fear. The real cost driver is forward-stationed combat troops. In the absence of a resurgent threat from Russia, stationing large numbers of combat troops in East Central Europe would be unnecessary. Thus, the costs should fall into the affordable range, somewhere between $30 billion and $50 billion over ten years, depending on the defence posture adopted – not a large amount by NATO standards.[26] Moreover, such costs need to be seen in a broader perspective. Making East Central Europe secure is part of the larger Alliance reform agenda. Done intelligently, enlargement can enhance NATO's overall ability to carry out Article 4 missions elsewhere – an important consideration often overlooked by critics and advocates alike.

The Baltic issue is also likely to play an indirect role in the debate.[27] While countries in this region are not likely to be in the first tranche of enlargement, any attempt to formally exclude them as possible candidates down the road would create tensions within the Alliance, particularly with Denmark. Sweden and Finland might also openly oppose a NATO enlargement that formally excluded the Baltic countries from consideration.

The final and most important factor will be the role played by the US: American action will be critical. Both the East Central Europeans and Washington's NATO allies will be looking to it for the political leadership and diplomatic energy to carry out enlargement. If the US falls short, much of the momentum could erode and enlargement could stall. This, in turn, could not only undermine prospects for the emergence of stability in East Central Europe in the long term, but might have a negative impact on US interests in Europe more broadly, provoking a crisis within the Alliance and opening the way for a serious erosion of transatlantic relations.

At the same time, NATO and EU enlargement require close harmonization. Conceptually, the two are closely linked. Both are part of a broader process of enlarging Europe and promoting stability eastward. However, this interrelationship does not necessarily mean that both must occur exactly simultaneously. In some scenarios, it may be preferable for NATO to take in new members first, since the EU will need time to sort out internal problems. Poland's security, for instance, should not be held hostage to the requirements of the Common Agricultural Policy. In other cases, it may be preferable for EU enlargement to occur first. The main point is that, in the end, these two processes should be harmonized as much as possible.

NOTES

1.   For the purposes of this essay the term 'East Central Europe' refers to Hungary, Poland, the Czech Republic and Slovakia.
2.   Kevin Dove and Anthony Robinson, 'EBRD praises "fast track" countries', *Financial Times*, 2 November 1995. See also 'Central Europe: The Winners', *Foreign Report*, 26 October 1995.
3.   See Wojciech Gebicki and Anna Marta Gebicka, 'Central Europe: A shift to the Left?', *Survival*, 37, no. 5 (Autumn 1995) 126–138.
4.   See José Maria Maravall and Julian Santamaria, 'Political Change in Spain and the Prospects for Democracy', in Guillermo O'Donnell, Phillippe C. Schmitter and Lawrence Whitehead (eds), *Transitions from Authoritarian Rule: Southern Europe*, (Baltimore: The John Hopkins University Press, 1986), pp. 93–94.
5.   For details, see Rudolf Andorka, 'Hungary: Disenchantment after Transition', *The World Today* (December 1994), 233–237.
6.   See 'Hungary Revived by Tough Medicine', *Financial Times*, 31 October 1995.
7.   The most recent differences have occurred over the draft of a language law that makes Slovak the only official state language. Hungary claims the law violates the spirit, if not the letter, of the Hungarian–Slovak bilateral treaty signed in March 1994. See 'Budapests schwieriges Verhältnis zu Bratislava', *Neue Zürcher Zeitung*, 1 November 1995.
8.   Vincent Boland, 'Slovakia Faces Uneasy Future as Reform Slows', *Financial Times*, 8 September 1995.
9.   In October of this year the EU issued an official warning to Slovakia, emphasizing the need to respect the norms of democratic pluralism. The

US also expressed a similar warning. See, 'Europäische Union mahnt Slovakei', *Frankfurter Allgemeine Zeitung*, 27 October 1995.

10. For a detailed discussion, see Thomas S. Szayna and F. Stephen Larrabee, *East European Military Reform After The Cold War: Implications for the United States* (Santa Monica, CA: RAND), MR-523-OSD, 1994.

11. For a detailed discussion, see Szayna and Larrabee, *East European Reform After the Cold War* (Santa Monica, CA: RAND, 1995), MR-523-OSD, pp. 17–26.

12. See Brooks Tigner, 'Czech Europeans Build Regional Defense Ties', *Defense News*, 2–8 October 1995. Also, Brendan McNally, 'Poles Mull Aircraft Swap with Czechs', *Defense News*, 8–14 August 1995.

13. *Security and Defence Strategy of the Republic of Poland* (Warsaw: National Security Bureau, July 1992) p. 13.

14. Previously, the majority of Polish forces had been located near the northern and western borders. In the east were mainly logistical bases and units in a low state of readiness.

15. See the interview with former Polish Defence Minister Zbigniew Okonski, *Defense News*, 13 November 1995, p. 70.

16. Figures provided by the Polish Ministry of Defence, March 1993.

17. The most notorious example of Walęsa's backstage manœuvring and intrigues to increase his control over the military was the so-called 'Drawsko affair' in October 1994, in which he reportedly met privately with a group of senior Polish officers and encouraged them to speak out against Defence Minister Piotr Kolodziejczyk. Kolodziejczyk, a retired military officer and ally, was fired shortly thereafter, largely because he resisted Walęsa's efforts to subordinate the General Staff to the President rather than the Defence Minister. For background, see 'Walesa fördert Verteidigungsminister zum Rücktritt auf', *Frankfurter Allgemeine Zeitung*, 11 October 1994.

18. Sebestyen Gorka, 'Hungarian Military Reform and Peacekeeping Efforts', *NATO Review*, 43, no. 6 (November 1995), 26–29.

19. See 'Die Länder Mitteleuropas wollen Aufbau Bosniens und Kroatiens unterstützen', *Frankfurter Allgemeine Zeitung*, 9 October 1995.

20. For a fuller discussion, see F. Stephen Larrabee, *East European Military Security after the Cold War* (Santa Monica, CA: RAND, 1993), MR-254-USDP, pp. 153–164.

21. See, Andrzej Ananicz, Przemyslaw Grudzinski, Andrzej Olehowski, Janusz Onyszkiewcz, Krzystof Skubiszewski, and Henryk Szlajfer, *Poland-NATO* (Warsaw: Euro-Atlantic Association and Stefan Batory Foundation, September 1995), pp. 11–12.

22. In February 1993, the two countries signed a military agreement that envisage an expansion of information exchanges and military training. The accord also calls for conducting joint exercises and developing joint activities in rear and technical supply of troops. However, both countries have emphasized that such co-operation does not constitute a security alliance and is not directed against other countries.

23. Separate association agreements were signed with the Czech Republic and Slovakia after the formal dissolution of Czechoslovakia on 1 January 1993.

24. See Lionel Barber, 'Brussels Keeps Shut the Gates to the East', *Financial Times*, 16 November 1995. Also, 'The EU Goes Well on Enlargement', *Economist*, 28 October 1995, pp. 57–58.

25. Vaclav Havel, 'New Democracies for Old Europe', *New York Times*, 17 October 1993.

26. For details, see Ronald D. Asmus, Richard L. Kugler, and F. Stephen Larrabee, 'What Will NATO Enlargement Cost?', *Survival*, 38, no. 3 (Autumn 1996) 5–26.

27. For a good discussion, see Ronald D. Asmus and Robert Nurick, 'NATO Enlargement and the Baltic States', *Survival*, 38, no. 2 (Summer 1996), 121–42.

6 Official Perspectives from Eastern Europe

In this chapter, a diplomatic representative to the United States from each of five countries directly affected by possible NATO enlargement summarizes his government's position on the issue.

DR. GYÖRGY BANLAKI, AMBASSADOR OF HUNGARY

The issue of integration, or, rather, reintegration into Euro- Atlantic structures is a topic very close to the hearts of Hungarians as our nation marks the eleven-hundredth year of her presence and, also, of her continuous statehood in Europe.

Hungary's stunningly quick peaceful transition to a working democracy, the genuine mental change, the gradual, although inevitably complex economic transformation, and the difficult but much-needed social reorganization, have all convincingly proven that it is again at the forefront of the Central European nations which finally succeeded in breaking with their painful past and which deserve to be counted among the reliable partners and loyal allies of the democracies of the West.

As anywhere else, such transition has been a politically costly, often uphill battle for Hungary's democratically-elected legislatures and governments. Gone is the euphoria of 1989–1990, gone are the illusions some of us might have had at that time, but not the conviction, the commitment and the determination to finally realize Hungary's age-old dream and present priority: to freely develop as a prosperous and respected sovereign member of the community of nations. This intention, this overall objective can be summarized in two words, closely interrelated, that one will often hear in Hungary or from Hungarians: *modernization* and *integration*, or, rather, modernization *through* integration. How else could we have access to know-how, so badly needed for the country; how else could we be constantly updated on technology; how else could we bring in capital investment, find reasonably-sized markets for our goods and – last but not least –

secure favourable exterior conditions for the country's peaceful development? Integration is our nation's 'manifest destiny', a must, and, at long last, an opportunity no longer hindered.

Hungary's objective in this field is to secure full membership in European and transatlantic institutions. We have already covered a certain distance in this direction: Hungary has been a member of the Council of Europe from as early as 1990, and she has been admitted to the Organization for Economic Cooperation and Development (OECD). The two-pronged objective now is to enter both the European Union (EU) including the Western European Union, and the North Atlantic Treaty Organization, so that Hungary might find her niche in the community to which she would naturally belong, had it not been for the adverse effect of establishing spheres of influence during and immediately after World War II.

Hungary's aspirations are not based exclusively on the projected benefits the country herself wishes to enjoy from integration. Our agenda is based not merely on our national interests, but rather on the communality of our interests with these of the Western countries, on the values we share with our partners in the West, and on the remarkably similar goals we all set for our societies.

In her drive for EU and NATO membership, Hungary puts equal emphasis on both processes. In our view, they should take a parallel course, although not in lockstep.

Hungary approaches NATO enlargement, the security aspect of consolidating the gains that the community of democratic nations has managed to achieve through so many sacrifices, as a means and not as an end in itself. Enlargement is just a part of the 'big picture' – that of a new European security architecture with interlocking pieces of systems, organizations and mechanisms, a system in which all countries of the region can make their contribution and in which security increases for each and every state to the degree it is ready and willing to participate.

Hungary knows how volatile a region Central and Eastern Europe can be. Yet, she sees no threat at present, merely risks, partly produced by the inability of governments of the region to meet the expectations of their respective electorates, possibly leading to frustration or the rise of extremism. In addition, some old expansionist habits seem to die very, very hard. Experience has shown that leaving 'grey zones' with questionable ties, unclear power relations and the potential for great power rivalry is definitely an inherently dangerous delusion in foreign policy. The 'grey zone syndrome' is nothing but an open invitation for tension and conflict to descend upon a region.

Unlike some of the decision makers further East in Europe who are still infatuated by the notion that military might can be the only entrance ticket to the international arena, we do not see NATO enlargement as a matter of geopolitics, but basically as an issue of integration. Hungary wants to join NATO *not* to win wars, but to prevent them.

In Hungary's approach, NATO integration is a process not *against* somebody else's interests, but rather *for* something: for deepening the stability and security of everyone in the region. And that 'everyone' does include the countries further to the east, for no one in his or her right mind could see the proximity of NATO as detrimental to the processes of democratization anywhere.

As we understand it, NATO is not merely a defence organization but goes much beyond that. It is a symbol standing for a shared vision, political co-operation, mutual understanding, firm commitments, and also for a culture of co-ordination, a tradition of reconciliation and a civilization of tolerance – the very same values on which Hungary's aspirations are based.

But will enlargement also serve the interests of NATO and its members? Will it bring benefits to the citizens of the United States? Our answer is a definite 'yes'. NATO has the chance to do today in Europe's East what it did fifty years ago for the Western half of the continent. Namely, it can prevent the return of local rivalries, strengthen democracy against future threats, and provide the conditions for market economies to flourish.

As a strategically sound and cost-effective security investment, enlargement will send just the right message to the region by encouraging democratic transformation there, discouraging archaic nationalism and deterring at an early stage any manifestations of aggressiveness. It will not be financially expensive if compared to the eventual costs of responding belatedly to possible contingencies – which would be almost inevitable without enlargement. On the other hand, anchoring the countries of Central and, maybe later, Eastern Europe, to the structures of the West will be economically very promising for our partners in the developed world, on both sides of the Atlantic. Increased stability will bring more investment; additional investment will result in greater profit, establish broader markets: they, in turn, will create demand for goods, and that will lead to more jobs – for example, in the United States.

Some claim that making additional commitments in Central Europe would be a dangerous course for the Atlantic Alliance, triggering countermeasures by old-time adversaries and increasing the possibility of American servicemen paying with their blood to defend faraway lands with no US interests at stake. This is simply not true.

In fact, the only way to ensure that no American should ever go into combat in Europe again is to enlarge NATO, to open it for those who want to enter and deserve to be admitted. Temporizing on enlargement will raise doubts about the commitment of the West to that region, while settling this issue once and for all will discourage any attempt to turn back the wheel of history. Left in limbo, the fate of Central Europe can cause major confrontations; if firmly determined and predictable, the future of this region can prove to be one of the great success stories of our generation.

The objective of Hungary is not to be a liability, but to become and remain an asset for the organization itself and, thereby, for European security. We envisage a Hungary that does not merely consume this security but is equally willing, ready and able to add to it, a Hungary that does not want to merely enjoy the apparent benefits of membership, but also wants to contribute to the common efforts. We do know that NATO membership is not a free ride. We do know that participation means burden- sharing as well. We do know that membership will increase Hungary's commitments, too. We are ready to pay this fair price.

The Bosnia Implementation Force (IFOR) is convincing proof of Hungary's ability and readiness to contribute to the evolving mission of NATO. The Alliance request for Hungary's permission to establish a staging area in our country shows the significance of its location. The prompt, positive response from the Hungarian side, and its readiness to support the operation, show the mutual usefulness of our co-operation. Finally, the smooth and virtually trouble-free implementation of the agreement about stationing thousands of US troops in Hungary shows how important it is to be committed to shared values and objectives, how easy co-operation can be on such a solid basis. Thus, as a result of IFOR activities, we have reached a situation whereby Hungary has not yet entered NATO, but NATO has already entered Hungary.

As for the methodology of enlarging NATO, one of the main requirements should be to make it a process, but also to keep the target in sight. Open-endedness may have a tremendous positive effect on the countries of the broader region, but keeping the would-be members waiting too long could lead to frustration on both sides. The 'giant tiny steps' of day-to-day Partnership for Peace co-operation give meaningful content to the period of preparation for membership, but changing the requirements, moving the goalposts, would be highly counter-productive.

Enlargement should also be made independent of short-term political considerations. It might be tempting to react to any election and other public event in, for example, Russia. But we all know that it is not NATO enlargement that will determine the future of that country. Therefore enlargement should in no way be determined by the position of Russia, either. Moreover, it is imperative for everyone to understand where legitimate security interests end and where aspirations of domination begin. Valid concerns are worth discussing; any right of veto over enlargement by any country outside the Alliance is and should be out of question.

Hungary wishes to be in the group of countries that gain entry in the first phase of enlargement. However, she has a strong interest in seeing other, additional countries joining the Alliance in a second, or a possible third phase. It is not merely about the precarious position that a front-line state has in any defence structure. It is also a profound conviction of Hungary's decision-makers that the more countries in the region join the Alliance, the better it will be for the whole of Europe.

With this in mind, Hungary is committed not to use her would-be membership for vetoing the accession of anyone else wishing to apply for membership and meeting the criteria for admission; at the same time, Hungary is not ready to wait for those lagging behind, either.

In short, we expect and encourage NATO to enlarge, to do it openly but firmly, gradually but consistently, flexibly but predictably, inclusively but without dodging differentiation when it is decision time.

Ever since NATO made the historic decision on enlargement in 1994, Hungary has called for such a resolute and responsible approach to this process. At the same time, it has understood that processes such as forging consensus within an alliance of sovereign states or deepening compatibility with armed forces brought up in a different tradition require time, patience and stamina. We have similarly been aware all along of the very special international responsibility of the United States, which makes it imperative for that country to avoid, if possible, burning bridges – at least as long as there is a reasonable chance to find a partner in combating the threats of nuclear war and arms proliferation. Hungary has appreciated the need and readiness to go beyond old Cold War clichés, just as it has appreciated caution and alertness.

We have always been realistic in our approach to enlargement, accepting the notion that decisions of this magnitude should be and will be made when they would already seem almost natural and self-evident. The process of enlargement is about to enter this stage. Enlargement, we are convinced, will happen, and new members will enter the Atlantic Alliance in the coming years. In 1999, NATO is to celebrate the fiftieth anniversary of its existence. In our opinion, there will be fifty candles on the birthday cake, but there will be more than sixteen members of the family around the table.

It has been most encouraging to see that our American friends fully share Hungary's aspirations and also my country's concepts. It is a reassuring thing in our present partnership, and a good omen for our future Alliance – a close relationship based on mutual trust, respect and dedication that will benefit both sides and the whole of our world.

MICHAEL ŽANTOVSKÝ, AMBASSADOR OF THE CZECH REPUBLIC

Communism was overthrown in Central Europe in the late 1980s. Since that time, just about everything has changed there: political systems, economic systems, laws, governments, even political geography. Even by the standards of the twentieth century, the rate and the scope of change have been unprecedented.

This political earthquake has destroyed the shackles of tyranny all over Central and Eastern Europe and ushered in an age of new opportunities for the nations of the region. However, this new world is also full of uncertainties and insecurities for the citizens of these countries. The situation of rapid change, economic upheaval and uncertain future is a ripe terrain for every shade of extremist, nationalist and ex-Communist retread to prey on these very insecurities. In the former Yugoslavia and in parts of the former Soviet Union, this has led to large-scale, bloody catastrophes. In other parts of the post-Communist world the results were 'mere' half-nostalgic election results, subtle but persistent tensions, and a permanent feeling of insecurity providing still more opportunities for the enemies of democracy.

The relative absence of any outside threat to Central and Eastern Europe during this period has certainly been a blessing that few people there would take permanently for granted. It was an invariable experience for centuries in this part of the world that whenever a security vacuum had been allowed to exist for some time, it would soon be filled, violently more often than not, by one or more of the neighbouring big powers. In this century alone, two world wars started in this part of the world, with seventy million dead as a result. The countries of Central Europe were among those who suffered the most. It is thus only natural that they would give a lot of thought to their own security, and to that of other countries in Europe as well. Europe is simply not big enough a place to contain local wars for too long.

Rather small and geographically exposed, the countries of Central Europe have traditionally seen their security in the context of European collective security or collective defence arrangements. Bilateral and even regional arrangements have proven too weak in the face of aggression by a big power.

The Czech Republic, in particular, in all its historical incarnations except for the forty years of Communism in this century, has always looked to the West – not only for its security, but for its cultural and political identity as well. Its learning, religion, art and diplomacy have always been influenced by – and have influenced in turn – events in Paris, Rome, London or Berlin. The only acceptable scenario for ensuring the continuing stability, security and identity of the country after the overthrow of Communism in 1989 was to reintegrate it into the West, which at the end of the century means the broad Euro-Atlantic Alliance of interests, values, principles and – certainly not least – defences.

On the security side, we have worked for several years to become full members of NATO. Once again, this is a logical consequence of our cultural and political self-identification as well as of our geographical position. It is also a consequence of our feeling of shared responsibility for European affairs and our willingness to make a contribution to European security. In 1990, our troops were a part of the coalition that reversed a brutal aggression against Kuwait. In sending soldiers to the Gulf, we were acting not on our immediate interest in the region but on the awareness that once the independence of a small country can be violated without fear of retribution, the independence of all small countries is threatened. In late 1995, a full combat battalion of Czech armed forces, one of the largest per capita contingents from any country, joined the Implementation Force (IFOR) coalition in Bosnia under NATO command. Once again, our participation was based on a feeling of shared responsibility for the security on the continent and on a determination to oppose the forces of tyranny, extreme nationalism, and intolerance, wherever they are.

Our determination to join NATO – an organization in which we would have been a founding member were it not for the fluke of postwar demarcation lines – is rooted in this shared system of values, principles and goals rather than threat-based. The expansion of NATO is not designed to threaten anyone in turn but, on the contrary, to expand the sphere of stability and cooperation in Europe. It is ultimately an open-ended process. At the same time, the right to join an alliance is, under the UN Charter, a sovereign right of any country and subject only to the willingness of such an alliance to accept it, not to any third party veto. Geographically, Prague is closer to Dublin than to Moscow. If Dublin does not object to the enlargement of NATO, there is no reason why Moscow should.

The absence of a discernible security threat in Europe at the moment does not mean that such a threat may not occur in future. The long and often painful history of Europe is the best warning against being careless in our optimism. There are and there will always be people to whom democracy represents an obstacle standing in the way of their dreams of superiority, purity and the one and only Truth. Such forces may sooner or later pose a new threat to European security. As Lady Thatcher has said, 'The unexpected happens, and when it does, you had better be ready'. We intend to be ready.

BRANISLAV LICHARDUS, AMBASSADOR OF THE SLOVAK REPUBLIC

The split of Czechoslovakia only three years after the 1989 'velvet revolution' put Slovakia on the political map of Europe as a truly independent country for the first time. This event, one of many profound changes in the former Eastern bloc, presented the West with a wide range of issues that were irrelevant in a previously simple bipolar arrangement. But the speed and scope of the changes from 1990 on have left former enemies at sea, seeking solutions amid a vast array of economic and security predictions, very few of which have come true. It is not all that surprising. The fall of communism has been rightly termed the third biggest security challenge in the world of the twentieth century, after the two world wars. To prevent a third crisis requires close, open-minded co-operation among former adversaries and allies.

The Slovak Republic is relatively new to this process, but has proved itself a contributor in the building of a new security system.

Its governments have unequivocally stated their commitment to European security, as well as their desire to become a fully-fledged member of the European and transatlantic security and economic structures. In 1993, the legacy of Czechoslovakia remained with the Czech Republic, and Slovakia was free to seek its new identity. Limited sources of information made many analysts and experts believe that the new Republic was just another disaster in the making. By the mid–1990s, three governments later, Slovakia is concluding a period of democratic and economic transition. It finds itself in the forefront of the movement for enlargement of, and membership in, the EU and NATO.

Despite an unfavourable start in 1993 and pessimistic predictions for its further development after separation from the allegedly more affluent part of former Czechoslovakia, Slovakias's macro-economic achievements by 1994 and 1995 ranked it among the most successful reforming countries of Eastern Europe. Robust growth and low inflation have stabilized the economy and encouraged its companies to go global. Slovakia is one of the founding members of the World Trade Organization and a post-COCOM regime known as the New Forum. The next step on the way to trade liberalization is meeting all criteria for membership in the Organization of Economic Cooperation and Development (OECD).

In transatlantic relations, the government of the Slovak Republic considers membership of NATO a fundamental prerogative. Central Europe thrives on the strong leadership of the United States in the process of NATO expansion, which is the top priority of Slovak foreign policy. The territory squeezed between Germany and Russia, stretching from the Baltic to the Mediterranean, is a unique place of a vast cultural diversity where nineteen languages are spoken. The peoples of this historically troubled region deserve a better role than that of merely another buffer-zone.

Representatives of Central European countries have come to the point where they publicly state that the pace and scope of economic and political changes taking place in their countries are not adequately reflected in the their security status. This delay may be viewed as a major destabilizing influence on developments in the whole region, particularly in those countries whose membership will be postponed indefinitely.

The search for new security models has not produced alternative scenarios in which NATO would cease to exist. Instead, the trend is more toward finding it new roles. One tangible example is the effective peacekeeping operation in Bosnia and Herzegovina, aimed at implementation of the Dayton Peace Accords. NATO, the Organization for Security and Cooperation in Europe (OSCE), the European Union (EU), the United Nations (UN), the Council of Europe and several non-governmental organizations have carried out specific peacekeeping and democracy-building tasks in the region's post-conflict period. The Slovak Republic reacted promptly to NATO plans for sending Alliance troops to the former Yugoslavia and officially offered its battalion of military engineers. Along with Belgian troops, a Slovak unit has also helped to reinforce UN peacekeeping operations in Eastern Slavonia (UNTAES).

The effectiveness of NATO's defence system is the reason why the Slovak Republic seeks fully-fledged membership in this collective security alliance. NATO has established ties to other co-operative security organizations, as well as ways and means for capable, timely reaction to new security challenges. The Individual Discussion Paper submitted to NATO in March 1996 moved Slovakia to a new level of candidacy. To reach this stage, the Republic also eagerly seized the opportunities offered by the Partnership for Peace (PfP) program. Its promise of closer ties with the Alliance has strengthened the hopes of military and civilian security experts in Slovakia. At present, the country spends annually four per cent (or 10.8 million dollars) of its military budget on PfP activities. About 128 events, up from 98 last year, were planned for 1996, including twelve military exercises, one to take place in the Slovak Republic.

The remaining tasks for Slovakia's military are challenging: the main focus lies in civilian control of military defence planning and budgeting, and inter-operability of the command and communication systems. Slovakia's army has its defence doctrine and plans for modernization of military forces set until 2010. These documents have been praised by many NATO experts, and provide evidence of the political commitments undertaken by Slovakia's government.

European integration and the Alliance remain popular in Slovakia, particularly among young and educated voters. In a survey by the Slovak Radio Polling Centre, some 52.6% of the population favored membership in NATO; 18.4% were against and 29.1% undecided. A further 51% agreed with the notion that NATO is the best-operating security organization in Europe.

The Central European region would not be complete without Slovakia. For it to become the odd-man-out would be a fatal mistake.

YURI SHCHERBAK, AMBASSADOR OF UKRAINE

One of the vital foreign policy tasks facing Ukraine is to ensure the external components of its national security. For Ukraine, as a European nation, that means active participation in the building of a new all-European security architecture. This process should include all interested countries of the Euro-Atlantic region, and should be based on the interaction of existing institutions such as the Organization for Security and Co-operation in Europe (OSCE), the European Union (EU), NATO, the West European Union (WEU), the Council of Europe, Partnership for Peace (PfP) and the North Atlantic Co-ordination Council (NACC).

Ukraine considers the NACC an important body for permanent political and security dialogue between NATO, on the one hand, and Central and Eastern European states on the other. As a specifically post-Cold War structure, NACC has in recent years already added its own valuable dimension to the existing European security landscape. That is why Ukraine has participated in NACC activities since March 1992. Co-operation within the framework of the NACC has also served an important practical role and – avoiding the domination of any one structure – assisted in finding an acceptable level of interaction between NATO, OSCE, WEU and the EU.

Ukraine considers PfP an important practical mechanism for co-operation between former adversaries. We strongly support the principle of equal rights for all partners laid down in the PfP Framework Document. The Minister for Foreign Affairs of Ukraine signed the PfP Framework Document on 8 February, 1994. On 15 May, 1994 Ukraine transmitted its Presentation Document to the NATO Secretariat. Since 1995, Ukraine's participation in the PfP Program has been defined in a yearly Individual Partnership Programme. With regard to military co-operation activities and disaster relief, Ukraine – taking into account its economic constraints – has been employing personnel and technical means to carry out joint training and exercises, as outlined in the Presentation document (and later expanded in each annual Individual Partnership Program). Ukraine is taking active an part in PfP activities in all spheres, such as military co-operation, disaster relief, and interoperability enhancement.

Ukraine does not oppose the expansion of NATO, the organization that unites democratic nations. Entering a military- political structure, including NATO, is the right of any nation, and no third party has veto power over that decision. In order to avoid new dividing lines in

Europe, the principle of the indivisibility of security should be observed, thus ensuring the primary national security interests of all interested nations. Ukraine should be no exception: its place in Europe demands that its interests be taken into consideration as fully as possible.

NATO expansion should be a gradual, transparent process, not a one-time action. Ukraine is also seriously concerned about the possibility of stationing nuclear weapons on the territory of new member states, and over territorial claims by certain candidates. It thus proposed to establish a nuclear-weapons free region in Central and Eastern Europe, from the Black Sea to the Baltic, fully capitalizing on a shrinking of the area where such systems are now deployed due to their withdrawal from Ukraine itself.

Though presently the largest non-bloc country in Europe, Ukraine will not necessarily retain that status in the future. By actively expanding its 'enhanced relationship' with NATO within the NACC/PfP framework and beyond, it hopes to establish a special partnership with the Alliance that should be reflected in the signing of a relevant political-legal document. Thus Ukraine is also ready to open a NATO Information Centre in Kiev as soon as possible, and – in the future – establish a Permanent Mission.

STASYS SAKALAUSKAS, COUNSELLOR, EMBASSY OF THE REPUBLIC OF LITHUANIA

Integration into NATO and the European Union (EU) is at the core of Lithuania's efforts to return to the Western community of nations, a community based on the values and ideals of democracy, individual liberty and the rule of law. Lithuania's drive to become a NATO and EU member is thus much more than merely a wish to be admitted to yet another international organization.

We have dramatically changed our geopolitical status from that of an occupied Soviet republic to a state that is once again part of Europe. As associate members in the European Union and the Western European Union (WEU), we enjoy the same status as the other countries of Central Europe, such as Poland, Hungary and the Czech Republic. The prospect and process of integration into Western structures has unified the Lithuanian people in pursuit of democratic and economic reforms, solidifying our pro-Western credentials.

With the ratification of an accord on co-operative relations with Belarus, Lithuania became one of the few countries in Central Europe to have implemented such an agreement with all of its neighbours. The historic rapprochement and close links with Poland are the best proof of Lithuania's capability and willingness to base its foreign policy on the principles of European integration. Lithuania has no territorial claims or border disputes with her neighbours. Her democracy and her respect for human rights and the rights of persons belonging to national minorities are based on internationally-recognized standards.

On the path to NATO and EU membership, Lithuania seeks to contribute to common Euro-Atlantic efforts directed at ensuring security and stability in Europe as a whole: concrete examples of this have been our active participation in the NATO-led Implementation Force (IFOR) mission in Bosnia and Herzegovina (platoon LITPLA–4 was replaced by company LITCOY–1 in October, 1996); our practical contribution to the implementation of the Dayton peace agreement; participation of Lithuanian police officers in the International Police Task Forces in Eastern Slavonia; and our financial contribution to reconstruction in Bosnia.

Lithuania's goal of achieving full membership in the North Atlantic Alliance is a major objective of our foreign policy. Our intention of joining NATO is guided by common values, historical experience, identity, and geopolitical situation, as well as the logic of the European integration process. We are making a bid for membership in NATO without fear of some immediate threat, the more so that we do not feel threatened.

NATO enlargement is the extension of security and stability to the East, and it cannot be carried out at the expense of the security of other countries. The inclusion of Lithuania in the Euro-Atlantic space would have a consolidating impact on our relations with neighbours, on our further progress, and on preventing tensions from emerging in this (until now) stable region. Stability and security in the Baltic states would have a beneficial impact on Russia by encouraging reforms and strengthening democracy there.

When the question of who will be admitted to NATO is addressed, it is vitally important for us that Lithuania be included in the accession process simultaneously with other Central European states. We are not speaking today about an exact time of accession, because we understand that, most likely, not all candidate countries will be admitted at once. The response to the question of 'when' will be determined by the practical preparation of candidate countries and their security needs.

European security is indivisible. In seeking to uphold and support democratic transformations in the newly democratic nations, it is paramount that all the new democracies should have the same starting point in terms of opportunities. It is particularly important to proceed with a consolidated integration of Central European states, including the Baltic nations, into NATO; it is equally important to avoid sending false and equivocal signals to our societies and our neighbours that we have been left outside, that our efforts to build a free market and democracy lack support. Including Lithuania in the NATO accession process would thus be an act of recognition that all of us together are members of the Western community of nations.

III
Questioning Broader Commitments: The Case for Caution

7 Reviving the West
Charles A. Kupchan[1]

FOR AN ATLANTIC UNION

The West has cause to rejoice as this century draws to a close. The fundamental ideological and geopolitical cleavages of past decades are no more. Democracy and capitalism have triumphed over Fascism and Communism, and this era's three revanchist powers – Germany, Japan, and Russia – are quiescent. Regional disputes that festered for years, such as those in Northern Ireland and the Middle East, are moving toward resolution. And the world economy is growing more liberal and vibrant as old markets expand and new ones come on line.

But the West is not celebrating. Without the Cold War to induce unity, politics among and within the liberal democracies are fragmented and disoriented. In the Bosnian conflict, the West remained paralysed until the United States wrested control of the diplomatic process. Voters across Western Europe and North America are in a foul temper, profoundly weakening their governments. Politicians and analysts alike bemoan the West's identity crisis and the breakdown of civic democracy; in September 1995, even President Bill Clinton admitted that America had descended into a funk.

To reverse this trend and breathe new life into the established democracies of the West, its leaders are seeking to broaden and deepen the collaborative institutions that served the Atlantic community so well during the Cold War. The European Union (EU) is persisting in its quest for a federal Europe while at the same time opening its doors to the continent's new democracies. The borders of NATO are expected gradually to stretch eastward, ensuring America's engagement in Europe and defending an enlarged democratic community.

Despite their good intentions, these leaders have embarked on a course that will lead to the demise, not the renewal, of the West. They are trying to broaden the community of peaceful, democratic nations even as they deepen it. But if enlargement is to be both politically feasible and strategically desirable, they must first loosen the West's structures. Were the Soviet Union still around to fuel integration, a federal EU might make sense, but plans for monetary union, a common foreign and security policy, and centralized governance of Europe are Cold War legacies that will founder as states resist further attempts to whittle away their sovereignty. Worse still, the futile push toward federalism will distract the EU from its most urgent mission: enlargement to the east. Meanwhile, NATO is misdirecting its energies into a heated debate over when and how to admit new members from Central Europe, failing to recognize that the problem lies in the very nature of the Alliance, not its membership. NATO's formality and the rigour of its territorial guarantees are no longer necessary or politically sustainable.

Unless the EU and NATO undertake fundamental reform, they risk coming apart just as they draw within reach of their historic mission to unite Europe under the banner of democracy and peace. The excessive ambition of the current policies will undermine the transatlantic community as member states attempt to escape unwanted responsibilities. To preserve and enlarge the West, leaders must scale back their vision and match institutional commitments to political realities.

The solution to the West's troubles is an Atlantic Union (AU) that would subsume both organizations. The EU would abandon its federal aspirations and concentrate on the extension of its single market east to Central Europe and west to North America. NATO would become the new group's defence arm, but its binding commitments to the collective defence of state borders would give way to more relaxed commitments to uphold collective security through peace enforcement, peacekeeping, and preventive diplomacy. The AU could then open its doors to the new democracies of Central Europe in a manner acceptable to both Russia and the commitment-weary electorates of the current NATO countries. Once democracy takes root in Russia and the other states of the former Soviet Union, the AU would include them in its security structures and single market. A looser but more comprehensive transatlantic union would ensure that the bridge between North America and an enlarged Europe rests on solid economic and political trestles, not just increasingly weak strategic ones.

An AU would sacrifice depth for breadth, but it would lock in, and eventually extend, perhaps the most profound transformation of this century: the creation of a community of democratic nation-states among which war is unthinkable. The Western democracies have built much more than an alliance of convenience among countries each out for individual gain. They enjoy unprecedented levels of trust and reciprocity and share a political order based on capitalist economies and liberal societies.[2] The consolidation and expansion of this democratic core holds the greatest promise for a stable peace in the Atlantic region and beyond, and it is a sensible and prudent starting point as the United States casts about for a new grand strategy.

BYE-BYE MAASTRICHT

Deeper European integration has lost not only its popular appeal, but its strategic purpose. A Europe-only single market, even if good for its member states in the short run, will likely harm the global economy. Although the North American Free Trade Agreement (NAFTA) and the Asia-Pacific Economic Co-operation (APEC) forum also aim to promote regional integration, they differ from the EU in one crucial respect: the United States links the two regions through its membership in APEC and its participation in NAFTA. As trade within North America and among the Pacific Rim countries increases and becomes more liberal, so will trade between the two regions. In contrast, if the EU forges ahead with a single market, single currency, and central bank, it jeopardizes Europe's integration into the global economy. The enlargement of the union would make this drift all the more likely as the influx of goods from Central Europe threatened producers in Western Europe, generating new pressures for protection from non-EU imports.

That the current plans for a deeper Europe are unravelling is, therefore, not all bad. Meeting the 1992 Maastricht Treaty's economic criteria for monetary union – particularly that each nation maintain a budget deficit not greater than three per cent of GDP – before the end of the century is becoming increasingly unrealistic for key EU members, including France and Germany. President Jacques Chirac has committed France to increased monetary and fiscal discipline, but his vow to reduce unemployment and bolster stagnant wages will likely take precedence, especially after the paralysing strikes of late 1995. Even in Germany, the engine behind integration, the budget deficit may remain above the Maastricht ceiling. Moreover, less than forty per cent of the German electorate favours currency union, largely because the deutsche mark remains a powerful symbol of national identity.

Even if France and Germany somehow clear Maastricht's hurdles, the costs of formally dividing the EU into the haves and the have-nots outweigh the gains. Proponents argue that monetary union will guarantee the integrity of the Paris–Bonn axis. But France and Germany are mature democracies, and their relationship is just fine despite separate currencies. Monetary union may even lead to new strains as the austerity measures it requires dampen sorely needed economic growth. As for the rest of Europe, a multi-tiered EU will create new fault lines and undermine the member states' sense of common destiny. Wealthier EU members will not bring along their poorer neighbours as they did in the past. The pie for aid is shrinking even as claims on it promise to balloon. Germany, for one, is unlikely to continue chipping in almost one-third of the EU budget as it absorbs the costs of reunification, seeks to remain competitive in the global economy, and accommodates an aging population. Despite the talk of concentric circles and widening cores, monetary union promises to leave Europe's poorer periphery just where it is.

Political integration has lagged considerably behind progress on the economic front, ensuring that the Maastricht agenda will be more a mantra than a map. Europeans are not, and may never be, ready to move from a fundamentally intergovernmental union to one that smacks of federalism. The hallmark of a federal system is a legitimate, representative political arena that operates above individual states. The European Parliament, however, is still without real legislative authority and remains a forum for speechmaking, not decision-making. The European Commission continues to churn out proposals for greater political integration, but most have to be approved at the national level. Opinion polls reveal that Europeans are at best ambivalent about further encroachments on national sovereignty, with less than half supporting a single currency.

The Maastricht Treaty envisioned a common foreign and security policy, but the outlook is bleak. The Western European Union (WEU), the Europe-only defence organization that has effectively lain dormant since its inception in 1948, is supposed to develop the capability to operate independently of NATO and intends ultimately to extend collective defence guarantees to states that have recently joined the EU or expect to in the future. But in the absence of a unifying Soviet threat, the security interests of European states are drifting apart, not coming together. The failure of Europe's security institutions to take effective and timely steps to stop the slaughter in Bosnia made clear that the continent's security is now divisible. Which EU members, for example, would today defend the Finnish border against a Russian attack, a task to which all should be committed in principle since Finland entered the EU last year?

The EU's plans for simultaneous widening make these obstacles only more formidable. Integrating the economies of the new democracies into the EU would bloat the organization's budget and pit Central and Southern Europe against each other in a competition for regional development funds. Because of Central Europe's sizable farming sector, the eastward enlargement of the union would, thanks to the Common Agricultural Policy's price supports and export subsidies, burden the EU with enormous outlays. Swelling the EU to twice its present membership would also, by complicating decision making, put an end to Maastricht's already unrealistic political agenda. A common foreign and security policy that would reconcile the interests of some thirty states, for example, would be out of the question.

By so overreaching, the EU risks two missteps of geopolitical consequence. Its pursuit of a federal Europe will come at the expense of the far more important task of eastward expansion. The tighter the internal structures, the higher the hurdles for entry. The more energy and resources expended in deepening, the less left over for widening. Enlargement would require reform of the EU's cumbersome decision-making procedures, expensive agricultural subsidies, and regional development programme. But delaying the inclusion of the new democracies in Europe's markets and councils while the EU pursues an illusory dream of federalism would miss a historic opportunity to widen the continent's zone of democracy and peace. States undergoing transition to democracy are particularly prone to instability and conflict, and the allure of acceptance into the West would provide East European leaders with a powerful incentive to keep political and economic reform on track. Though less urgent, the westward expansion of the single market to include North America would serve as a bulwark against Europe's drift from the global economy.

The EU's unrealistic objectives could also jeopardize Western Europe's significant progress toward an integrated community of democracies. Trying to do more risks overburdening institutions and triggering a backlash among nation-states bristling at what electorates will view as unjustified and unwanted infringements on national sovereignty. If it continues to cling to a vision its member states will summarily reject, the organization will suffer irreparable damage. The EU should consolidate its achievements rather than gamble for more and risk Europe's undoing in the process.

THE LIMITS OF NATO

Current schemes for NATO enlargement are equally fanciful and dangerous. Because NATO is a traditional military alliance – a concentration of power against a common external threat – its extension would impel Russia to marshal a countervailing coalition. NATO enlargement would resurrect, not erase, the dividing line between Europe's east and west. It would also erode NATO from within as current members balked at assuming new responsibilities in the face of shrinking strategic threats. As for the argument that NATO assures American engagement in Europe, the declining importance of defence policy means that if the transatlantic partnership is to remain intact, America's primary institutional tie to Europe cannot be merely an outmoded military alliance.

NATO must take the lead in consolidating a democratic peace in Central Europe and incorporating the region into a meaningful security structure. But this initiative need not and should not entail its eastward expansion as a Cold War military alliance. The formal extension of the mutual defence provisions of Article 5 of the 1949 North Atlantic Treaty would irk Russia and leave in limbo those states to the east of NATO's new boundary. An America that is increasingly turning inward will also take exception to the formality and potential cost of extending NATO's territorial guarantees to the new democracies of Central Europe.

The risks of enlarging NATO as a traditional military alliance might be justified were a major external threat to the Central European states to arise. But Russia is neither interested in nor capable of mounting such a threat. Moscow does not protest against NATO's increasing engagement with Europe's east. It has joined NATO's Partnership for Peace – the 1994 initiative that promoted military cooperation with the former Warsaw Pact nations but stopped short of offering them formal membership – watched passively as NATO troops conducted exercises with local forces in Poland and the Czech Republic, sent its troops to the United States to train with American forces, and agreed to put its soldiers under NATO command in all but name to enforce the Dayton accord in Bosnia. But Russia justifiably objects to the formal enlargement of a Western military bloc from which it would be excluded.

Electorates in the NATO countries are happy to see their militaries collaborate with former adversaries. However, in light of the rancorous debate that followed President Clinton's decision to send US troops to Bosnia, the American people and their representatives are not likely to respond favourably when asked to extend ironclad defence guarantees to countries they could not locate on a map. If it stakes its future on moving east, only to have its plans shot down by the public, NATO would be dealt a crippling blow.

LOCKING IN THE DEMOCRATIC PEACE

America belongs in Europe, and Central Europe belongs in the West. But if Western leaders are to achieve these aims, they must first strike a balance between an institutional structure that demands too much and falls prey to overextension and one that delivers too little and atrophies from irrelevance. They must also make sure that strategic matters are no longer divorced from economic considerations. The strategic link between America and Europe will wither if it is not embedded in a broader political and economic framework.

An Atlantic Union that would incorporate the EU, the WEU, and NATO fulfils these criteria. The initial members of the AU would be the current members of these three organizations. The AU would then expand at a steady pace not just to Central Europe, but also to Russia and the other states of the former Soviet Union. The infrastructure of the EU and NATO would serve as a ready foundation for the AU. States joining the AU would take on three basic commitments: to introduce a single market, to uphold collective security, and to expand political engagement at the transnational level.

Calls for the negotiation of a free trade area encompassing North America and Western Europe have already surfaced on both sides of the Atlantic. Part of the impetus comes from economic prospects; the removal of today's barriers would, by 2000, increase transatlantic trade by at least twenty per cent.[3] The introduction of a single market would likely be accompanied by an investment protocol and more convergence on regulations and standards, increasing the flow of capital and prompting industrial restructuring in Europe and North America. It would also prevent both areas from drifting toward protectionism and emerging as regional trade blocs. The United States would then serve as the pivot of an integrated global economy, connecting the transatlantic free trade zone with that of the Pacific Rim.

The most potent appeal of the Atlantic Union's single market is, however, its political significance. The conclusion of the Uruguay Round of negotiations of the General Agreement on Tariffs and

Trade reduced trade barriers in most sectors to minimum levels, and the EU and the United States agreed at their 1995 summit in Madrid to pursue a host of follow-up measures. The elimination of all impediments would threaten powerful sectors such as agriculture and textiles and thus would call for heavy lifting. But just as the introduction of a single market in Europe made borders more porous, facilitated political integration and promoted a sense of common identity, so would the creation of a single Atlantic market strengthen the underpinnings of the community of North American and European democracies. Winning congressional approval of a transatlantic free trade zone would not be easy, but a high-profile debate that connected America's prosperity to Europe's fate would drive home to Americans that they share a unique political space with Europeans.

The Atlantic Union's commitments to collective security would be looser and less automatic than NATO's assurances, removing the key stumbling block to a broader Western security community. The organization would replace NATO's emphasis on collective territorial defense with a focus on peacekeeping and peace enforcement; confronting external threats as well as those that might arise from within, it would co-ordinate multilateral operations across Europe. Members would affirm their intention to solve conflicts peacefully whenever possible and, when necessary, to use military force to defend against common threats. Case-by-case decision-making and a broad mandate to preserve peace in the Atlantic area would be the organizing principles of a new US-European security bargain and a revamped NATO. The elimination of NATO's Article 5 guarantee would weaken the Alliance's deterrent power, but as long as Russia continues to pose no danger to Central or Western Europe, the trade-off makes sense.

Under the guise of the AU, a transformed NATO could soon take in the new democracies of Central Europe without appearing anti-Russian. Limited collective security commitments would provide Central Europeans with some, but not all, of the assurance they seek. American troops would stay in Europe. NATO's existing infrastructure would be preserved. Militaries in the new democracies would continue the planning and exercising already begun through the Partnership for Peace, furthering their integration into the Western security community and their ability to co-operate with the forces of current NATO members. But this steady integration would occur quietly, avoiding the political histrionics that would make the admission of new members to today's NATO so problematic. To be sure, the new arrangements would involve a sleight of hand. Central Europe, via AU membership, would secure a place under the West's protective umbrella. But couching new commitments in a broader political context and making them contingent on strategic circumstances and less formal would render Central Europe's early inclusion in the West far more palatable to Russia as well as to electorates in the NATO countries. Central European states would get to join the club, even if that club proves to be less exclusive and selective than the new entrants would like.

Merging NATO and the EU also permits a broader definition of Europe's boundaries. Because NATO is still a formal military alliance, only countries deemed to be of sufficient strategic value will ultimately be eligible for membership. Therefore, some argue that NATO expansion should not extend beyond Poland and the Czech Republic, the two countries that occupy the main corridor between Russia and Western Europe. But this approach would leave much of Central Europe out in the cold. In contrast, states would join the AU as they demonstrate a commitment to democracy, markets, and international norms of behaviour, offering the prospect of inclusion to all of Central Europe as well as the former Soviet Union. A pan-European collective security system could become a reality, not just rhetoric to placate Russia as Poland enters a NATO everyone knows will never go farther east. At the same time, should Russian democracy falter, the AU's military infrastructure could serve as the foundation for a new, enlarged anti-Russian alliance.

Finally, merging NATO with the EU and the WEU avoids a looming crisis over the responsibilities of these institutions. The three already have incongruent memberships that will grow only more inconsistent should they pursue their respective enlargement plans. If, as in the most likely scenario, the EU and the WEU incorporate ten or more Central European countries while NATO stops after accepting only three or four, the United States and its main European partners would no longer share parallel strategic commitments on the continent. The AU, on the other hand, would keep American and European commitments in step, preserving the sense of common purpose that undergirds the Atlantic community.

Regardless of how far east the AU ultimately reaches, its major powers should form a directorate that will prevent the body from becoming unwieldy. A small, flexible forum in which the major powers could forge a consensus, this directorate would guide the AU on both military and economic matters. The absence of a formal mechanism for great-power leadership has prevented the Organization for Security and Cooperation in Europe (OSCE) from fulfilling its potential. More-over, an informal concert of major states already calls the shots on the continent. The Contact Group formed to seek a settlement in Bosnia comprised the United States, Germany, France, Britain and Russia. In practice, both NATO and the EU function through the fashioning of agreement among their leading members. A major-power directorate at the core of the AU would only formalize present realities, while making possible effective decision making and timely collective action.

The final pillar of an Atlantic Union is deepened civic engagement on the transnational level. Civic society among nation-states emerges from political participation and community association, just as it does within nation-states. If the Atlantic community is to survive and prosper, its citizens must share a sense of belonging not only to their national states, but also to a transnational political space that the Western democracies inhabit. The legitimacy that the institutions of the EU enjoy in member states, for instance, is not just a function of the services they provide. It is also a reflection of the degree to which Europe has come to compete with the nation-state as a defining element of individual identity and allegiance.

The Cold War bequeathed to the West a rich network of public institutions and associations as well as private enterprises and groups that transcend national boundaries. Thickening this network so that it becomes the enduring social and political fabric of an Atlantic Union entails several tasks. The European Parliament should be enlarged into an Atlantic Parliament and charged with providing legislative over-sight of the union. National parliaments would retain the lion's share of legislative authority, but handing a substantive portfolio of respons-ibilities to a transatlantic parliament would nurture a Western political identity that would complement national loyalties. The Atlantic Parliament's duties would include designing the AU's budget, aligning American and European social policies, and developing union-wide laws and regulations.

Public and private groups should encourage the flowering of the many forms of transatlantic association – business contacts, religious and cultural activities, social causes, and leisure activities. These asso-ciations will intensify citizens' engagement in and identification with a transatlantic polity. Educational and vocational exchanges and scient-ific and industrial co-operation should also be promoted. Finally, Western governments should launch ambitious education campaigns to inform their electorates of the importance of public engagement in preserving and widening the transatlantic community. The West is unravelling in part because it lacks the defining images and projects that galvanize domestic polities. Constructing an Atlantic Union of democracies will not call up the same sense of collective commitment and sacrifice as the struggle against communism. Yet it need not. Bold leadership in laying out a vision of a peaceful, prosperous union of Atlantic democracies and proceeding with the necessary institutional innovations will suffice to wean citizens away from domestic preoccupations and inspire them to construct a new West.

A CONSERVATIVE REVOLUTION

To make the renovation of the West a priority of US foreign policy is not to demote other regions or indicate that the Western democracies should prepare to do battle against them. On the contrary, consolidating the transformation of the Atlantic area into a zone of peace will free the Western powers to address challenges and promote stability elsewhere. As they work to build an Atlantic Union, the United States and the EU members should endeavour to augment co-operation with powers outside the Atlantic area. Although its results were less substantive than symbolic, the EU–Asia summit in Bangkok in 1996 was an important step in the right direction. As long as the Western powers make clear that their partnership will not come at the expense of their relations with others, a strong Atlantic coalition will lead to greater co-operation with other areas.

While strengthening its ties to other regions, the AU should also foster regional integration elsewhere. Linked by global trade and co-ordination among the great powers, regional unions along the AU model in Asia and Africa could eventually consolidate new zones of peace and provide the foundation for a more stable international order. The main reason for not inviting Japan, one of Asia's most democratic and prosperous nations, to join the AU is that a focus on the Atlantic community would distract Japan from facilitating further integration in its own neighbourhood. The AU is the first step toward the creation of a global concert of democratic great powers that would co-ordinate relations among and within regional organizations.

The AU would also serve as the driving force behind the liberalization of global trade. Through successive accessions to NAFTA, a transatlantic free trade zone would gradually extend throughout Central and South America. Because the EU is already looking south as well as east, an Atlantic single market might eventually include the

Middle East and North Africa. Fearful of being excluded from the AU's widening trade zone, other areas would feel pressure to open their markets in return for access. The geoeconomic move toward globalization would balance the geopolitical move toward regionalization.

Constructing an Atlantic Union is a conservative enterprise. Plans that call for further sacrifices and increased responsibilities, like monetary union and NATO expansion, have little public appeal in this era of waning internationalism. A more modest set of objectives is needed to fashion a new consensus. Rather than deepen existing institutions, the AU would merely extend their reach, reasonably asking electorates on both sides of the Atlantic to form a single market, uphold collective security and send representatives to a common parliament. By solidifying a transatlantic community of peace, an Atlantic Union would do much more for the West and the rest of the world than monetary union for Germany, France, and Luxembourg or tank traps on the Poland-Belarus border. If the AU successfully consolidates the democratic peace, what appears mundane today will, in the longer course of history, prove revolutionary.

NOTES

1. This chapter was originally published in *Foreign Affairs*, 75, no. 3 (May-June 1996), 92–104.
2. See Daniel Deudney and G. John Ikenberry, 'The Logic of the West', *World Policy Journal*, Winter 1993/94, 17–25.
3. Clyde V. Prestowitz, Jr., Lawrence Chimerine, and Andrew Szamosszegi, 'The Case for a Transatlantic Free Trade Zone', in Bruce Stokes (ed.), *Open for Business: Creating a Transatlantic Marketplace* (New York: Council on Foreign Relations Press, 1996), p. 22.

8 Russian Perspectives on the Expansion of NATO

Susan Eisenhower

Perhaps the biggest news of the post-World War II era has been the collapse of Soviet Communism and the disintegration of a centuries-old empire. The 'Evil Empire', which the West spent trillions of dollars to contain, is gone. Unflagging Western vigilance played a role, but considerable credit must also be given to the Soviets, who finally understood that their system had led them to a dead end. This realization brought about a fundamental change in their policies that eventually ended the Cold War.

Implicit in the foreign policy shifts of the Gorbachev era was a desire and a determination to join the 'community of civilized nations'. Mikhail Gorbachev's 'new thinking', and the concept he advanced of a 'common European space', were evidence that the Soviet President and his reform-minded colleagues recognized a series of concessions would be the necessary cost for being welcomed into this 'community'. Under his leadership, the Soviet Union was prepared to take unilateral steps, if necessary, to end its international isolation. To demonstrate its seriousness, Moscow departed from the traditional Soviet script, dropping its intransigent manner and initiating a broad set of reform measures. As Hannes Adomeit has written,

> The crux of the matter was that Russia wanted a 'special status' in any security arrangement in Europe that would reflect its position in world and European affairs and its military might and nuclear status....The complete departure from Soviet conduct in international affairs and the ambition to forge a 'strategic partnership' both economically and militarily with the United States was emphasized also by Yeltsin.[1]

Many concessions have been made during the last ten years, including Soviet, then Russian willingness to open military facilities to the West for inspection; to de-link the Strategic Defense Initiative (SDI) from the negotiations on the Intermediate Nuclear Forces (INF) agreement; to reduce their superior conventional forces in Europe, resulting in the Conventional Forces in Europe (CFE) Treaty; to adopt a hands-off policy with respect to the collapse of Communism in Eastern Europe; to allow Germany to reunify, acquiescing to its membership in NATO; to allow the dissolution of the Warsaw Pact and refrain from turning the Commonwealth of Independent States (CIS) into an effective military bloc; to support UN sanctions against Iraq; to accept the American formula for nuclear force ceilings in the START II treaty; to join the American-sponsored Missile Technology Control Regime (MTCR); and to work with NATO peacekeepers in Bosnia.

Most of these concessions – the biggest of which may have been the Soviet Union's acquiescence in Germany's unification and the latter's membership of NATO – were agreed to with the expectation that the international community would reciprocate by recognizing Russia's rightful place in Europe and her role as a global partner in the fullest sense of the word.

Furthermore, the Soviet and then Russian desire to become what they call a 'normal country' motivated them to show restraint and persistence in securing significant internal changes. Moscow should be given credit for the peaceful dissolution of the Soviet empire. During this process, hundreds of thousands of troops were withdrawn from foreign and former-Soviet soil; manpower and military assets were reduced, reorganized and reassigned to new former-Soviet states. Since then, vast arsenals of conventional weapons have been and are being destroyed, and the former Soviet states of Belarus, Ukraine and Kazakhstan have joined the Nuclear Non-Proliferation Treaty (NPT). Just as important, many of the former Soviet states, including Russia and Ukraine, have established independent parliaments, elected in free competitive elections.

Perhaps because of these advances during the 1990s, the West has had a tendency to take Russia's concessions for granted, just as it has assumed that internal developments would continue to go as smoothly as they have done to date. Ironically, though, because of Western attitudes, the opportunities presented by the peaceful deconstruction of the Soviet bloc have been largely squandered, and the West is now in serious danger of destroying its unique chance to establish a new partnership with Russia.

FOSTERING A SENSE OF BETRAYAL

The West's great sin after the collapse of the Soviet Union did not lie in doing too little, but in promising too much, raising expectations and then dashing them. The Soviets imagined, for instance, that after the Cold War massive foreign investment would be forthcoming; it was not. Despite Russian hopes, the country was not admitted fully to the G–7 group of industrial states; and the Jackson-Vanik Amendment withholding 'most favoured nation status', while still waived annually, has not yet been repealed. The Russians also thought that aid would be just that – aid, and not rigid inducements to orchestrate their economic transition according to theoretical Western models that do not even correspond to Western experience, let alone Russian reality.

The West's failure to address Russia in its internal debates without condescension or hypocrisy has been deeply felt in Moscow. In the years that followed the dissolution of the Soviet Union, advice, if not money, flowed freely. Western economic gurus set up shop in Moscow, advising the Russian government on the fine points of macroeconomics – which often had damaging 'micro' results. Aid was tied to Russia's adopting world prices for many commodities, pricing them beyond the means of most Russian industry. International financial institutions insisted that 'cheap credits' to ailing enterprises be curtailed, even though they were responsible for providing the country's workers with their only social safety net. The West pushed privatization even though the process was mafia-ridden and susceptible to an unconscionable level of official corruption.

Today, most Russians view aid to the former Soviet Union as either a welfare program for the US Agency for International Development (AID) contractors, or as a way to support socially devastating austerity programs. Money distributed under the Nunn-Lugar risk reduction programme has also been greeted with mixed feelings. Money to defray the costs of disarmament, they say, has not only benefited the American contractors but has required an unacceptable level of intrusiveness – indeed, one that would be unacceptable to the United States under reversed circumstances. 'We have been treated as if the United States thinks we have unconditionally surrendered,' one Russian complained. Andrei Kokoshin, First Deputy Minister of Defence, a civilian, also recently lamented that there have been 'quite a few mistakes and failures' perpetrated by 'the advice and actions of those [in the West] who sincerely want to help us', creating 'a very heavy burden to our people'.[2]

In international trade, Western policy has not matched its talk of free markets and free trade. Almost immediately after the Soviet collapse, the United States and Europe set about imposing quotas on, for example, aluminum, uranium, aerospace and rocket-launch technology – areas in which Russia actually had a hope of competing internationally. In space technology, for instance, Western interests demanded quotas restricting Russia to one rocket launch annually, for hard currency commercial purposes, until the year 2000. Despite the economic implications for their industry and country, the Russians conceded, hoping that the agreement would open the door for further co-operation with the United States. At that time, Russia was launching about one hundred rockets a year in a programme recognized to be the safest, most reliable and cost-effective in the world.[3]

Aside from the joint work on the space station, other promises of significant economic co-operation were not fulfilled. Moreover, the United States surged ahead in the international market place in arms exports, while continuing to apply pressure on Russia to cancel deals worked out with India to sell cryogenic rocket technology, and with Iran for the sale of nuclear reactor technology.[4] Boris Yeltsin himself worried aloud that Russia would be unable to sell its technology and know-how abroad because of protectionist walls, prompting one Russian diplomat to observe that 'the Americans are frankly driving us into a corner'.[5]

But perhaps the most unfortunate and long-lasting mistakes have been made in the international political sphere. It was unreasonable to expect a country of Russia's size and power to walk in lockstep with the West over every issue, yet when Moscow showed signs of developing its own policies, heavy-handed threats were often made, like the one to impose sanctions if it honoured the deal with India. At the same time, Russia received virtually no recognition for its sacrifice in co-operating with Western policy, in real-dollar terms something it could ill afford. By some estimates, for instance, Russia's observance of the sanctions against former allies – Iraq, Libya and former Yugoslavia – have, to date, cost more than $30 billion in lost contracts.[6]

Russia is deemed 'no longer a superpower', yet until recently little thought has been given to the psychological reaction in Moscow to this reduced status, and the role the West has played in exacerbating it. For instance, the Russians – once an integral part of the Middle East peace process – have essentially found themselves shut out of participating in any meaningful way in recent years, just as they were marginalized during the Dayton peace negotiations. On a more specific level, the United States made no effort to inform Moscow about the 1993 air strikes against Iraq or NATO air strikes in Bosnia. As former Foreign Minister Andrei Kozyrev recalled, Russia was presented with that decision, in February 1994, as a fait accompli, despite its active participation in the efforts to settle the Bosnian crisis and its traditional influence on one of the conflicting parties.[7]

The West's tendency to ignore Russia has fostered a sense of humiliation that is increasingly defiant. Wrote one Russian military journalist: 'Previously nobody could ignore Russia. Now Moscow can cry out for two weeks without anybody reacting. This is a situation Russia is not prepared to accept.'[8] The result is that Russians are now writing about the 'period of hope' in the past tense. 'Russia attempted to become part of Europe by renouncing military instruments of conducting policy and sharply curtailing its geographic presence on the continent (by granting independence to the Baltic countries, Belorussia, Ukraine, Moldova etc...),' Russian analyst Alexei Pushkov wrote in 1995; 'This unprecedented attempt to become an integral part of Europe through geopolitical self-disarmament is ending in failure.'[9]

While no conspiracy existed, much of Russia's humiliation resulted from the unco-ordinated pursuit of Western special interests. Then in 1994 came one more development: the expansion of NATO became a major priority of the Western Alliance. This plan has led Russia to assume that, despite democratic advances and painful efforts to turn the corner economically, it has been 'written off' by the Western world. What other conclusion could Moscow reach as its former allies prepared to join the ranks of its former Cold War nemesis, the United States, in a military alliance founded during the Stalin era? Furthermore, the Two Plus Four Settlement, which provided for the unification of Germany, had excluded the stationing of foreign troops and nuclear systems on the territory of the former German Democratic Republic, an assurance, in the Russian view, that NATO would not extend beyond the borders of Germany. After the Alliance declared its intention to expand eastward, the Russians felt further humiliated by the unilateral nature of the decision.[10] 'It is significant', writes analyst Michael Mandelbaum, 'that *all* the modifications in Europe's security arrangements from 1987 to the present, the net effect of which has been dramatically to reduce Russian power, have occurred with Russian consent. NATO expansion would make a departure from that pattern'.[11] Under these circumstances, it is not surprising that Vladimir Lukin, prominent reformer and currently Chairman of the Duma's Foreign Affairs Committee, wrote: 'In thousands of Russian cities and villages, the reaction of Russia's people [to the expansion of NATO] will be the same "We have been betrayed".'[12]

THE NET EFFECT OF NATO'S NEW MISSION

An outside onlooker might ask why Russia, a country in the midst of a desperately difficult transition, must face the overwhelming pressure of an expanding NATO at this delicate time. The answer rests with perceptions within NATO itself. Like many other Cold War institutions, the Alliance feels it needs a new mission to remain relevant in the post-Soviet era.

Regrettably, the Clinton administration's decision to advocate enlargement was made before public discussion of the issue. Since the Alliance announced its intentions, however, the resulting foreign policy debate has sparked more passion and exposed more divisions than any issue in recent memory. Some advocates, like Peter Rodman of the Nixon Center, speak eloquently about 'consolidating the gains of 1989' by swiftly bringing the Visegrad countries – Poland, Hungary, the Czech Republic and Slovakia – into the Alliance. Still others see the new, revamped NATO as the principal organization to further democratization and market values for the qualifying countries of Eastern and Central Europe. Deputy Secretary of State Strobe Talbott, apart from the President himself perhaps the most visible spokesperson for this approach, has declared, 'if NATO is to continue to be useful, it will have to adapt to the post-Cold War era, and that, in turn, means that NATO must promote and consolidate democratic and free market values'.[13]

Michael Mandelbaum, a critic of expansion, has responded by noting that 'if the promotion of democracy is NATO's new mission, then the expansion under consideration does not reach far enough to the east.' Mandelbaum goes on to explain, 'It is in Russia and Ukraine that the development of Western political and economic systems will be the most difficult, where failure would be the most costly for Europe, and where, therefore, success would have the greatest benefit.'[14] Even though the Clinton administration has cited the need for a bulwark of stability in East Central Europe, a function they expect Russia to applaud, the requirements for entry into the Alliance are sufficiently stringent to assure that only countries already stable can join. Because of the transparency of this approach, many experts believe that the 'democratization and stability' argument is in fact a ruse, and that the expansion of NATO is really about Russia. Senator Sam Nunn summed it up this way: 'Are we really going to be able to convince the East Europeans that we are protecting them from their historical threats, while we convince the Russians that NATO's enlargement has nothing to do with Russia as a potential military threat?'[15]

Strobe Talbott, however, refutes the notion that NATO is still 'threat-based'. Such an idea 'has two flaws', he says. 'First it emphasizes the most punitive and "anti-Russian" reason for NATO's enlargement; and it diminishes the other equally valid less provocative reasons for enlargement, which Russia should accept and even support: the promotion of democracy.'[16] At the end of the day, however, even Talbott himself is mindful of the impact the issue of expansion has had on the internal Russian debate. 'Suspicions and warnings reverberate across its political spectrum,' he concedes. 'They are exploited by conservative, reactionary and fascistic elements who use the prospect of enlarging NATO as proof that the West is bent on humiliating Russia, keeping it weak, plotting its demise.'

If that is the effect – and it is, unfortunately – neither Talbott nor anyone else in the administration has adequately justified the damage already done to Russia's democratic reform movement.

The West's policies – and specifically its intention to pursue enlargement – have had a destabilizing effect on Russian internal affairs by marginalizing pro-Western pro-reform intellectuals. It has already claimed victims, including former Foreign Minister Andrei Kozyrev, and it threatens more. By ignoring Russia's positions on economic and security issues, the West has underscored the weakness of its democratic leadership on the international stage, thereby inflaming nationalist feelings on both the right and the left, while giving a platform to the 'bad guys' who would use the growing mistrust against the West for the re-establishment of a garrison state. 'For some', says Sergei Kortunov, a Russian assistant national security advisor, 'this [issue] is the only available way to power, for others, this is the means to strengthen their hold on power with "an iron hand"'.[17]

Most important, expanding NATO makes a mockery of the Russian liberals' dream of bringing their country into the 'common European space'. Whether the West wants to acknowledge it or not, an Alliance stretching to Russia's borders will create a new dividing line in Europe, isolating the country and antagonizing a full range of forces within this newly developing democracy.[18] In a sense, the Russian perception of this line will be the reality, making first-class European citizens out of those who are 'in' and second-class citizens of those who are 'out'. 'NATO is preparing not merely for the admission of several new members [into NATO], but for a radical geostrategic shift that would make this bloc the undoubted dominant force in world politics,' Alexei Pushkov wrote in *Moskovskiye Novosti*. As he added,

> For Russia, this means that the doors to full fledged participation in European affairs will be virtually closed....The new Europe will extend not from the Atlantic to the Urals, as Charles de Gaulle once proposed, but from San Francisco to Brest. The bloc's expansion will preserve and strengthen the American presence in Europe while at the same time squeezing out Russia, which is geographically part of Europe.[19]

Other Russian political figures perceive the expansion of NATO as a 'grab for allies' in Eastern Europe, all part of a pattern they see beginning with the expanded influence and continuing presence of American armed forces in the Persian Gulf region since the war against Iraq ended in 1991. Newly prominent Russians are increasingly convinced that moving NATO to the borders of the former Soviet Union, and their own country, is part of a concerted US strategy to exploit its weakness for geopolitical gains. As evidence, they cite the dominant role of the United States and NATO in settling the crisis in the Balkans, combined with the previous use of NATO air strikes against their traditional allies, the Serbs. 'NATO's undeclared war against the Serbs means that it has already gained practical experience, schooled the world public, and mentally prepared NATO soldiers for conducting combat operations against Slavs with impunity,' the Commander of the Black Sea Fleet, Admiral Eduard Baltin, observed in 1995.[20] Russian Major General Viktor Gomenkov concurred:

> NATO's muscle-flexing policy, the arbitrary expansion of the bloc's zone of responsibility, the policy of its eastward enlargement, are primarily spearheaded against Russia. Moreover, the North Atlantic Alliance, as a result of its intervention in the Balkan events, has obtained first-hand experience in conducting offensive operations on foreign territory. It has tested the effectiveness of its troops and armaments on an enemy which uses Soviet-type tactics and armaments. All this shows that NATO is not our possible partner but is a direct threat to Russia's security. It does not ensure Europe's security.[21]

As stated above, sentiments expressed by those just quoted are bound to have some resonance throughout the country. Alexei Arbatov, a pro-reform liberal with experience as the Deputy Chairman of the Duma's Armed Services Committee, has had to work with people of this view. He confirms that the expansion of NATO has 'undermined' the pro-Western forces in Russia. 'We are attacked now because we were the ones who were fighting to end the Cold War and the arms race. We were the ones who were advocating the "Common House of Europe". [NATO enlargement] has undercut everything we were working for, it has provided great ammunition for discrediting everything we were trying to achieve.'[22] Russian progressives are concerned that paranoid feelings will re-inspire the political leadership in Moscow to push for – and receive – public acceptance of renewed military spending. They also worry that it will provide legitimacy for large, powerful foreign and domestic intelligence agencies. In that respect, this issue has been a godsend for hardliners only too happy to unify the country under their firm control using the spectre of an external enemy.

A point worth stressing once more is that initial reaction to NATO enlargement might have been more tempered had this issue not come as the last straw for a country that feels humiliated and ignored, increasingly convinced that the Western community has thwarted its interests.

EXPANDED NATO AND A CHANGING STRATEGIC POSTURE

This developing sense of profound mistrust toward the West in Russia is disturbing enough, but plans to expand NATO could also trigger a dangerous deterioration of current conventional and nuclear postures, one of the chief gains from the end of the Cold War. Western experts, including former Ambassador Jonathan Dean, argue that extending the nuclear umbrella to points further east will 'increase the scope of current US nuclear guarantees and complicate the strategic nuclear relationship with Russia'.[23] Andrei Kokoshin, Russia's civilian First Deputy of Defence, warned in 1996 that 'many spheres of arms limitations and reduction would be severely and maybe mortally affected by NATO expansion to the East'.[24]

This issue has moved to the front burner since NATO released its study on 'the principles and objectives of NATO expansion' in September 1995. In it, NATO leaves open the decision of placing troops in the new member countries, and states that prospective new members 'must be committed to developing, manning, and supporting NATO's new force structures'. It also states that NATO reserves the right to 'modify its nuclear posture as circumstances warrant'.[25] Responding to the document, Minister of Atomic Energy Viktor Mikhailov warned that any such future deployment 'means that you are officially carrying out a policy of nuclear weapons proliferation'.[26] And presidential candidate Gennady Zyuganov, leader of the rechristened Communist Party and victor of the 1995 parliamentary elections, declared that expansion of NATO jeopardizes the START II and CFE treaties: 'If one speaks about NATO's enlargement then it is necessary to sum up all countries which will join the Alliance. [NATO enlargement] violates the balance of conventional forces, destroys the achieved agreements and raises the issue of how to compensate for this.'[27] Yeltsin's pledges made at the 1997 summit with Clinton may thus face opposition in a parliament dominated by hardliners.

Two top nuclear specialists at Arzamas–16 have indicated how such compensation may be handled. If NATO expands, they said in 1996, Russia will have to deploy 'nuclear air defence and sea-defence weapons on its western borders, as well as tactical and operational missile systems, including Pioneer [SS–20] and Oka [SS–23]' – weapons banned under the INF agreement. The two also proclaimed that if NATO enlarges, Russia would not sign the Comprehensive Test Ban Treaty.[28] In summing up Moscow's reaction to the NATO study, Pavel Felgengauer, a reform-minded analyst in Moscow, argues that an international crisis could be provoked.

> Russia's future reaction to any attempt to deploy foreign troops near its border (including such a move under the guise of conducting manœuvres) is quite predictable. It will be exactly the same as Washington's reaction in 1961, when our troops landed in Cuba. First there will be blockade (if the geographic location of the future conflict allows this), then an ultimatum demanding an immediate withdrawal, and, if the ultimatum is not complied with, a preventive strike that would deprive the adversary of offensive capabilities.[29]

Short of Felgengauer's scenario, plans to carry forward the enlargement of NATO will most certainly put Russia's 'near abroad' under excruciating pressure. In 1996, Minister of Defence Pavel Grachev declared that with the expansion of NATO, Russia would have to 'start to look for partners in Eastern and Central Europe and in the CIS with a view to getting up a military–political alliance'.[30]

Candidates for such a new bloc would surely be the countries of the former Soviet Union and perhaps some nations west of Russia, like

Bulgaria and Romania, whose membership of NATO is not even in the cards. While there is very little support for joining a new bloc that might have some features of the Soviet era, military co-operation is becoming increasingly likely as Russia pushes for deeper economic, even military, integration of the former Soviet states, using economic leverage to do so.

NATO expansion could hasten this process, and cautionary statements have already been issued by many of the countries in the 'near abroad', the most important of which include Ukraine and Kazakhstan. Eitrydas Bajarunas, an official of the Lithuanian Foreign Ministry, has also worried aloud about the impact enlargement will have on the Baltics. If NATO expands, he noted, the countries that are not members will need some kind of commitment from the Alliance, perhaps in the form of 'associate status'. 'Enlargement will reduce, not improve stability in Europe as a whole,' he cautioned.[31]

THE FUTURE ROLE OF NATO AND WHAT RUSSIA AND EASTERN EUROPE REALLY NEED

Unless the whole concept of NATO is altered, the Alliance will have to provide security guarantees to its new members. But despite its unilateral assurances to the contrary, NATO may also be pressured to forward-station troops and possibly nuclear weapons in Eastern Europe. 'The extension of an empty or half-hearted security guarantee will not only do nothing for Central and Eastern Europe', said NATO's former Secretary-General Willy Claes, 'it will mean the end of NATO'.[32]

Furthermore, such commitments will not come without cost. A rough estimate by RAND analyst Richard L. Kugler, who supports expansion, is that 'the Alliance-wide, ten year "out-of-pocket" cost for a satisfactory programme probably will fall in the range of $10–50 billion'. Some estimates for the enlargement program are as high as $100 billion.[33] 'The lack of financial resources [among the prospective new NATO members]', says Joseph C. Kun, Director of Central European Studies at the Potomac Foundation, also makes it difficult for these countries 'even to contemplate purchasing expensive Western military equipment without foreign assistance'. At the same time, Kun reports, opposition is growing among grassroots organizations in Eastern Europe who believe that military 'compatibility with NATO' will siphon off precious resources needed for social, educational, cultural and environmental priorities – at a time when it is recognized by all Central European countries, even in their military doctrines, that no imminent threat exists.[34]

If the price tag is so steep for the expansion of NATO membership, why is it that economic integration, which is what Eastern Europe really needs, is not more aggressively pursued? Presumably German unification demonstrated the enormous costs of economically integrating the former socialist world into Western structures. This concern, and pressure from protectionist forces within the EU, are perhaps responsible for its reluctance to place a priority on preparing the most advanced Eastern European countries for accession to the Union. Arnold Horelick of the RAND Corporation questions this logic: 'If the leading members of the European Union, who are also our principal NATO allies, are unwilling to make the economic sacrifices that may be required to accelerate EU membership for East Central European states within the time frame now being suggested for NATO expansion, then the seriousness of our allies about the urgency of stabilizing (East Central Europe) has to be questioned.' Horelick labels it a 'strategically bankrupt policy' to advocate NATO expansion, with its accompanying political–military costs, 'as a "cheap" substitute for a more relevant and much less politically costly way of accomplishing similar ends'.[35]

IS EXPANSION OF NATO THE WAY TO SAVE IT?

While some believe that the expansion of NATO will give the Alliance the raison d'être it has lacked since the dissolution of the Warsaw Pact, other experts are of the view that it could only undermine NATO's effectiveness. In an article in the *New Republic*, Michael Lind asserts that in the Gulf War and Bosnia, difficulties associated with 'governance' have arisen because of genuine conflicts of interest among member countries. 'In the absence of an overwhelming threat, the interests of NATO allies are naturally diverging,' he says, warning that 'to invent a threat in order to reunite these interests is an act against the grain of both history and sanity.'[36] In testimony before the United States Senate, Arnold Horelick also expressed the same doubts, using a simple analogy to describe current thinking: 'To expand NATO's membership absent a new understanding of what the Western Alliance is all about displays the same kind of logic that leads a couple in a deeply troubled marriage to forgo marital therapy and have a new baby instead.'[37]

Many believe, as this author does, that NATO has played a valuable – indeed indispensable – role, and that it fulfils an essential purpose in keeping the United States fully engaged in Europe; providing a deterrence against expansionism, much as it did during the last forty-odd years; and sustaining a framework in Europe into which an increasingly dominant Germany can fit. Or as a German colleague put it, 'to assure that Germany is not left alone on the continent of Europe'.

Despite irritation with NATO's dominant role in the Balkans, even Russians, across the political spectrum, understand and appreciate the valued role the Alliance has played, specifically in keeping the United States engaged in Europe. Andrei Kortunov, Chairman of the Russian Science Foundation, wrote that without American political, economic and military potential, 'the ability to control or contain, at least, to counterbalance the power of a united Germany [would be impossible]'. From that, he concluded, 'a Europe "closed" to the US is bound to be a "German" Europe, which is unacceptable even to the most fervent partisans of the idea of a "Europeanized" security system on the continent'.[38]

Even though NATO, in co-operation with Russia, can play a crucial role in Europe, by definition the Atlantic Alliance, a military bloc, is an inappropriate framework for overall European security. The latter can only be provided by an organization that can encompass all of the peaceful countries of the region. Furthermore, the expansion of NATO should not take precedence over the survival of US relations with Russia, and the nuclear and conventional forces framework so painstakingly negotiated. As Sergei Rogov, Director of the Moscow-based Institute of United States and Canadian Studies asserted, in the final analysis, 'The security of Eastern Europe depends on good relations between the United States and Russia.'

CONCLUSION

Not long after the euphoric early post-Soviet period had ended, a Russian colleague lamented: 'We put ourselves up for adoption and there were no takers.' In looking at the road ahead, many Russians feel a profound sense of sadness – that is, after the anger has subsided. Among the West's friends and spiritual allies in Moscow, an intense frustration is also palpable. Before their very eyes, the integration with the West that they had worked for – even prospects for future reform – have been threatened by fear, and by what Sergei Kortunov calls a growing 'complex of the besieged'.

Despite the deferral of any specific decisions on who would join an expanded NATO, considerable damage had already been done. On a trip to Eastern Europe and Russia, Secretary of State Warren Christopher 'firmed up the US position', declaring 'We are determined to move forward,' and adding 'NATO made a commitment to take in new members, and it must not and will not keep new democracies in the waiting room forever.'[39] Christopher said this just three months before the 1996 Russian presidential election. The result? Boris Yeltsin – the man whom Washington hoped would win – was placed on the defensive, while suspicions about the United States and its allies' true intentions were fostered anew.

What is required now, if it is not too late, is leadership; the courage to step back and then aggressively seek an over-arching *inclusive* security framework, acceptable not only to East Central Europe, but also to Russia and the European states of the former Soviet Union. Time is increasingly short, and if this ill-advised, even provocative plan for enlargement proceeds, it could create a self-fulfilling prophecy, eliminating the gains of the Cold War's passing, including those related to nuclear arms reductions.

The search for an effective security mechanism begun at the 1997 Clinton-Yeltsin summit in Helsinki should be given top priority, and negotiations should identify an appropriate vehicle. 'The prospective opening of NATO–Russian discussions, although a move in the right direction, fails to allay the concern,' General Andrew Goodpaster, NATO's former Supreme Allied Commander, has written. '[The Russians] do not see this move as measuring up to the attention being given to expansion of NATO membership.' Goodpaster adds,

> Partnership for Peace, which Russia now joined, will – if made the future centrepiece of NATO – provide a much superior alternative. It responds to today's real security needs for Poland, the Czech Republic, Slovakia, and Hungary, rather than bowing to vague fears and historical enmities that would perpetuate past divisions. Just as those were overcome in the case of Germany by the Western allies after World War II, the West should take advantage of the same opportunities now with Russia.[40]

The Organization for Security and Cooperation in Europe (OSCE) has also conducted a study on a European-wide security structure for the twenty-first century. This venue and others should be considered. It is possible, however, that the most effective framework has yet to be created. If so, this generation, like the postwar generation before it, will have to devise an innovative structure, reflecting the most crucial current political, social and economic challenge of our time: the integration of the former Communist world into the West. While the West cannot afford a new Marshall Plan, some sacrifices will be necessary to open markets to the former Soviet bloc. The West will also have to find renewed ways to co-operate – as full partners – with Boris Yeltsin and whoever succeeds him as Russian president.

We cannot fail in this process, for no one can afford another Cold War – a stand-off that would create not only a dangerous nuclear stalemate, but reduce the opportunity to address deferred domestic problems and ensure peace and security in Europe. One hopes that we have the leadership and the creativity to find a new way. If not, and the West's current strategy goes forward, it will isolate and alienate Russia, an outcome that Ambassador Jonathan Dean has warned would be 'the worst possible mistake in US policy toward Europe since the end of World War II'.[41]

NOTES

1.   Hannes Adomeit, 'Russia as a "Great Power"', *International Relations*, 71, no.1 (January 1995), 44,49.
2.   Rick Atkinson, 'Russian Official Assails NATO Expansion Plans Warning of Sharper Conflict', *Washington Post*, 4 February 1996, p. A30.
3.   In early 1996, some of those quotas were relaxed at the behest of potential Western partners, but a good deal of damage in terms of bad will has already been done.
4.   Russia was not a member of the Missile Technology Control Regime at the time of the deal with India but, nevertheless, volunteered that the details of the deal be opened to the West. Non-governmental experts say that the cryogenic rocket technology had none of the proliferation qualities asserted by US officials, as the regime did not make a distinction between peaceful rockets for space vehicles and live missiles. Regarding the nuclear reactor technology, US demands were made after US–Russian relations had already deteriorated. The Russians have refused to give up the sale of nuclear reactors to Iran, citing its legality under the Nuclear Non-Proliferation Treaty and the fact that the United States is providing similar reactors to North Korea.
5.   Susan Eisenhower, 'A Troubling Chill in US-Russian Relations: How US Actions Look in the Russian Press', *Perspectives on Change*, 16 July 1993, p. 14.

6. Adomeit, 'Russia as a "Great Power"', p. 57.
7. Andrei Kozyrev, 'Partnership or Cold Peace', *Foreign Policy*, 99 (Summer 1995), 10.
8. Aleksandr Golz, *Krasnaya Zvezda*, in *Foreign Broadcast Information Service-Central Eurasia*, 24 October 1995.
9. Alexei Pushkov, 'NATO Begins its "Eastern Set"', *Moskovskiye Novosti*, no. 67 (1–8 October 1995) 11, cited in *The Current Digest of Russian Press*, 47 (3 November 1995), 9.
10. The Two Plus Four Settlement states that 'units of German armed forces assigned to military alliance structures...may...be stationed in that part of Germany (GDR), but without nuclear weapons carriers...(but) foreign armed forces and nuclear weapons or their carriers will not be stationed in that part of Germany (GDR) or deployed there'. An 'Agreed Minute' clarified the point by saying that 'the word "deployed"...will be decided by the Government of the united Germany in a reasonable and responsible way taking into account the security interests of each Contracting Party as set forth in the preamble'. While the agreement did not specifically say that Eastern and Central Europe was subject to these restrictions – a loophole any lawyer would love – the spirit of the agreement excludes such a possibility. Settlement cited in Stephen S. Szabo, *The Diplomacy of German Unification* (New York: St Martin's, 1992), pp. 129–37.
11. Michael Mandelbaum, 'Preserving the New Peace: The Case Against NATO Expansion', *Foreign Affairs*, 74 (May–June 1995), 12.
12. Vladimir Lukin, *Foreign Affairs*, 12 May 1995, 3.
13. Strobe Talbott, 'Why NATO Should Grow', *New York Review of Books*, 10 August 1995, p. 5.
14. Mandelbaum, 'Preserving the New Peace', p. 9.
15. Senator Sam Nunn, 'The Future of NATO in an Uncertain World' (speech presented at a seminar sponsored by Supreme Allied Headquarters, Atlantic, Norfolk, VA, 22 June 1995).
16. Talbott, 'Why NATO Should Grow', p. 5.
17. From an informal memorandum to the author.
18. Under current plans, Kaliningrad, part of the Russian Federation, will be bordered by a new member of NATO, Poland.
19. Pushkov, 'NATO Begins its "Eastern Set"', p. 9.
20. Zhanna Kasyaenko, 'Black Sea Fleet Commander: Velvet War Has Been Lost', *Sovetskaya Rossiya*, 31 October 1995, p. 3, from *Foreign Broadcast Information Service-Central Eurasia*, 1 November 1995.
21. Interview with Itar-Tass, 21 November 1995.
22. Interview with the author, 15 February 1996.
23. Jonathan Dean, 'Losing Russia or Keeping NATO', *Arms Control Today*, (June 1995), 3–7.
24. Atkinson, 'Russian Official Assails NATO Expansion', p. A30.
25. NATO, *Study on NATO Enlargement*, 20; Pushkov, 'NATO Begins its "Eastern Set"', p. 9.
26. Lee Hockstader, 'Russian Vows to Attack if NATO Expands East', *Washington Post*, 16 February 1996, p. A29.

27. Remarks reported by Interfax, 'NATO Enlargement Threatens START II Ratification', 29 January 1996.
28. ITAR-TASS, 'Banned Missile Would Counter NATO Expansion', *OMRI Daily Digest*, 1, no. 62,2 (27 March 1996).
29. Pavel Felgengauer 'NATO Expansion – An Unsuccessful Compromise', *Sevodnya*, 28 September 1995, cited in *Current Digest of Russian Press*, 47 (3 November 1995).
30. From a 9 February 1996 press conference reported by Itar-Tass, from *OMRI Daily Digest* 1.
31. Elaine Sciolino, 'Yeltsin Says NATO Trying to Split Continent', *New York Times*, 6 December 1994; Stanley Kober, 'NATO Expansion and the Danger of a Second World War', Cato Institute, Foreign Policy Briefing, no. 38 (31 January 1996), 14.
32. Kober, 'NATO Expansion', p. 8.
33. R. L. Kugler, 'Defense Program Requirements', in Jeffrey Simon (ed.), *NATO Enlargement: Opinions and Options* (Washington D.C.: National Defense University, 1995), 192; Kober, 'NATO Expansion', p. 4.
34. Joseph C. Kun, 'In Search of Guarantees, The Elusive NATO: Is Enlargement in Sight', *The Potomac Papers* (November 1995) 1, 11, 13.
35. Arnold Horelick, in Senate testimony, Congress, Senate Committee on Foreign Relations, Subcommittee on European Affairs, 104th Congress, 27 April 1995.
36. Michael Lind, 'Let's Appease Russia!' *The New Republic*, 9–16 January 1995, p. 31.
37. Horelick, Senate testimony.
38. Cited from an informal e-mail memorandum from Andrei Kortunov to the author, February 1996.
39. Christine Spolar, 'Christopher Assures Aspirants on NATO Expansion', *Washington Post*, 21 March, p. A26.
40. General Andrew J. Goodpaster, from an Atlantic Council memorandum, 13 July 1995.
41. Dean, 'Losing Russia or Keeping NATO', pp. 3–7.

9 Is NATO Still Relevant?
William G. Hyland

It is fashionable to describe the current international scene as the 'new world disorder'. Not only is the world in great turmoil, but allegedly it is even more dangerous. Such sentiments are not entirely wrong, but they are nevertheless misleading. The world is disorderly, but surely no more so than five, ten, or twenty years ago. And it is clearly far less dangerous.

The difference from earlier periods is the source of such disorder and the reaction to it. In the Cold War the significant disorders came from the East–West conflicts. The Cold War provided clarity, a vantage point for viewing, analysing and interpreting events. The policies that flowed from this view were not necessarily the best or most effective ones, but at least there was a perspective that could be explained and justified, and a platform around which to rally public support. The Cold War also provided a framework for setting priorities. So the world seemed dangerous, but less volatile. In fact, a great deal of turmoil was ignored if it did not impinge on the central conflict.

Since the end of the Cold War, especially since the Gulf War of 1990–91, that perception of a global order has changed. Conflicts that were critical, such as Afghanistan, have been relegated to lesser importance. Others that are incredibly tragic, including Rwanda, command sporadic attention. Still others go on seemingly forever, without arousing great international concerns – Sri Lanka, for example. There are the usual contradictions and inconsistencies. The invasion of Kuwait produced a major war; the 'aggression' against Slovenia and Bosnia produced years of hand-wringing indecision.

A number of new theories have sprung up to explain international affairs. They, too, are testimony to a new intellectual vigour and diversity, but they remain unconvincing, and are quite pessimistic. Thus, some see the future in terms of a 'clash of civilizations' between of the West and Islam. Others see a further decline of the West. Still others anticipate a coming era of anarchy. And those such as John Lukacs, for example, even see the end of the 'modern age', which they say began with the expansion of Europe; now, he argues, we are seeing the end of the Atlantic community as the world's centre.[1]

The current confusion was provoked in some part by the sudden end of the Cold War. Between 1989 and 1991 the core structure of international politics collapsed, a transformation more complete and quick than any comparable change in modern history. When George Bush took office in January 1989, the world was not radically different than when Ronald Reagan took office. By the time President Bill Clinton took office, international politics was unrecognizable. Inside or outside of Washington there was little or no intellectual preparation for the end of the Cold War. Many pundits were still predicting the defeat of the democracies; the Washington bureaucracy was still debating whether to 'help' Soviet leader Mikhail Gorbachev when he fell. Gradually, the United States lost its bearings. Washington not only failed to devise a cohesive foreign policy, but its policies aggravated the sense of international disorder.

The end of the Cold War and Communism's demise created illusions that the failure of communism meant that: (1) democracy was inexorably on the rise; (2) market economies would prevail; and (3) collective security would replace national security. This would be the so-called new world order. The Gulf War loomed as a test of that order, and especially as a test of collective security. And, indeed, there seemed to be a new international consensus and a new international coalition built around the UN. A week after the war ended, President Bush said:

> Now, we can see a new world coming into view, a world in which there is the very real prospect of a new world order ... a world where the United Nations – freed from Cold War stalemate – is poised to fulfil the historic vision of its founders; a world in which freedom and respect for human rights find a home among all nations.[2]

But the Gulf War was an aberration. Nationalism was a far more potent force than internationalism, and collective security was a casualty of wars in the former Yugoslavia. Obviously, the interests of the Great Powers were not necessarily congruent. Moreover, there was little progress in building new democracies, and in a number of newly-liberated countries of East Europe the economies remained a mix of socialism and capitalism.

In several major countries the old domestic order was challenged. Consider the struggles of the Liberal Democrats in Japan, the disappearance of Canada's Conservatives, the rise of the Greens in Germany, the revival of neo-Fascists in Italy, the emergence of ultra-nationalists and neo-Communists in Russia, and the return of post-Communist parties to government in Poland, Hungary and Lithuania. In the United States there was increasing social discontent and political turmoil. For only the third time since 1945, a sitting president was defeated for re-election. For the first time since 1912, a significant third-party candidacy, that of Ross Perot, wrecked the political structure. The anti-Washington rebellion of the November 1994 elections seemed to portend further upheavals.

On key national security issues, the consensus in the United States was weakening, as reflected in the close Senate votes on President Bush's request for authorization of the Gulf War, and later House votes on Bosnia – 318–99 for lifting the arms embargo, for example, despite opposition from the Clinton administration. Signs of isolationism and protectionism began to reappear. In the 1992 campaign, candidate Clinton accused President Bush of 'fuelling' isolationism by failing to produce a clear strategy for national security. In the 1996 campaign the same charged would be levelled at President Clinton. Moreover, in the US there seems to be a growing feeling that the traditional institutions can no longer be trusted to confront the new agendas. The old political class is being challenged, if not rejected. Thus another era of anxiety may well be dawning.

For a time it was also thought that the United States could disengage from some of its responsibilities in favour of regional groups such as the European Union (EU), the Organization for Security and Co-operation in Europe (OSCE), or the organizations of the Asian-Pacific Basin. It has become apparent, however, that both major governments and regional organizations were weaker than any one could have foreseen.

In any case, many still believe that the current period is comparable to previous postwar periods, i.e., 1919 and 1945. In effect, the US has been given its 'third chance'. It would therefore take some years to work out a new post-Cold War settlement. George Bush and Bill Clinton said much the same thing, and several think tanks drew similar conclusions. In 1993, the Trilateral Commission concluded: 'World history is at a cross roads where political leaders have an opportunity to alter courses and set new directions. Such opportunities come rarely – only three times in this century.' In 1992, the Carnegie Endowment National Commission claimed, 'Now America once again faces a rare opportunity, an open but fleeting moment in world history.'[3] This is a dubious and misleading analogy. The present is almost certainly not a 'fleeting moment'. As of 1996, seven years had passed since the Berlin Wall was breached; relative to the two earlier

turning points in this century, that is the equivalent of 1925 or 1952. It is more likely that we are involved in a long historical process that may stretch over decades. We are not only at the end of the Cold War, but at the end of a period of modern history that dates back to 1914, if not to 1870. Claims of a 'third chance' are misleading, because they create expectations that a clear and clean post-Cold War settlement can be achieved in the foreseeable future. The reality is certain to be quite different.

In sum, there has been intellectual confusion over the nature of the post-Cold War world, and, therefore, over what the aims of American foreign policy should be.

Unfortunately, the Clinton administration fell back on clichés. We have to be 'fully engaged' abroad, to pursue ambitious goals on a global scale, and of course, provide global leadership. In the first phase of his administration, President Clinton reverted to a kind of neo-Wilsonianism. He elevated the UN to the core of his security policies, mysteriously described as 'assertive multilateralism'. The result was a string of setbacks and failures, so that by the spring 1994 a *Time* magazine poll showed that a majority, some 58 per cent, believed that the US had lost power and influence. Another poll at this time showed that only thirteen per cent believed that the administration had a 'clear' foreign policy. And 66 per cent of the public wanted to reduce America's international involvement. Clinton was in danger of bringing about the very foreign policy orientation he railed against – isolationism.[4]

Gradually, since then, we have seen the emergence of a new pragmatism, but still quite ragged, uncertain, and to a great degree reflecting the pressures of domestic politics. Current policy was summed up by the President: 'We have to drop the abstractions and dogma, and pursue, based on *trial and error and persistent experimentation*, a policy that advances our values of freedom, democracy peace and security (emphasis added).'[5]

WHERE DO WE GO FROM HERE?

In the early 1990s, we were preoccupied by Somalia, Haiti and Bosnia, but they do not affect our vital interests. What matters, or should matter, are relations among the Great Powers. In a disorderly world, the Atlantic Alliance should have been an island of reassurance. It could have consolidated its historic success. It had the opportunity to become the principal political organ in Europe. But NATO, too, lost its bearings. It sought to create new roles, first as a peacekeeper, and then as the new guarantor of the eastern marches. Both options threaten the very basis of the Atlantic bargain. Indeed, NATO's relevance is increasingly questionable.

Peacekeeping in Bosnia came about not because of NATO cohesion, but because of a quite belated American intervention. Even a military success could not mask the political failure. NATO is an ideal mechanism for fighting the last war (that mercifully never came), but it is ill suited to peacekeeping. Acting out of false pride and anti-American arrogance, the Europeans insisted on dominating the diplomacy of the Yugoslav crisis. Washington acquiesced, and the result was a disaster. Forces were indeed sent to Bosnia under the Dayton accord, but the debate in the United States had already begun over whether the American troops could or should be withdrawn as promised.

Bosnia is far overshadowed, however, by the proposal to expand NATO to the east. It is difficult to imagine worse strategic circumstances for expanding the Alliance.

For the United States the positive results of the Cold War were (1) the conversion of two great nations, Germany and Japan, into stable democracies, economic giants and American allies; (2) the encouraging movement toward the economic and political unification of Western Europe; and, of course, (3) the collapse of Soviet empire in Eastern Europe, the collapse of Soviet Union itself, and the shrinking of the old Russian empire. These changes have left the old order in Europe in a shambles.

The two countries most directly and dramatically affected were Germany and Russia. Both countries are still haunted by their own history: Germany by the ghost of Hitler, Russia by that of Peter the Great. It may be that Western successes in the Cold War will wreck the old idea of a united Europe, for the roles of the new Germany and Russia are not yet clear.

Germany is still absorbed in the questions flowing from unification, while Russia is confronted by the task of trying to keep the new federation together in face of nationality conflicts. The most worrisome question is whether Russia will revert to its imperial vocation. Such a concern has been fuelled by the shift to a more aggressive Russian foreign policy, especially more assertive claims against the 'near abroad', neighbouring former Soviet republics. It was this concern over the revival of Russian expansion, as well as the prospect of renewed German hegemony, that provoked the idea of enlarging

NATO to embrace most of the former members of the Warsaw Pact. Not surprisingly, this idea has provoked a growing if erratic Russian resistance.

In the United States, two schools of thought are contending: (1) the 'Russia-firsters', who want try reach accommodation with Moscow, and thus would restrain NATO; and (2) the 'neo-containers' who want to deter potential Russian expansion by tilting toward Ukraine and pushing NATO eastward. Both hope for same result – a mellowing process inside Russia that will lead to a benign foreign policy. But the arguments are an eerie rerun of Cold War debates.

To be sure, Europe is expanding eastward. Ideally, it should be a relatively benign expansion of economic interdependence, cultural affinity and political co-operation. The overriding issue, however, has become how to deal with the 'grey zone' between Germany and Russia – put another way, how to reassure the new democracies in this area and, at the same time reconcile Russia to a new European order based on restraint and independence. President Clinton's initial answer was to defer a choice, creating the halfway house of the Partnership for Peace, which envisages an evolutionary expansion of the Alliance. 'Not whether, but when' became the catchphrase. The East Europeans remained neither in nor out, not reassuring them, but still challenging Russia.

The expansion of NATO is a massive new security undertaking for the United States that needs to be thought through carefully. First of all, there is the question of genuine security. The prospective new members, the Visegrad Four (Poland, Hungary, the Czech Republic and possibly Slovakia), will create an area that cannot be defended, but must be protected especially if NATO still pursues the doctrine of forward defence. To defend this area would require a large contingent of foreign troops, or the threat of the early use of nuclear weapons. But even proponents of NATO expansion are wary of stationing foreign troops in these new areas, and nuclear weapons have now become weapons of 'last resort'.

Thus we are left acting like France between the wars, promoting alliances in the 1920s to contain the revival of German power, guaranteeing the security of its smaller allies in Eastern Europe. France's allies then welcomed such assurances. But at the same time, France was adopting a defence strategy with the Maginot line that made it either unlikely or impossible to come to the aid of its allies when they were threatened. Something similar will be NATO's position in the 1990s and beyond.

Some propose a selectivity, taking in certain new members nearby, but deferring admission for or excluding others further off. This is puzzling if the motive is to deter Russia. Why exclude those most immediately threatened – the Baltic republics and Ukraine? But extending the NATO guarantee and the American nuclear umbrella to these additional areas, so far from NATO's traditional area, is mind-boggling in its implications for an effective defence. Moreover, why de-nuclearize Ukraine, if the United States intends to guarantee its security?

The most controversial aspect of NATO expansion is that it puts the cart before the horse. The main aim of American policy should be to strengthen democracy in Russia. If this can be achieved, everything else will fall into place. Yet the expansion of NATO challenges the Russian democrats, including Boris Yeltsin, when they are fighting for their survival against the resurgence of totalitarian parties and ideologies.

It is surely not beyond the wit of American and European diplomats to square the circle: to reassure both the Eastern European states *and* Russia. Proponents suggest banning foreign troops from the territory of new members and excluding nuclear weapons. This, however, would not only stigmatize them as second-class members, but would suggest they will not in fact be defended. Administration officials have also negotiated an accord with Russia parallel with Alliance expansion. But such negotiations about compensating Russia for NATO's expansion invite bargaining and compromises that would make east Central Europe virtually a demilitarized cordon. A new pan-European treaty – perhaps modelled on Locarno – with American and Canadian participation, seems a better answer. Such a collective guarantee, if combined with vigorous European Union (EU) expansion, is more likely to promote stability and democracy in the area that expanding NATO in the teeth of Russian objections.

CONCLUSION

For the United States these questions about NATO are part of a larger issue. It is often said that the United States has no real 'vision'. It is a valid point. We have been trying to replace containment with some new doctrine – for example, 'enlargement'. Thus far the effort has been unsuccessful. It is not likely to be successful because devising a new doctrine is no longer just a matter of defining a threat and marshalling the resources to meet it. We will have to define ourselves as a nation. Demographic projections indicate that the white, non-Hispanic European majority in the United States is declining. In thirty or forty years, blacks, Hispanics and Asians will make up over forty per cent of the population. What this will mean for the nation's international orientation no one can say.

In a moment of pique, Secretary Christopher has said Western Europe was no longer the dominant area of the world. Indeed, there is a new round of 'Asia-first' talk. There are promises of an expanded free trade area oriented toward the Pacific basin, including Latin America, by the year 2005. Are we indeed backing away from the Eurocentrism established by Roosevelt during World War II, and supported by every president since then? Even such Europeanists as Henry Kissinger have advocated treating Asia and Europe on the same level of importance.

For the present we have to recognize that we are in a major historical transition. There is no major threat to America from abroad. It would be wise to use this transitional period to solve domestic problems rather than be diverted into foreign debates. Sooner or later the United States may have to deal with new security issues. Better to face them from a stronger domestic base. As for NATO, it would also be wise to use this period to transform the Alliance into a new mechanism for creating a concert of Europe, including Russia, rather than trying to act as the region's policeman or its hegemon.

NOTES

1. John Lukacs, *The End of the Twentieth Century and the End of the Modern Age* (New York: Tickner & Fields, 1993).
2. President George Bush, 'The New World Order', (speech presented at the Joint Session of Congress, Washington, DC, 6 March 1991).
3. Carnegie Endowment National Commission, *Changing Our Ways* (Washington DC: Carnegie Endowment, 1992) p. 1.
4. George Church, 'Dropping the Ball', *Time*, 2 May 1994.
5. President Bill Clinton, 'US Foreign Policy' (speech presented at conference sponsored by Freedom House, Washington DC, 6 October 1995).

10 Wishful Thinking and Strategic Evasions: The Campaign for NATO Enlargement
Ted Galen Carpenter

A telling characteristic of the campaign to enlarge NATO is the tendency of proponents to speak in nebulous terms about fostering co-operation and promoting stability throughout the continent.[1] Indeed, many of them downplay NATO's military significance, preferring to portray the Alliance as primarily a political association in the post-Cold War era. That rationalization enables them to skirt discussions of the tangible costs and risks of enlargement.

The gossamer nature of the expansion proposals coming from Western policy-makers and pundits is worrisome. Those who favour enlarging NATO to include some or all of the nations of Central and Eastern Europe are evading a number of crucial substantive issues. NATO is first and foremost a military alliance created to protect its members from armed attack. Although the organization does have a political dimension, it never has been exclusively – or even primarily – a political association. Consequently, if NATO moves eastward, the United States and the other current members will be undertaking new and potentially far-reaching security obligations. No amount of 'feel-good' rhetoric about encouraging stability and incorporating the Central and East European countries into the Western community of nations should be allowed to disguise that reality.

The need for intellectual rigour stands in contrast to the flippant attitude of a 'senior administration official' who explained why Washington wanted to go beyond the Partnership for Peace programme and enlarge the membership of the Alliance: 'Partnership for Peace (PfP) is like getting guest privileges at the club – you can play golf once in a while. Now we want to send the bylaws and ask "Do you want to pay the dues?"'[2] But NATO is not a country club – or even a geopolitical honour society; it is a military association with serious obligations.

There are numerous problems and dangers associated with the enlargement of NATO. Critics have already addressed some of them at length, including the likelihood that expanding the Alliance to the borders of the Russian Federation will fatally undermine pro-Western democrats in Russia, and the potential danger of NATO's becoming entangled in parochial quarrels among the various Central and East European countries.[3] Three additional issues warrant closer examination. First, do the United States and the West European powers really comprehend that Russia's neighbours are seeking tangible protection, not merely the status symbol of Alliance membership? Second, if security guarantees are extended to the Central and East European states, how can the Western powers make good on those promises if the commitments are ever challenged? Third, can any amount of conciliatory rhetoric convince Moscow that NATO's expansion is not directed against Russia? A failure on that score could poison Russia's relations with the West and create the self-fulfilling prophecy of a second Cold War. On all of those points, advocates of enlargement have engaged in a mixture of wishful thinking and outright evasion.

THE EAST EUROPEAN SECURITY AGENDA

It is true that the Central and East European countries may not view NATO in exclusively military terms. There are indications that several governments, most notably that of the Czech Republic, consider inclusion in the Alliance important evidence that their nations are finally and irrevocably part of 'the West'.[4] Some may also see NATO membership as a way of entering other important Western institutions – especially the European Union, with all its economic benefits – through the back door.

Nevertheless, the central goal of the East European countries seeking NATO membership is unambiguous: they want the protection of the Alliance's security guarantees. Czech President Vaclav Havel expressed the view of many of his colleagues when he urged NATO leaders to make his country, Poland, Hungary, and Slovakia – the four Visegrad powers – full members of the Alliance as soon as possible, and bring the other 'post-Communist countries' in at a later date.[5] Although the East European states continue to hope for an affiliation more substantial than the Partnership for Peace, they embrace even that limited measure as an important step toward full membership.

During the initial post-Cold War years, most East European leaders avoided publicly identifying specific potential enemies, preferring instead to cite general security concerns. Laslo Kovacs, then Chairman of the Hungarian parliament's Foreign Affairs Committee, typified the tendency to address the issue obliquely when he stated, 'The security risk we now face stems from the instability of the region rather than a traditional military threat.'[6] The ominous political developments in Russia, however, have changed the tone of statements from Central and East European capitals. Although there are still occasional diplomatic circumlocutions about NATO's guarding against the vague spectre of instability, East European officials increasingly have definite security threats in mind.[7] The comments of Poland's Deputy Minister of Defence, Andrzej Karkoszka, are typical. Citing statements by Russian officials that they considered Belarus's borders nonexistent, Karkoszka noted that such a policy meant that Poland's defensive frontier 'is no longer hundreds of kilometres from Russia, but right next to us. If the political situation in Russia deteriorates, we are at risk.'[8]

The East Europeans' fear of a new wave of Russian expansionism was evident even before the resurgence of hard-line political forces in Russia's last two elections for the Duma and the March 1996 Duma resolution advocating the restoration of the Soviet Union. Not surprisingly, those developments have intensified the desire of the East European countries for NATO protection from a neo-imperial Russia. Those nations believe that membership in NATO would give them a reliable security guarantee, since Article 5 of the North Atlantic Treaty declares that an attack on one member shall be considered an attack on all, and obligates every signatory to render assistance to the treaty partner under assault.

There is a conflict between the agendas of Western proponents of expansion and the Central and East European governments that seek to join NATO. The former seem to regard enlargement primarily as a political exercise to enhance European 'stability'. The latter, however, regard NATO as a lifeline to secure their independence from powerful adversaries – especially a revanchist Russia. To those governments and populations, NATO's great appeal is precisely the obligations of mutual assistance set out in Article 5.[9] Apprehensive Central and East European nations want reliable protection, not merely membership in a political association and 'consultations' in the event of trouble.[10] It is also apparent that at least some officials see Article 5 as a specific guarantee of *US* protection. When asked whether his country would 'accept a lower level of NATO membership for itself that does not require US troops to assist it if attacked', Romania's Foreign Minister, Teodor Melescanu, replied bluntly, 'This is unacceptable.'[11]

The cool reception that some East European officials initially gave the Partnership for Peace underscores the point that they want something more substantial. Former Hungarian Defence Minister Lajos Fur's reaction to the PfP was typical. 'Hopefully it's a step toward NATO integration, which is our aim. But unfortunately it does not give us what we need – a guarantee of security'.[12] During President Clinton's visit to Prague in January 1994, Havel also made that point, stating that while the Central European powers welcomed the PfP as 'a good point of departure', those countries 'do not regard the Partnership for Peace as a substitute for [full NATO] membership, but rather as a first step toward membership'.[13] Slovakia's government adopted a similar position in its memorandum formally accepting the Partnership for Peace, stating, 'the Slovak Republic deems it necessary to stress that it will proceed in its initiatives aimed to achieve full membership in NATO and the security guarantees which are a prerequisite for the successful accomplishment of its economic transformation and strengthening of its democracy.'[14]

Such desires on the part of Russia's former Warsaw Pact allies create difficult enough problems for NATO, including the potential for embroiling the Alliance in nasty confrontations with Moscow. Similar goals on the part of several former Soviet republics are even more troublesome, since NATO's acquiescence would require an Alliance presence in Russia's 'near abroad' – a step that Russian leaders have made clear would be highly provocative. That is not merely a hypothetical problem; the three Baltic states express the same eagerness as Poland, Hungary, the Czech Republic, and other Russian neighbours for NATO membership and Article 5 guarantees.[15] Moreover, the Baltic republics are receiving support from some Central European countries, especially Poland, several West European officials (most notably leaders of the Scandinavian countries), and influential Americans both in and out of Congress.[16]

THE COSTS AND RISKS OF DEFENDING EASTERN EUROPE

The East European nations may not be satisfied with the paper guarantee of protection that comes with NATO membership, even if it includes Article 5 commitments. Sooner or later – and probably sooner – they will want NATO, including US, tripwire forces. Poland's former President, Lech Wałęsa, spoke repeatedly of the need for a US military presence in his country.[17] A senior Hungarian official also expressed his government's willingness to accept NATO nuclear weapons on Hungarian territory, if the Alliance so desired.[18]

It would hardly be surprising if the East Europeans wanted NATO tripwire forces. American proponents of expansion who argue otherwise ignore the history of the Alliance during the Cold War. One of the earliest and most consistent aspirations of the West Europeans was to obtain and keep a US troop presence on the continent.[19] Without that presence, European leaders stated privately – and sometimes publicly – that they could never be certain that the United States would honour its pledge to defend them if war actually broke out. Not only did the allied governments want US forces stationed in Europe, they wanted them – along with nuclear weapons – deployed in forward positions so that they would be certain to be caught up in the initial stages of a Soviet offensive. A persistent theme of the transatlantic relationship throughout the Cold War was the West European effort to deny US policy-makers the luxury of choice.[20] If the West Europeans were unwilling to trust the US treaty commitment to aid them, despite the importance to America's own security of keeping Western Europe out of Moscow's orbit, the East Europeans, who recognize that their region has never been as important to the United States, would have an even greater reason to want the tangible reassurance provided by a NATO tripwire force that included US military personnel.

Yet for NATO to take that step would entail serious risks. University of Chicago political scientist Charles L. Glaser, a cautious advocate of NATO expansion, concedes that a war between Russia and one or more of its neighbours is probable at some point, and 'because war in the East is likely, Western commitments would likely be put to the test'.[21] Yet most proponents of new NATO missions in Eastern Europe act as though there is no serious prospect that the security promises embodied in Article 5 will ever have to be honoured.

It is on that issue that NATO expansionists of all types tend to be the most evasive. They insist that Alliance security commitments would prevent a repetition of Russian expansionism and thereby enhance the stability of the region. Yet, with the exception of Glaser and a few others, they downplay both the likelihood and the severity of the risks the United States and its Alliance partners would be incurring if NATO moved eastward. Such a position is inconsistent if not disingenuous. Either the Alliance intends to afford the nations of Eastern Europe reliable protection against Russian expansion or it does not.[22] If the former is true, the commitment involves grave risks – including the prospect of a confrontation with a nuclear-armed great power. If the latter is the case, NATO's leaders are engaging in an act of deceit that could prove fatal to any East European nation foolish enough to rely on the Alliance. A retreat under pressure would also devastate NATO's credibility – and the credibility of NATO's leader, the United States – on other issues.

It is a problem that cannot be finessed, however much enlargement advocates might try. William E. Odom, former Director of the National Security Agency, argues that NATO could constrain Russia's 'imperial reconsolidation' if the Alliance moved its boundary to the eastern borders of Poland, Slovakia, and Hungary. 'It would also reassure the Baltic states by bringing NATO forces closer to them. And it might even affect the capacity of Ukraine to sustain its independence.' Having NATO 'close at hand', Odom insists, 'would affect the political psychology in the belt of states between the Baltic and the Black Seas'.[23]

Odom's argument has some validity, since a NATO presence would probably dampen intramural quarrels among the East Europeans and act as a deterrent to Russian adventurism by raising the level of risk. On balance, though, it is an insidiously dangerous case of wishful thinking. Odom's analysis implicitly assumes that the United States and the other NATO members can issue promissory notes of security to the nations of Central and Eastern Europe, largely for the purpose of reassurance, without having to worry that those notes will ever be presented for payment. But to be effective, a military alliance must be a credible security shield, not merely a psychological security blanket. Expansion based on the latter assumption is little more than an irresponsible bluff that Russia, given its extensive interests in Eastern Europe, might someday decide to call.

But creating a credible defence of Central and Eastern Europe would be a difficult and expensive undertaking. A March 1996 Congressional Budget Office report estimated that bringing just Poland, Hungary, the Czech Republic, and Slovakia under the Alliance's defensive umbrella would cost more than $60 billion. Moreover, the CBO estimate was merely for upgrading the quality of the armed forces of those candidate members. The report noted that far more substantial expenditures would be required to mount a serious defence against a resurgent Russia. Indeed, just preparing bases to handle NATO air and ground units in the event of a crisis, pre-positioning materiel, and permanently stationing a small number of NATO troops in the Central European countries would increase the tab by another \$64 billion.[24] The CBO declined to study the option of stationing large numbers of NATO troops in the new member states.[25] It is therefore impossible to attach a specific figure to that alternative, although it would undoubtedly add tens, and probably hundreds, of billions of dollars to the cost.

The financial burden is not the sole, or even the primary, problem associated with making an expanded NATO security role credible, however. Relations between Russia and several of its neighbours are tense, as disputes continue over boundaries, resources, and the treatment of Russian minorities in the other independent republics of the former Soviet Union. The risk of a collision between Russia and NATO might well be greater than it was during the Cold War. The chance that the Kremlin would challenge the US commitment to Western Europe's security was always rather remote, but a challenge to NATO's military intrusion into Russia's geopolitical 'back yard' is more probable.

That point is especially worrisome given the desire of the more aggressive proponents of NATO enlargement to incorporate the Baltic states. It is at least possible to argue that the Alliance could mount an effective conventional defense of the Visegrad countries. Indeed, the most practical argument for any form of NATO enlargement is that including the Central European powers would give the Alliance the strategic depth that it lacked during the Cold War (that consideration, however, is based on the implicit assumption that a second Cold War is virtually inevitable – a line of logic that creates the risk of a self-fulfilling prophecy). One would be hard-pressed, however, to find a military expert willing to argue that NATO could mount a conventional defence of the Baltic republics.[26] That means that any meaningful NATO security commitment to those countries would have to entail a nuclear guarantee – specifically, a US nuclear guarantee. As NATO's leader, the United States would incur the same grave risk that it accepted to keep Western Europe out of the Soviet orbit during the Cold War. Only this time Washington would be doing so to protect countries that are not, and have never been, important to America's security.

MAKING RUSSIA SWALLOW THE BITTER PILL

The multiple tensions along the perimeter of the Russian Federation underscore the potential dangers entailed in expanding NATO into Eastern Europe. *National Interest* editor Owen Harries sharply questions the wisdom of enlargement:

> [T]he proposal takes no account at all of Russian susceptibilities and interests and envisages no role for Russia in Eastern Europe. NATO is simply to take over responsibility for the stability of a region that has been in Russia's sphere of influence for centuries. The 45–year interlude of the Soviet bloc was merely an episode in a much larger history, and its demise should not be taken as marking the end of Moscow's involvement. Strategic interests, traditional motives of prestige, the 'historic mission' of freeing the Greek Orthodox population from infidel rule, and the pan-Slavism that had a varying but real impact on policy – all these combined to make Eastern Europe... a matter of intense concern for Russia long before Lenin and Stalin appeared on the scene.[27]

Harries warns that to 'ignore all this history and to attempt to incorporate Eastern Europe into NATO's sphere of influence, at a time when Russia is in dangerous turmoil and when that nation's prestige and self-confidence are badly damaged, would surely be an act of outstanding folly'.[28]

Certainly, Moscow's reaction to NATO enlargement proposals has been hostile. President Boris Yeltsin's blunt warning in December 1994 that an enlargement of NATO threatens to again split the continent into hostile military blocs and create a 'cold peace' is only one of many ominous rumblings by Russian officials.[29]

The angry rhetoric emanating from Moscow is hardly surprising. Even the most democratic, peaceably inclined Russian leader would find it difficult to tolerate a US-dominated military alliance perched on his country's western frontier. It is the US connection and the extent of NATO's current military capabilities, not the marginal addition to that strength that would be provided by the new members, that concern the Russians. Enlargement advocates such as the Heritage Foundation's Ariel Cohen habitually miss this point. 'Despite the fact that neither Poland, Hungary nor the Czech Republic threaten Russia, Moscow still hopes that the West can be intimidated or cajoled into preventing enlargement,' Cohen concludes.[30] But the Russians do not fear Polish, Hungarian, and Czech forces; they fear the prospect of forward-deployed German, British, French and especially US divisions – and forward-deployed US nuclear weapons. A NATO presence in Eastern Europe would inevitably be regarded as a threatening, anti-Russian policy, however much Western officials might reassure Moscow that the enlarged Alliance sought only to promote peace, democracy, and stability.

The post-Cold War changes that have already taken place in NATO's overall mission are likely to heighten Russian apprehension. Throughout the Cold War, Western leaders could credibly argue that the Alliance existed solely to defend the territory of member states from attack. But as NATO has ventured into 'out-of-area' missions in recent years, most notably in Bosnia, and such prominent supporters of the Alliance as former Secretary of State James Baker advocate NATO intervention 'anywhere and under any circumstances' when peace and stability in Europe are threatened, the Alliance now clearly has an offensive as well as a defensive orientation.[31]

Clinton administration officials and other supporters of NATO expansion profess to be baffled at Moscow's negative reaction. US leaders repeatedly assure the Kremlin that the enlargement of the Alliance is not meant to be a bellicose act. National Security Adviser Anthony Lake's comments during a speech delivered, appropriately enough, on April 1, 1996 are typical. 'As we have stressed to our Russian colleagues, NATO enlargement is not directed against anyone.'[32] Secretary of Defence William Perry exemplified the administration's relentless optimism when he predicted, 'Russia will come to understand that NATO enlargement means enlarging the zone of security and stability that is very much in Russia's interest.'[33] But Deputy Secretary of State Strobe Talbott inadvertently underscored the contradiction at the heart of the enlargement policy when he emphasized that NATO must convince the Russians that expansion is not aimed at them, but at the same time argued that NATO must expand to protect Europe from possible turmoil in Russia and to preclude the prospect of a new Moscow-led military bloc in Eastern Europe.[34]

Some West European officials have been more sensitive to Russian concerns and are worried about the consequences if NATO takes in new members despite Moscow's objections and warnings. 'We do not think NATO should enlarge against Russia's wishes,' one Italian official stated. But the sense of resignation among worried and sceptical West European leaders was also evident when he added that 'it depends on Clinton, not on us'.[35]

A few advocates of enlargement also seem to realize, at least implicitly, that Russia might well be suspicious of NATO's incorporation of the Central and East European countries. American University political scientists William Kincaid and Natalie Melnyczuk caution that the form and extent of the Alliance's expansion could be crucial. Even the Partnership for Peace risks 'creating a Europe not from the Atlantic to the Urals but to an extended Curzon Line – the border between Poland and Russia drawn by the Western Powers in the 1919 Versailles Peace Treaty without Russian participation. Such a division of the region would create a new and troublesome fault line.'[36]

Policy experts who are concerned about an adverse reaction from Moscow have typically sought to neutralize the problem by advocating simultaneously strengthening the West's security links to Russia. Leslie H. Gelb, president of the Council on Foreign Relations, attempts to be both hard-line and conciliatory toward the Russians:

> If stability and democracy in Eastern Europe require a NATO security shadow, it should be lengthened with or without Moscow's blessing. To be sure, Russian leaders should not be made to feel left out of European security arrangements. Nor, more importantly, should they be left with the idea that they can intimidate their European neighbors once again.[37]

How the tension between such competing objectives can be resolved, Gelb does not say.

Zbigniew Brzezinski offers a more substantive scheme to overcome the dilemma, suggesting 'a far-reaching NATO proposal for a treaty of alliance with Russia' to accompany an expansion of NATO's membership.[38] Brzezinski strives even harder than Gelb to have it both ways:

> The deliberate promotion of a larger and more secure Europe need not be viewed as an anti-Russian policy, for the inclusion in NATO of several Central European democracies could be coupled with a simultaneous treaty of alliance and co-operation between NATO and Russia. It is altogether unlikely that Russia could be assimilated into NATO as a mere member without diluting that alliance's special cohesion – and that is certainly not in America's interest. But a treaty between the Alliance and Russia (even if Russia falls short of US hope for its democratic evolution) would provide the Russians with a gratifying recognition of their country's status as a major power while embracing Russia within a wider framework of Eurasian security.[39]

Such schemes may deserve high marks for creativity, but they are unlikely to convince suspicious Russians that a powerful military alliance poised on their country's western border is not threatening. Given Russia's weakened condition, the United States and its allies may be able to force Moscow to accept NATO enlargement accompanied by such sops as statements that the Alliance has no plans to station nuclear weapons or large numbers of conventional forces in the new members – plans that can easily be changed at a later date.[40] A country that is unable to subdue Chechnya is in no position at the moment to challenge NATO's military might. But the probability is that Russia will someday recover politically, economically, and militarily. And Russians will likely remember that the West exploited their country's temporary weakness to establish hegemony throughout Central and Eastern Europe. NATO enlargement, therefore, has the potential to become the 1990s' equivalent of the Treaty of Versailles, which sowed the seeds of revenge and an enormously destructive war.

Moreover, even in the short term Moscow can take a number of disagreeable actions short of a direct military confrontation. For example, the Russian Duma could reject the START II arms reduction agreement, a danger stressed by Mikhail Gorbachev.[41] Moscow can also seek closer strategic relationships with China and other powers outside Europe. The rapprochement between Moscow and Beijing at the April 1996 summit between Yeltsin and Chinese President Jiang Zemin was one indication of Russia's possible response.[42] Although the 'constructive partnership' announced at the summit fell short of heralding a Moscow–Beijing axis (much less a formal military alliance), it ought to serve as a warning to Western policy-makers. The implicit assumption of the NATO expansion advocates has been that Russia will ultimately have no choice but to accept enlargement gracefully or risk international isolation. The warming of relations with China illustrates that Moscow does have other options.

Most disturbing, as NATO expands eastward, Russia can create its own political–military bloc among those nations that are not included on the roster of new Alliance members.[43] There are indications that that may already be occurring. The 1996 agreement between Russia and Belarus that makes the latter virtually a wholly-owned subsidiary of Moscow suggests an intent to construct such a bloc. It is unlikely that the move was solely a reaction to the campaign for NATO enlargement, but statements by Russian officials and foreign policy experts indicate that such concerns were a factor. Irina Kobrinskaya, a researcher at the Carnegie Endowment's Moscow office, aptly described the pact as 'preventive diplomacy' and a reaction to NATO's plans for expansion.[44] It is also interesting that two years earlier Moscow had rejected an overture from Belarus for a more limited, largely economic, association.

Russia's ability to move westward as NATO moves eastward creates a particularly thorny dilemma for the Alliance. If enlargement comes in stages, with only the Visegrad countries offered membership in the first round, Moscow has an incentive to pre-empt further rounds by creating its own sphere of influence. Yet a single, massive expansion that incorporates not only the Central European countries but Moscow's other erstwhile Warsaw Pact allies and the Baltic republics would be so provocative as to virtually guarantee a second Cold War.

The East European countries are acutely aware of the dilemma, but they have reacted in sharply different ways. The three Baltic states and Romania are terrified that they will be left out of an initial round of expansion and will then be vulnerable to Russian domination; they are lobbying feverishly to be included in any enlargement process.[45] Conversely, Ukraine and – until recently – Belarus have been critical of proposals to enlarge NATO and have repeatedly warned against again dividing Europe into hostile blocs. Having concluded that NATO leaders will never be so reckless as to move the Alliance that far eastward, they justifiably fear being consigned to Russian hegemony – or at least to an uncomfortable 'grey zone'. Ukrainian Prime Minister Yevhen Marchuk expressed that apprehension when he asserted that the main task facing his country was to avoid 'turning into a buffer' between NATO and non-NATO countries.[46]

As they do on so many other issues, the NATO governments respond with evasive generalities to the problem of which nations are to be included. The communiqué issued by the ministerial meeting of the North Atlantic Council on December 1, 1994, stated that the Alliance would 'expect and welcome NATO enlargement that would reach to democratic states to our East, as part of an evolutionary process, taking into account political and security developments in the whole of Europe'. The communiqué added, however, that it was 'premature to discuss the timeframe for enlargement or which particular countries would be invited to join the Alliance'.[47] A much-touted internal NATO study, completed in September 1995, which was to clarify the issue, provided surprisingly little clarity. Former Secretary-General Willy Claes emphasized that 'the study addresses the "why and how" of enlargement and what NATO and possible new members will need to do to prepare to join'. But, he added, 'the "who and when" of enlargement have not been addressed and are subjects for future discussion and decision'.[48] Matters had not become appreciably clearer when Secretary of State Warren Christopher addressed a meeting of East European foreign ministers in March 1996. Christopher stated that 'NATO has made a commitment to take in new members and it must not and will not keep new democracies in the waiting room forever.'[49] But he did not even provide a hint about whether some of those democracies had an earlier appointment than others.

The issue obviously cannot be evaded forever. At some point NATO will have to decide which nations will receive membership invitations and which will not. Equally important, the Alliance will have to decide what it is prepared to do, if anything, should Russia move to dominate those countries that are not added to NATO's roster.

A DANGEROUS 'ALTERNATIVE MISSION'

Proposals for NATO enlargement are symptomatic of a desperate effort to find a new mission – almost any new mission – to justify the Alliance's continued existence following the collapse of the Soviet Union. But NATO was never designed for, nor is it well suited to, addressing the security issues of post-Cold War Europe. NATO is the quintessential Cold War institution. It was the product of a specific era to deal with a unique set of problems. Put bluntly, NATO's primary purpose was to provide an institutional framework within which the United States could help shield a demoralized, war-devastated Western Europe from an aggressively expansionist totalitarian great power, the Soviet Union. Its initial secondary purpose was to be an insurance policy against the possible reemergence of a revanchist Germany. As those fears receded – and it became evident that West German military manpower was needed to enhance NATO's conventional deterrent – the Alliance became a useful multilateral mechanism to harness German military strength without alarming neighbouring countries.

Neither purpose is terribly relevant today. The spectre of an aggressive Germany again running amok in Europe is scarcely more credible than a renewed Napoleonic menace. Western Europe is no longer demoralized and war-ravaged. On the contrary, the nations of the European Union collectively have an economy and population larger than that of the United States. More to the point, they have a population more than twice as large as that of Russia and an economy twelve to fourteen times as large. The European Union, therefore, is fully capable of being a strategic counterweight to Russia and playing the role of stabilizer in Central and Eastern Europe that Atlanticists have in mind for an expanded NATO.

The current incarnation of NATO is a bad idea from the standpoint of America's interests. It is needlessly expensive and perpetuates an unhealthily dependent mentality on the part of the West European countries. But an enlarged NATO is not merely a bad idea; it is a dreadful, potentially catastrophic idea.

NOTES

1. Examples of articles and studies advocating NATO enlargement include Jeffrey Simon, 'Does Eastern Europe Belong in NATO?' *Orbis*, 37 (Winter 1993), 21–35; Ronald D. Asmus, Richard L. Kugler and F. Stephen Larrabee, 'Building a New NATO', *Foreign Affairs*, 72 (September–October 1993), 28–40; Asmus, Kugler, and Larrabee, 'NATO Expansion: The Next Steps', *Survival*, 37, no. 1 (Spring 1995), 7–33; Zalmay M. Khalilzad, 'Extending the Western Alliance to East Central Europe', RAND Corporation Issue Paper, May 1993; Zbigniew Brzezinski, 'The Premature Partnership', *Foreign Affairs*, 73 (March–April 1994) 67–82; William S. Cohen, 'Expand NATO Step by Step', *Washington Post*, 7 December 1993, p. A25; Charles L. Glaser, 'Why NATO Is Still the Best', *International Security*, 18 (Summer 1993), 13–14; William E. Odom, 'NATO Expansion: Why the Critics Are Wrong', *National Interest*, 39 (Spring 1995), 38–49; and Ronald D. Asmus, Robert D. Blackwill, and F. Stephen Larrabee, 'Can NATO Survive?' *Washington Quarterly*, 19, no. 2 (Spring 1996), 79–101.
2. Quoted in Elaine Sciolino, 'US Wants to Expedite Entry of Eastern Nations into Alliance', *New York Times*, 27 October 1994, p. A1.
3. See Ted Galen Carpenter, *Beyond NATO: Staying Out of Europe's Wars* (Washington: Cato Institute, 1994) pp. 49–55, 71–86; Jonathan G. Clarke, 'Beckoning Quagmires: NATO in Eastern Europe', *Journal of Strategic Studies*, 17 (December 1994), 42–60; and Hugh De Santis, 'Romancing NATO: Partnership for Peace and East European Stability', ibid., 61–81. Other analyses sceptical or critical of NATO enlargement include Owen Harries, 'The Collapse of "the West"', *Foreign Affairs*, 72 (September-October 1993), 41–53; Charles A. Kupchan, 'Expand NATO – And Split Europe', *New York Times*, 27 November 1994, p. E11; Ted Galen Carpenter, 'Conflicting Agendas and the Future of NATO', *Journal of Strategic Studies*, 17 (December 1994), 143–164; Fred C. Iklé, 'How to Ruin NATO', *New York Times*, 11 January 1995, p. A21; Michael Mandelbaum, 'Preserving the New Peace', *Foreign Affairs* (May-June 1995), 9–13; Michael E. Brown,

'The Flawed Logic of NATO Expansion', *Survival*, 37, no. 1 (Spring 1995), 34–52; Jonathan Dean, 'Losing Russia or Keeping NATO: Must We Choose?' *Arms Control Today* (June 1995), 3–7; Sam Nunn, 'The Future of NATO in an Uncertain World', *Vital Speeches of the Day*, 15 July 1995, pp. 583–86; Susan Eisenhower, 'Why Bait the Bear?' *Washington Post*, 18 July 1995, p. A21; R. T. Davies, 'Should NATO Grow? – A Dissent', *New York Review of Books*, 21 September 1995, pp. 74–75; Martin Butcher, Tasos Kokkinides and Daniel Plesch, 'Study on NATO Enlargement: Destabilizing Europe', British–American Security Information Council Report 95.2, 29 November 1995; Benjamin Schwarz, 'The NATO Empire', *New York Times*, 5 October 1995, p. A29; Bill Bradley, 'Eurasia Letter: A Misguided Russia Policy', *Foreign Policy*, 101 (Winter 1995–1996), 81–97; Stanley Kober, 'The United States and NATO Expansion', *Transition*, 15 December 1995, 6–10; Kober, 'NATO Expansion and the Danger of a Second Cold War', Cato Institute Foreign Policy Briefing no. 38 (31 January 1996); and Stephen J. Cimbala, 'NATO Enlargement and Russia', *Strategic Review* (Spring 1996), 51–57.

4. That motive was evident in the informal remarks of Czech prime minister V clav Klaus at a Cato Institute luncheon, 4 December 1995. Bulgaria's president, Zhelyu Zhelev, likewise has argued that his country should join all European and Euro-Atlantic organizations, including NATO. Such integration is necessary, Zhelev contends, to confirm a set of values that would guarantee Bulgaria's transition to a market economy. Embassy of Bulgaria News Bulletin, Washington, DC, 27 March 1996, 1. See also the interview with Tibor Tóth, deputy state secretary for international affairs in Hungary's Ministry of Defense, *Jane's Defence Weekly*, 7 February 1996, p. 32.

5. Václav Havel, 'New Democracies for Old Europe', *New York Times*, 17 October 1993, p. E17.

6. Quoted in Celia Woodard, 'Hungary Winces as West Defers Its NATO Membership', *Christian Science Monitor*, 28 October 1993, p. 3. See also Pavel Bratinka, 'The Challenge of Liberation: The View from the Czech Republic', Svetoslav Bombik, 'Returning to Civilization: The View from Slovakia', Jerzy Marek Nowakowski, 'In Search of a Strategic Home: The View from Poland', and Tamas Waschler, 'Where There's a Will . . . : The View from Hungary', in *NATO: The Case for Enlargement* (London: Institute for European Defence and Strategic Studies, 1993), pp. 13–35.

7. In addition to concerns about Russia, some leaders privately still express fear of Germany's long-term ambitions, although even the most paranoid concede that the notion of a Fourth Reich is rather far-fetched at the moment.

8. Interview with Andrzej Karkoszka, *Defense News*, 21–27 August 1995, p. 30. See also 'Fear of Russia Cited in Polish NATO Bid', *Washington Times*, 6 February 1996, p. A12; and Michael S. Lelyveld, 'Vote on Soviet Union Sparks Demand for NATO Expansion', *Journal of Commerce*, 25 March 1996, p. 3A.

9. See, for example, the comments of Romanian foreign minister Teodor Melescanu in 'Bucharest Treads Line between Moscow, West', inter-

view, *Washington Times*, 6 February 1996, p. A12; and Estonian president Lennart Meri, 'President Says NATO "Firm Safeguard" of Security', *Foreign Broadcast Information Service Daily Report-Central Eurasia*, 18 September 1995, p. 68.

10. A failure to understand that point is also the root problem with Charles Kupchan's proposal to do away with Article 5 guarantees altogether and subsume both NATO and the European Union under a new Atlantic Union. Charles A. Kupchan, 'Reviving the West', *Foreign Affairs*, 75 (May–June 1996), 92–104. According to Kupchan, 'NATO would become the new group's defense arm, but its binding commitments to the collective defense of state borders would give way to more relaxed commitments to uphold collective security through peace enforcement, peacekeeping, and preventive diplomacy. The AU could then open its doors to the new democracies of Central Europe in a manner acceptable to both Russia and the commitment-weary electorates of the current NATO countries' (93). The reason that such a scheme might be acceptable to Russia and the existing NATO members is that there is no substance to it – although the West European countries are not enthusiastic about giving up *their* Article 5 guarantees. The lack of any meaningful security obligations is also why the proposal has received a generally chilly reception in Central and East European capitals.

11. 'Bucharest Treads Line between Moscow, West', p. A12.

12. Quoted in David Ottaway and Peter Maass, 'Hungary, NATO Grope toward New Relationship', *Washington Post*, 17 November 1993, p. A32.

13. Quoted in Ann Devroy and Daniel Williams, 'Clinton Boosts A-Arms Pact in Ukraine', *Washington Post*, 13 January 1994, p. A1.

14. Press Release, Memorandum of the Government of the Slovak Republic on Joining Partnership for Peace, Bratislava, 1 February 1994, p. 1.

15. Officials in Latvia and Estonia are quite candid about the desire for NATO membership to protect their countries' independence from a neo-imperial Russia. See 'Minister on "Partnership for Peace" Expectations', 4 February 1994; 'Foreign Affairs Minister on Plan', 4 February 1994; 'Official: Bilateral Ties with NATO Needed', 7 February 1994, *Foreign Broadcast Information Service Daily Report-Central Eurasia*, 7 February 1994, pp. 70, 72; and Lennart Meri, 'Estonia, NATO and Peacekeeping', *NATO Review*, 42, no. 3 (April 1994), 6–8.

16. Chyrstia Freeland, 'Poland and Lithuania Fuel NATO Row', *Financial Times*, 18 September 1995, p. 2; 'Foreign Minister, Danish Counterpart on EU, NATO', Tallinn Radio Network, 19 September 1995, *Foreign Broadcast Information Service Daily Report-Central Eurasia*, 20 September 1995, p. 101; 'Officials Comment on US Security Act', Tallinn BNS, 17 February 1995, ibid., 21 February 1995, p. 100; 'Latvia Welcome in NATO, Oslo Leader Says', *International Herald Tribune*, 24 April 1996, p. 5; and George Melloan, 'If Russia Wants Another Cold War, Fine', *Wall Street Journal*, 18 September 1995, p. A19. For a detailed argument in favour of offering NATO membership to the Baltic republics, see Vejas Gabriel Liulevicius, 'As Go the Baltics, So Goes Europe', *Orbis*, 39 (Summer 1995), 387–402. Central European support

for including the Baltic republics and other East European countries goes only so far, however; the Central Europeans are not about to jeopardize their own chances for admission by insisting on a comprehensive enlargement. Hungarian Foreign Minister Laslo Kovacs underscored that point: 'It is also in our interests that as many neighbours as possible get the chance to join NATO. At the same time, we do not feel Hungarian admission should be postponed because of being handled together with the applications of other countries.' Quoted in 'Kovacs: Hungary Wants Full, Not Part, NATO Membership', *News File*, Embassy of Hungary, 25 April 1996, p. 3. West European leaders seem the most wary of bringing the Baltic states into NATO's fold, recognizing that such a step would be extremely provocative to Russia. See, for example, Lionel Barber, 'Kohl Draws Line across Europe', *Financial Times*, 14 December 1995, p. 1.

17. Paul Bedard, 'Wałęsa to Clinton: Russians Coming', *Washington Times*, 7 July 1994, p. A11.

18. 'Ready to Accept NATO Nuclear Weapons on Territory if Asked', *New Europe*, 29 October–4 November 1995, p. 17.

19. For discussions of this point, see Lawrence S. Kaplan, *NATO and the United States: The Enduring Alliance* (Boston: Twayne, 1988), passim; Christopher Layne, 'Atlanticism without NATO', *Foreign Policy*, 67 (Summer 1987), 22–45; Ted Galen Carpenter, 'United States NATO Policy at the Crossroads: The Great Debate of 1950–1951', *International History Review*, 8 (August 1986), 389–415; and Carpenter, 'Competing Agendas: America, Europe, and a Troubled NATO Partnership', Ted Galen Carpenter (ed.), *NATO at 40: Confronting a Changing World* (Lexington, Mass.: Lexington Books, 1990), pp. 29–42.

20. Christopher Layne, 'Continental Divide; Time to Disengage in Europe', *National Interest*, 13 (Fall 1988), 13–27, and Layne, 'Atlanticism without NATO'.

21. Glaser, 'Why NATO is Still the Best', p. 10.

22. On the improbability of NATO's willingness to wage war to defend the nations of Central and Eastern Europe, see Stephen Blank, 'New Challenges to European Security', *Strategic Review* (Summer 1994), 40–49.

23. William E. Odom, 'Strategic Realignment in Europe: NATO's Obligation to the East', in *NATO: The Case for Enlargement* (London: Institute for European Defence and Strategic Studies, 1993), pp. 8–9.

24. Congressional Budget Office, 'The Costs of Expanding the NATO Alliance', March 1996, pp. xiv, 28, 54.

25. Ibid., p. 52.

26. The *Economist* complained that 'there is a tendency at NATO headquarters to say the Baltic states are "indefensible".....' 'Partners for What?' *Economist*, 14 September 1994, p. 49.

27. Harries, 'The Collapse of the West', p. 42.

28. Ibid., p. 43.

29. See, for example, the comments by (then) Foreign Minister Andrei Kozyrev, arguably the most pro-Western member of Yeltsin's government. Andrei Kozyrev, 'Partnership or Cold Peace?' *Foreign Policy*, 99 (Summer 1995), 3–14. Kozyrev's opposition to a NATO presence in

Eastern Europe was mild compared with the attitudes of Russian military leaders. See the statements by Deputy Defence Minister Andrei Kokoshin and Defence Minister Pavel Grachev. *Foreign Broadcast Information Service Daily Report-Central Eurasia*, 4 April 1995, 7, and 8 May 1995, p. 31. The hostility of Russian leaders has grown rather than diminished. See 'NATO Expansion Could Prompt Czech, Polish Targeting', *Moscow Nezavisimaya Gazeta*, 7 October 1995, ibid., 10 October 1995, p. 34; Charles Aldinger, 'Russian Defense Chief Warns NATO Not to Expand', *Washington Times*, 5 January 1996, p. A15; and Ed Reavis, 'Russian Foreign Minister Bristling over NATO Plans to Expand East', *European Stars & Stripes*, 9 February 1996, p. 4. For a thoughtful discussion of Russian attitudes on the NATO enlargement issue, see Anatol Lieven, 'A New Iron Curtain', *Atlantic Monthly*, January 1996, pp. 20–25.

30. Ariel Cohen, 'Bill Clinton Gambles Big on Mr. Yeltsin', *Washington Times*, 3 May 1996, p. A21.

31. James A. Baker III, 'Drawing the Line at Macedonia', *Los Angeles Times*, 2 May 1995, p. 2. NATO, Baker contends, 'remains an organization in search of a mission. It need only look as far as preventing a broader Balkan war.'

32. 'Stability in Russia Is Vital to US, Lake Says', text of speech by Anthony Lake to the US-Russia Business Council, Washington, DC, 1 April 1996, *Washington Times*, 7 April 1996, p. A10.

33. Quoted in Laurinda Keys, 'Perry Sees Bosnia Duty Easing Moscow's Fears', *Washington Times*, 5 February 1996, p. A15.

34. Martin Sieff, 'Talbott Now Backs Expansion of NATO', *Washington Times*, 20 September 1995, p. A1.

35. Quoted in Bruce Clark, 'NATO Hopefuls Let Their Impatience Show', *Financial Times*, 7 May 1996, p. 3.

36. William Kincaid and Natalie Melnyczuk, 'Unneighborly Neighbors', *Foreign Policy*, 94 (Spring 1994), 102.

37. Leslie H. Gelb, 'Can Clinton Deal with the World?' *Washington Post*, 6 March 1994, p. C1.

38. Zbigniew Brzezinski, 'A Bigger – and Safer – Europe', *New York Times*, 1 December 1993, p. A23.

39. Brzezinski, 'The Premature Partnership', pp. 81–82.

40. Reflecting Russia's weak position, Yeltsin has already hinted at a face-saving compromise that might be acceptable to Moscow. The former Warsaw Pact countries could join NATO's political institutions but not the alliance's military structure. John Thornhill, 'Yeltsin Suggests Compromise on NATO Expansion', *Financial Times*, 26 March 1996, p. 2. See also Jim Mann, 'Yeltsin NATO Plan Attracts Interest from Clinton Aides, Central Europe', *Los Angeles Times* (Washington edition), 15 April 1996, p. 3.

41. Mikhail S. Gorbachev, 'NATO's Plans Threaten Start II', *New York Times*, 10 February 1996, p. A23.

42. Although the Sino-Russian rapprochement seemed to catch many Western officials by surprise, there had been indications of that development for months. See John Thornhill and Bruce Clark, 'Russia Waves China

Card in NATO's Face', *Financial Times*, 16 November 1995, p. 4. For analyses of the summit outcome, see Steven Mufson, 'China, Russia Swap Support, Sign Array of Agreements', *Washington Post*, 26 April 1996, p. A27; and Joseph Kahn, 'China, Russia Flaunt New Camaraderie in an Apparent Warning to the US', *Wall Street Journal*, 26 April 1996, p. A8.

43. Grachev stated that intention explicitly. Nenad Sebek, Harriet Martin, and Bruce Clark, 'Moscow to Seek Own Allies if NATO Grows', *Financial Times*, 10–11 February 1996, p. 2.

44. Quoted in Peter Ford, 'Troubled Neighbors Watch Belarus Rush into Moscow's Arms', *Christian Science Monitor*, 29 March 1996, p. 31.

45. In September 1995, the presidents of the three Baltic republics issued a joint statement calling for the admission of their three countries 'at the earliest possible time'. Quoted in 'Baltic States Call for Entry to NATO', *Financial Times*, 8 September 1995, p. 2.

46. Quoted in 'Marchuk Reaffirms Ukraine's Non-Aligned Status', Kiev Radio, Ukraine World Service, 13 September 1995, *Foreign Broadcast Information Service Daily Report-Central Eurasia*, 14 September 1995, p. 49. Also see 'NATO Membership Seen "Not Practical"', interview with Vladimir Mukhin, chairman of the Supreme Council of Ukraine Commission on Issues of Defence and State Security, *Most* (Kiev), no. 38, 25 September–1 October 1995, *Foreign Broadcast Information Service Daily Report-Central Eurasia*, 13 October 1995, p. 42; and Hennadiy Udovenko [Ukraine's minister of foreign affairs], 'European Stability and NATO Enlargement: Ukraine's Perspective', *NATO Review*, 43, no. 6 (November 1995), 15–18.

47. Communiqué Issued by Ministerial Meeting of the North Atlantic Council, Brussels, 1 December 1994, text in *NATO Review*, 42, no. 6/ 43, no. 1 (December 1994–January 1995), 26.

48. 'Study on NATO Enlargement', *NATO Review*, 43, no. 6 (November 1995), 10.

49. Quoted in Carol Giacomo, 'Christopher Tries to Reassure Eastern Europe', *Washington Times*, 21 March 1996, p. A14.

IV
Assessing Future Prospects

11 Political Options and Obstacles
Clay Clemens

In their own detailed, at times even passionate, analyses of NATO's possible venture into uncharted territory, this volume's contributors reflect the wide array of opinions about 'functional' and above all 'geographical' enlargement. On the latter concept in particular, differences among proponents or among opponents often seem as great as those between the two camps, for this debate cuts across other, more familiar schools of thought, at times making for strange political bedfellows.

How far NATO ultimately goes with either form of enlargement will rest not only on a calculation of strategic interest, but on how the body politic in key countries perceives that equation. Traditionally, even democratic governments have felt able to shape security policy without first ensuring broad support, counting on a generally prevailing climate of passivity or permissiveness, and indifference toward the often seemingly esoteric, even abstract issues involved. To some extent that remains true, yet the trauma of debate over nuclear weapons in the 1980s taught policy-makers a lesson: that it pays to look beyond defence planning seminars and war games before taking major steps. Certainly further action on either form of NATO enlargement warrants such attentiveness to political and public opinion: such steps would be on an order of magnitude well beyond that of most more routine decisions on weapons procurement or deployment.

This conclusion surveys the state of debate in countries that will ultimately decide how far NATO actually goes beyond its previous mission of collective defense for current members. While all of the West European allies are formally equal in this decision-making process, three medium powers are 'more equal' than the rest – Britain, France and above all the Federal Republic of Germany, which has taken a rare leadership role – while the pivotal player in every respect remains the United States.

THE DISCUSSION IN WESTERN EUROPE

West European member governments all endorse NATO's movement towards functional and geographical enlargement. In this they enjoy broad, usually bipartisan, formal parliamentary support and backing from members of their foreign policy establishments.

Part of this consensus reflects an overall feeling that the Alliance remains essential to European security. Polls taken in all major NATO countries bear out that trust, as do the positions adopted by leading political parties – and not just those of the centre-right. In Britain, for example, moderate leaders like Neil Kinnock and Tony Blair have softened Labour's previous hostility to the Alliance. After ruminating about possible pan-European or even EC-related alternatives, the German Liberals and Social Democrats have likewise endorsed NATO as the primary agent of security on the continent. Similar views are expressed even by foreign policy spokesmen in the largely pacifist, anti-nuclear Greens, a party that was originally formed in part to help resist NATO's perceived militarism.[1] Perhaps most striking is the emergent pro-Alliance consensus among the parties of three straight French presidents – from the remnants of François Mitterrand's Socialists, to a centrist bloc associated with his predecessor Valéry Giscard D'Estaing, and the Gaullist Rally for the Republic of incumbent Jacques Chirac. And despite a sense that America's role should diminish somewhat, the share of French citizens who see NATO as vital to their own security has doubled since the 1980s, from thirty per cent to over sixty per cent – nearly the same level of public approval it enjoys in Great Britain and Germany.[2]

Similarly broad, diffuse support can be found elsewhere as well. That sentiment even intensified somewhat in countries like Denmark and the Netherlands during the early 1990s when left-wing groups that had long considered the Alliance a militaristic anachronism came to regard it as a good means of keeping America engaged on the continent, thus obviating any need for a newly-united Germany to seek security unilaterally. To the extent that leaders in Rome can focus on anything beyond their chronic political crisis, Italy joins other Mediterranean members in seeing NATO membership as evidence of their inclusion in Europe and as a hedge against instability spilling over from North Africa.

Functional Enlargement

This pro-NATO consensus has helped facilitate plans for its functional enlargement. But to what extent are member states themselves prepared for sending troops on *any* non traditional peacekeeping or peace enforcement missions outside Western Europe? And how fully do they agree that the Alliance is best suited for collective 'out-of-area' action? After all, many long favoured assigning such tasks to the European Union's nascent defence arm, the West European Union (WEU). Do NATO's Implementation Force (IFOR) and Stabilization Force (SFOR), set up to enforce the Dayton accord for a ceasefire and elections in war-torn Bosnia, offer a general model for future 'coalitions of the willing'? Does the answer lie in the North Atlantic Council's 1996 Berlin ministerial decision, which envisages WEU members of the Alliance deploying forces out-of-area in Combined Joint Task Forces (CJTF) with US assistance and facilities, even if America itself chooses not to take part?

Based on its postwar record, Britain has been the European country most ready and best equipped for projecting power, as well as the one most likely to accept doing so within a NATO framework. UK defence officials have grown accustomed to working closely with Pentagon colleagues on out-of-area contingencies. For many politicians as well, notions of the Alliance as a police force fit well with residual sentiment for the Anglo-American special relationship – a tradition of collaboration bolstered by broad British support for Operation Desert Storm, in which the two countries took a lead role, if then diminished somewhat by often-bitter transatlantic differences over Bosnia. Even many of those in both major parties less nostalgic about Anglo-American ties and favourable to European unity have still come to see NATO as the preferred vehicle for security, especially out-of-area; few have shown enthusiasm for shifting major responsibility in this realm to an EU-dominated defence apparatus, and right-wing Tories hostile to integration have resisted such proposals even more strongly. To be sure, British leaders have come to accept that the WEU can play a more active role *alongside* NATO: after transatlantic friction over Bosnia, some feel more comfortable with bolstering the European pillar, especially now that Washington no longer strenuously objects. And even Conservative 'Eurosceptics' can stomach a new role for the WEU so long as it remains merely intergovernmental and does not constrain British latitude. Above all, most still see any steps toward a European defence identity as facilitating, not obviating, the Alliance's own functional enlargement. Thus London favoured structural reforms approved in 1996, allowing for WEU members of NATO to deploy forces out-of-area in CJTFs with extensive US help, if not direct American participation. Based partly on tradition and the more recent Gulf experience, public opinion could also be expected to accept NATO out-of-area missions, in principle.[3]

For much of the early 1990s, French opinion remained sceptical about charging the Alliance with new tasks. Officials in Paris continued holding out hope that a souped-up WEU alone could provide EC (then EU) countries with a vehicle for managing out-of-area crises. They pushed the organization into an oversight role for European forces protecting Kurdish rebels in northern Iraq and monitoring sanctions compliance in the Adriatic. At La Rochelle in 1992, French and German leaders approved a new, if vague, WEU out-of-area mandate. Paris-Washington friction over Bosnia and the ways in which Alliance forces should be used there seemingly intensified French resistance to a larger role for NATO in peacekeeping or peace enforcement. The then Foreign Minister Alan Juppé insisted such tension showed 'the necessity of moving beyond NATO...'.[4] As late as 1995, President Chirac challenged the Alliance with a proposal to send a European rapid deployment force to help protect besieged Bosnian enclaves.

And yet during this time events also nourished French scepticism about Europe's ability to act as a unit in such new missions. The Gulf and, ultimately, Bosnia seemed to show the necessity for extensive US participation. Moreover, the Chirac government also concluded that a European-only out-of-area force lacked the necessary sea-or air-lift capabilities, and could not procure them soon: its hopes of meeting the criteria for admission to European Monetary Union required budget austerity, including major cuts in defence. Only the US could provide the requisite support. Greater American readiness to see a larger role for the WEU alongside the Alliance also opened the way for compromise. In later 1995, France's Defence Minister thus met with his colleagues at NATO for the first time in three decades; Paris announced that it would rejoin the Military Committee, if not yet the integrated military command. That modus vivendi cleared the way for both IFOR and, on a longer-term basis, the Berlin compromise allowing future formation of CJTFs.

Germany's cautious support for NATO's functional enlargement rests on a similar mix of general support for the Alliance and scaled-back expectations of a European pillar, as well as some considerations unique to the Federal Republic's post-unification effort to address its own role in international security affairs.

Given its traditional middle position between Washington and Paris, Bonn rarely echoed French talk in the early 1990s about turning out-of-area tasks over to a WEU under EU authority, preferring to see the former remain linked in some way with NATO. But Chancellor Helmut Kohl's centre-right governing coalition and even moderate leaders of the opposition Social Democrats (SPD) did hope that prospects of a more integrated, active European role in non-traditional operations like peacekeeping – and even peace enforcement – could help them overcome opposition to their own country's involvement in such missions. Bonn's political establishment had long claimed that the Basic Law banned military activity outside the traditional NATO area, an interpretation that served and reflected a 'culture of self-restraint' in divided Germany. Even Kohl's coalition worried about evoking charges of revived militarism, and proved hesitant about testing domestic opinion that had grown weary of things military at home yet comfortably unaccustomed to the risks or costs of upholding peace or stability abroad. But the government also conceded that Germany's credibility required changing that mood – a sense that became more urgent after its isolation from Western partners who took part in the Gulf War. Kohl pinned his hopes heavily on the argument that Bonn could neither shirk its duty to help the post-Cold War United Nations and the EC or EU, take on more in the security realm, nor default on its obligation to join partners in doing so. Linking a seemingly sensitive cause to more broadly accepted ones, he argued that complete abstention from out-of-area peacekeeping and even military missions could hinder efforts both to strengthen the UN and to advance European integration. Bonn thus supported larger security roles for the world body and the EC or EU – through the WEU – in part aiming to help transform attitudes about military security at home, and thus to widen its own latitude abroad and in turn gain more credibility as an equal partner. Kohl's government even planned to send military units abroad on what it thought would be relatively non-controversial, multilateral *humanitarian* missions under UN and EC auspices – helping citizens grow accustomed to seeing their sons in uniform helping their comrades. If challenged by opponents, it also hoped to win a ruling from the constitutional court that would sanction even bolder future steps. Given NATO's Cold War image and Bonn's own long-restricted definition of the North Atlantic Treaty's area of operations, Bonn did *not* at first try to persuade public opinion to accept out-of-area missions by arguing that they might take place under the auspices of a functionally enlarged Alliance.

This tactic worked, if perhaps not quite as planned. The German military's biggest overseas humanitarian commitment came in

Somalia, but the criticism that mission drew dimmed enthusiasm for further, large-scale UN operations. European caution and discord over peacekeeping in the Balkans, along with a domestic backlash against integration and logistical shortcomings likewise limited support for and momentum towards a more active WEU. Moreover, contrary to expectations, the occasions on which Bonn joined non-traditional out-of-area missions came primarily under *Alliance* auspices – in 1992, as part of Adriatic naval forces monitoring compliance with sanctions against Serbia (though confusingly, the German ship shuttled back and forth between NATO-and WEU-patrolled waters); in 1993, on AWACs flights patrolling no-fly zones, even to the delicate extent of directing fire against violators; and in 1994–95, with indirect support of raids against Serb targets. Most importantly, after some debate, the government, top SPD moderates and even many Greens approved deploying German Tornado fighters to help assist a NATO plan for extricating peacekeepers in mid-1995. Late that year, this same bipartisan majority approved not only flying air missions but dispatching supply units and a field hospital to Croatia as part of IFOR. By the originally-planned withdrawal deadline of December 1996, most parliamentarians were even ready to extend that commitment for another eighteen months and had swallowed a technical reclassification of those units as 'combat forces'.

In sum, German attitudes toward involvement had indeed begun shifting. Yet despite some initial difficulties, it was NATO rather than the UN or WEU that proved to be best suited to out-of-area tasks, at least in Bosnia, and thus public opinion came to accept Bundeswehr participation out-of-area under Alliance auspices. Moreover, the constitutional court did finally offer a flexible reading of Basic Law limits: it allowed participation in collective security missions under UN, WEU *or* NATO authority.

One reason for the surprisingly brief domestic discussion of and broad consensus for missions once considered off-limits lay in the Bosnian conflict itself. Centre-right leaders argued that 'an end to the suffering of Bosnia-Hercegovina is not possible without the Dayton accord and without NATO's contribution...'.[5] Even left-wing politicians felt Germans in particular could no longer abstain from efforts to help end the bloodshed, whatever their fear of moving toward a more 'militarized' foreign policy. As a result, they overcame most qualms about a direct, albeit modest Bundeswehr role in an Alliance mission – at least one on the periphery of Europe – that entailed some risk of combat.

Indeed, some on the left have even begun to talk of 'a new transatlantic partnership in the age of globalism,' precisely because they do not trust EU-only organizations, let alone Germany itself, to ensure the stability and peace of a more united, but still conflict-prone continent.[6] Polls show that four out of five Germans want NATO to help tackle crises on Europe's fringes, and that most cite this role as the main reason for backing a continued US military presence in their country.[7]

Yet even most West European government and political leaders who endorse expanding NATO's tasks do so conditionally or cautiously. Some worry about transatlantic friction over which crises outside Europe warrant what degree of NATO involvement. Some see the Bosnian episode's bitter, discordant first chapter as likely to be more typical than its less-acrimonious second – that is, the Dayton accord, IFOR and SFOR. Nor did the 1996 Alliance restructuring agreement on CJTFs end all European debate over NATO as the vehicle for out-of-area operations; as one editorial observed, 'Plainly [it] hides fuel for political conflict'.[8] As late as mid-1996, French leaders still preferred an entirely separate WEU reaction force. Their persistent desire for some independence from Washington also surfaced in a refusal to go further toward re-integration into NATO – not joining the Alliance Nuclear Planning Committee, for example – and in a spat over which nation should control its Southern Command in Naples.

Despite having cleared away constitutional obstacles to out-of-area ventures and arrived at a consensus on NATO's role in Bosnia, German leaders also remain cautious. Kohl's government, let alone one of the centre-left, might find that Bonn's campaign to change the 'culture of caution' has not yet crossed its Rubicon – that political and public opinion remains unready for prospects of Bundeswehr troops being shot, or having to shoot. While Bosnia's proximity to East Central Europe, German antipathy towards the Serbs, horror at what many have labelled genocide and a sense of moral obligation generated by Nazi crimes in the Balkans *did* all help spawn bipartisan domestic accord on sending a limited force under strict rules of engagement to help NATO allies, such conditions are unlikely to obtain in future crises beyond Europe. For example, given that Bonn does not share either Washington's hostility towards the Iranian regime or its approach to terrorism, agreement on any Alliance involvement in southwest Asia would prove elusive. Moreover, many politicians on the left – the sizable number who, after all, resisted involvement in Bosnia and even those who backed it – have drawn a line, refusing to see IFOR as a precedent for future missions. As prominent German Greens have declared, 'multinational peace forces under NATO leadership [offers] ... no model for the future'.[9] And concrete Alliance plans for CJTF notwithstanding, even government supporters would have reservations or outright objections to US-led 'coalitions of the willing' using Alliance bases in their country to support out-of-area missions where Bonn's and Washington's views differ – again, for example, on the Middle East.

Geographical Enlargement

If Europe's broad post-Cold War honeymoon with NATO has helped generate support for functional enlargement, it has likewise bolstered the case for opening the organization to new members from the former Soviet bloc – especially the so-called Visegrad states of East Central Europe (Poland, Hungary, the Czech Republic and perhaps Slovakia), as well as possibly some Balkan countries (Slovenia and Romania) and the small Baltic republics (Latvia, Estonia and Lithuania). Many policy elites see the continent as incomplete without its eastern half, and regard the inclusion above all of its new, nearby democracies – Poland, the Czech Republic and Hungary – as just and natural. A certain guilt for the past plays a role as well, given the West's general indifference to the fate of those countries before World War II and during Soviet occupation. Residual concern about Russia motivates some, but not all; indeed, a desire for inclusion trumps any nervous quest for containment of Moscow.

Much the same profile also fits that share of public opinion inclined to back enlargement, at least in three major countries. There too the emphasis lies on inclusion rather than on defence. Members of focus groups in Germany, France and Britain, for example, generally agreed that a larger NATO 'would be like the United Nations for defence,' and thus 'can't be a bad thing'; some added 'a common alliance is always better than establishing a counterpart, an opposite pole'. On average, two-thirds of those polled in each country even favoured admitting Russia as well.[10]

Support for opening NATO to new members has proven especially strong among German leaders. Such sentiment reflects in part an innate desire to atone for the past – especially Nazi occupation and atrocities – along with a general belief in the virtue of inclusion. But geography also helps explain why so much of the enlargement discussion began in Bonn. Chancellor Helmut Kohl stresses that his country does not again want to be on democratic Europe's periphery, while others warn against a 'security vacuum' in their region – both points reflecting the broad bipartisan desire for stable surroundings, a view that undergirds German support for extending *all* Western institutions.[11] Alliance enlargement specifically received a big early boost from its late Secretary-General Manfred Wörner, previously Defence Minister in Bonn, and from one of his successors in that post. Volker Rühe notes that the proposal would serve German security interests, an argument most politicians in Bonn still avoid as too unilateral – and stresses that the East Central European countries do not again want to be 'left in the lurch as in 1938 and 1939, as in 1945 and 1956, as in 1968 and 1981...They want to belong to the family of free Western democracies.'[12] After NATO introduced its Partnership for Peace, Rühe took a lead in pushing to ensure that PfP did not slow, let alone block enlargement. In 1995, his boss, Chancellor Kohl, even promised Poland admittance as early as the year 2000.

NATO enlargement also finds support among leaders and security specialists on the left. Social Democratic Party spokesman Karsten Voigt has argued that 'we must act quickly to open the door for new members,' explaining that the plan 'will complete Germany's multilateral integration,' and is also motivated 'by the search for stability through integration'.[13] Even some prominent Greens agree. Their stance rests less on calculations of national interest than on a more diffuse, general desire to erase old Cold War divisions, along with reluctance to abandon neighbours brutally victimized by Nazi Germany.[14]

History and geography in part also feed *public* backing for enlargement in Germany, consistently somewhat higher there than in France or Britain. These factors also help explain why support for admitting Poland and the Czech Republic runs at sixty per cent, for Hungary – which played a key role in unification – 72 per cent. Enthusiasm for Slovakia, the Baltics, and Bulgaria is a bit less, while opinion divides on Ukraine, Slovenia and Romania.[15]

Germany is not the only member state with specific reasons for embracing enlargement. On NATO's northeastern periphery, Denmark and Norway share concerns about stability in the Visegrad states, but have an even more direct stake in enhancing security for their Baltic neighbours, Latvia, Estonia and Lithuania. For similar reasons, Italy embraces Slovenia's candidacy.

Though less intense than in Germany, support for NATO's geographical enlargement exists in Britain and France. In the UK it also rests somewhat on a residual uneasiness about Russia, especially among Conservatives, along with broad sympathy for East Central Europe. That sentiment may at least in part reflect lingering guilt about Britain's failure to honor security guarantees for Poland in 1939, or to support it again in 1944–45 (in any case, eventual Polish admission to NATO wins backing from 79% of those polled – a level clearly higher than the support for any enlargement candidate by any other current NATO member).[16] For France, some residual Russo-phobia, as well as cultural or political ties with countries like Poland and, above all, Romania – links in its prewar East European *cordon sanitaire*, but later abandoned to Nazi conquest – feeds some sympathy for extending Alliance membership to them. Reinforcing such motives is a tacit yet evident wish to preserve French influence in a region where the US and German role is growing.

Yet even many of those West Europeans formally on record in support of NATO's geographical enlargement also evince caution. For German leaders the major reason is reluctance to provoke Russian nationalists. As early as 1994, Kohl overruled Rühe in the defence minister's dispute with foreign minister Klaus Kinkel over the pace of enlargement, and at times seemed to link extension of Alliance membership with admittance to the EU, an even more intricate, gradual process. The Chancellor himself also remained vague about whether PfP would speed admission to NATO, and in 1996 warned American politicians against outbidding each other in their haste for enlargement for fear it might endanger Yeltsin's re-election. Uneasy that pressing for admission of the Baltics could intensify Russian resistance to membership for the nearby Visegrad states, Kohl began to balk on, even reportedly resist, early membership for Lithuania, Estonia and Latvia.[17] In short, despite Rühe's avid support, NATO enlargement, especially at a rapid pace and on a broad basis, evokes ambivalence, even among centrists. A top security policy analyst at the think tank closest to Kohl's party has called the idea 'folly'.[18] And with vivid memories of the 1980s debate and what it almost did to NATO's popularity in their country, centrist leaders may grow ever more cautious about enlargement if discussion turns – as at some point seems inevitable – to whether new members would come under US nuclear protection. Having cleared the country of missiles and fudged some aspects of Alliance military strategy, Bonn has no desire for more political and public debate over exactly what a worst-case scenario would mean for Central Europe.

Despite their official stance, politicians and officials in other allied countries have displayed even greater scepticism. Many worry in particular about Moscow's reaction. As one official in Rome observed, 'We do not think NATO should enlarge against Russia's wishes.' Without Germany's proximity to East Central Europe, they lack the natural sense of concern about that region that animates even cautious advocates in Bonn. Indeed, worried about the cost and practicality of new commitments, some politicians and publicists in London have even depicted enlargement as Germany's effort to have allies help secure its periphery or even carve out a sphere of influence. Many officials in Paris share that view, and also worry that expansion will unduly expand the US role in Eastern Europe. French officials even initially tried using the discussion of membership criteria to argue for a rewriting of the North Atlantic Treaty aimed at making the EU and US equal partners in a broader, looser league.

In short, support for enlargement even in Germany and especially in other West European allied countries is broad but shallow. And always in the background of deliberations or debate, feeding resignation but also to some extent concern and resistance, is a sense that the real decision about Europe's future ultimately lies elsewhere – in Washington. As one Italian official sighed, 'it depends on Clinton, not us'.[19]

THE DISCUSSION IN AMERICA: STRANGE BEDFELLOWS

Most of America's traditional foreign policy establishment and political elite officially regard NATO's double enlargement as a settled issue. The Clinton administration, along with both major party leaderships, is on record as fully in support of extending the Alliance's tasks and opening its ranks, initially at least to the three larger Visegrad states. At Helsinki in early 1997, he made this case to Boris Yeltsin and seemed to win the Russian leader's grudging acquiescence.

Yet as Ronald Asmus notes, if there is major contention over enlargement, it is mainly 'an American debate'. For uncertainty persists over how far the world's only remaining superpower will ultimately commit to expanding the Alliance's functions, or to guaranteeing the security of any new members. Such confusion about NATO's future reflects a broader indecision and some deep, if often still implicit, differences about the country's own overall post-Cold War international role. At the same time, discussion of the

Alliance or even America's place in the world at large has not engaged a broad spectrum of opinion. Such controversy as has occurred, moreover, often involves odd and shifting alliances, underscoring the near-irrelevance of older categories like 'hawk' or 'dove' – even of broader, time-honored labels like conservative or liberal – to post-Cold War era discussions of American foreign relations. As a result, the balance of opinion about any actual commitments that Washington may ultimately make to advance NATO's double enlargement remains far from settled. Largely unforeseeable developments – above all abroad – may yet affect, even effect, the outcome.

Functional Enlargement

To the extent George Bush's talk of a 'new world order' meant anything specific, it called for going beyond Cold War structures, building broader, UN-based coalitions against rogue states and other new or old agents of instability. His administration hoped that a broader, looser framework would permit, even encourage, greater co-operation with Gorbachev's USSR and other key partners abroad. Operation Desert Storm thus rested on Security Council resolutions, and brought together a loose team of two dozen states, including some NATO members, if by no means restricted to these allies. On the other hand, the administration acknowledged that Alliance infrastructure and 'habits of co-operation' proved valuable (some said invaluable) in its successful Gulf operation. Moreover, US resistance to upgrading the WEU in 1991–92 reflected a reluctance to see the Alliance displaced – in Europe itself, but also in any future role in Western peacemaking or security missions elsewhere.

Others close to the Republican administration articulated an even more clearcut case for functional enlargement. Fearing that a rising tide of post-Cold War neo-isolationism might cut the US off from its transatlantic allies if the vital transatlantic link – NATO – came to be seen as shaky and outdated, Senator Richard Lugar argued that the Alliance needed new missions. While stressing its traditional task of collective defence, he worried that American politicians might find the price of continued engagement too high unless they saw other benefits: by popularizing the now-familiar phrase 'out-of-area or out-of-business', he admonished Western leaders to make the Alliance a vehicle for co-ordinated responses to regional security crises beyond Europe or risk seeing US support for the entire organization, including even in its traditional roles, erode.

Almost inadvertently, the Clinton administration solidified official American support for NATO's functional enlargement. Initially even more favourable than its predecessor to an expanded UN role, including perhaps a standing force at the Secretary-General's disposal, it backed away from such ideas after – rightly or not – blaming the world body for a disastrous end to international efforts at stabilizing Somalia. The Balkans war accelerated this reversal. At first the administration conditionally approved having the UN use NATO forces to help monitor sanctions compliance and punish isolated no-fly zone violations, but again grew unhappy with the result. At home, an emergent Republican majority in Congress attacked Clinton for allegedly surrendering authority over US forces to the Secretary-General, decrying the arrangement as an infringement of national sovereignty. Critics also charged that the UN's caution about using force and confused, overlapping lines of authority could damage both American *and* Alliance credibility. In early 1995, Congress passed the National Security Restoration Act, which – among other things – called on the administration to reaffirm that 'NATO military planning includes joint military operations outside of NATO jurisdiction'. In 1995, Washington also pushed for new rules of engagement in Bosnia and new missions that gave the Alliance more latitude. The Dayton accord then in effect put a seal on NATO's primary role in that region. At the same time, the administration backed plans for CJTFs that would allow more European defence collaboration with or without direct US involvement, yet still rely on Alliance infrastructure and thus shield its pre-eminent role in any such out-of-area operations.

America's establishment politicians have thus made plain that they would prefer entrusting any such missions to NATO, the popular flagship of postwar US foreign policy. Yet at the same time there have been growing indications that the Alliance would also face an intensifying current of unilateralist sentiment, a mood reaching even into the political mainstream.

Early in the Bosnian crisis, when the administration – under Republican pressure – upheld NATO as a way of damning the UN, transatlantic differences flared. US insistence on air strikes and pressure to lift the arms embargo on Moslem government forces revealed a fundamental difference in approach to the handling of an out-of-area conflict, at least one on Western Europe's fringes. Clinton's November 1994 declaration that the US would no longer stop weapons being brought into Bosnia, made necessary by Congressional vote, marked the first open break with set Alliance policy in decades. The then

Senate majority leader Robert Dole remarked that transatlantic differences over Bosnia had brought NATO to its worst crisis ever. It seemed that such strains were compelling even longtime Atlanticists to adopt, or at least placate, unilateralist sentiment at home.

American politicians in both parties have also shown growing readiness to push harder than their allies in dealing with rogue states and terrorism, even at the risk of intra-NATO rifts. Again under Republican pressure, for example, Clinton signed the D'Amato act permitting sanctions against European firms investing in Iran and Libya. Transatlantic differences over US action against Saddam Hussein further suggest that agreeing on joint *NATO* action in a future crisis in an area like the Middle East could run afoul of sharply different views on and approaches to 'Western' interests. Moreover, given a reflexive sense on Capitol Hill and in the public that America's allies already shirk their share of the financial burden for collective efforts, and the fact that they are actually scaling back their own military establishments even faster than the Pentagon, future CJTFs in which the US lends assets to NATO partners could prove divisive.

For the same reason, seemingly unrelated frictions raise some doubts about the real depth of American support for functional enlargement. Speaker Newt Gingrich's reminder that 'NATO's military policy cannot be discussed in isolation [because] trade, diplomacy, defence and dealing with terrorism all go together,' ends with a blunt warning: 'we cannot be happy with our allies on the military side if they are gouging us in our trade relations.'[20] In sum, despite respect for the NATO tradition, politicians on both sides of the aisle reflect a steadily-rising public sense that partnership should mean sharing US priorities, and an unshakable assumption that America too easily allows itself to do favours for freeloading friends. For most, the Alliance is only one value among many, and by no means so sacred as it might have been for a previous generation.

Thus, while some advocates of functional enlargement hope that giving NATO new tasks abroad may help bolster its image in the United States, few wholly discount the potential risk involved – the prospect that such non-traditional missions might instead also feed a backlash *against* the organization.

Geographical Enlargement

While the Bush administration talked in general terms of opening NATO to Eastern Europe, the issue did not draw attention until late

1993, when the Visegrad countries pressed their case more urgently. Advocates like Lugar argued that Alliance credibility required such a step, while analysts at the Rand Corporation insisted that consolidating democratic stability in the region made enlargement vital, with or without any future Russian threat. But beset by hardliners, Boris Yeltsin's Kremlin bluntly warned Bill Clinton against it. Though reluctant to dash East European hopes altogether, the president was also cautioned by his Joint Chiefs against expecting too much from rapid Alliance expansion and by State Department officials – particularly Deputy Secretary and close friend Strobe Talbott – against destabilizing reform in Russia. Thus Clinton opted for a compromise: Partnership for Peace.

But critics complained of PfP's vagueness, above all on whether and when it might lead to actual enlargement, or on who might be admitted; some called it a mere delaying tactic or a weak substitute for the real thing. Polish, Czech and Hungarian officials voiced disappointment. Lobbying groups claiming to represent some twenty million US citizens with ethnic ties to those countries, five per cent of the electorate concentrated heavily in key industrial states, went into action. The Polish-American Congress, speaking on behalf of nine million Americans, put out a legislative alert, flooding Congress and the White House with telegrams, faxes and calls to warn against a 'new Yalta', another betrayal of their ancestral homeland. Some of the few Republican leaders still deeply interested in foreign policy generally and Europe particularly, like Lugar, also depicted enlargement as necessary – not simply as reinsurance against a future Russian threat and fulfilment of an obligation to East Central Europe, but as another new, relevant post-Cold War role that might sustain American domestic support for NATO. They charged that the administration's deference to Russia risked leaving a dangerous security vacuum at the continent's centre: far from drawing a new dividing line further east, they insisted, enlargement could erase such partitions or make them meaningless.

Caught off-guard, the President stood by PfP – which became official NATO policy in January 1994 – but pledged that it represented a commitment to and preparation for membership. Enlargement was no longer a question of 'if', but 'when', he stated. Yet as pressure for clarification mounted in early 1994 from (for example) German Defense Minister Rühe, Lugar, Henry Kissinger, and experts at such think tanks as Rand or the Hudson Institute, administration officials remained ambiguous, vaguely depicting enlargement as an evolutionary process. Talbott's emphasis on allaying the concerns of a still-shaky Russia took precedence. Washington continued pursuing a double-track approach – holding the door open for new members, yet not naming a date or concrete membership plans. That summer and into the early autumn, administration officials contradicted Rühe and other at home or abroad who favoured rapid enlargement. Defence Secretary William Perry noted that no applicant was yet ready for membership.

But domestic pressure also mounted. A bipartisan three-fourths Senate majority endorsed the 'NATO Participation Act' in July, 1994, granting the Visegrad states weapons export privileges traditionally reserved for Alliance members. Lobbied by the newly-founded Central and East European Coalition, House Republican aspirants included a call for enlargement in their 'Contract for America', one of its few foreign policy planks. Opposition leaders increasingly raised charges that Clinton's administration took too soft a line on Russia, evoking a residual Cold War suspicion of Moscow. Yet even Democrats, above all those with ethnic East European populations in their states like Illinois's liberal Paul Simon, as well as others such as Joseph Biden and Joseph Lieberman, joined the call for enlargement.

The autumn of 1994 saw administration policy grow more specific, a concentration of mind due in part to the spectre of an imminent hanging – the Republican sweep of Congress (even if foreign policy would play only a minor role). But after months of intra-Alliance friction over Bosnia, Clinton also wanted to defuse any potential rift over enlargement. Fearing further ambiguity might send false signals, some top officials – most notably the newly-named Assistant Secretary of State for Europe, Richard Holbrooke – talked of membership in the near future. Soon Talbott joined him in this call, reversing his earlier stance. Yet administration calls for Alliance plans to prepare a study laying out details on enlargement still struck critics as equivocation.

After the worsening Chechnya crisis in early 1995 revived concern among Clinton advisors about Yeltsin's position, a reported US offer of NATO membership for *Russia* sparked still more confusion abroad and new partisan attacks at home. Polls showed that voters favoured admitting Poland and Hungary, and Clinton's Republican foes seemed set to make that case in the next presidential race, arguing that he had put these countries' security at risk in the effort to placate Moscow. By passing the National Security Restoration Act in early 1995, they aimed at underscoring his alleged weakness on this issue (as well as his readiness to put US troops under UN command). As a presidential candidate, Dole charged Clinton with taking a 'deliber-ately slow' approach to opening NATO; he called for action rather than continual study and planning.[21] Thus, even after the Alliance in late 1995 published its study calling for enlargement, the administra-tion faced opposition criticism for equivocating.

Yet Clinton could also remain at the centre ground between those favouring what his advisers labeled imprudent speed and others at home or abroad who were dragging their feet. That confined his differences with rivals like Dole to a question of timing, and increas-ingly compelled the latter to adopt bolder rhetoric and argue for ever quicker action, regardless of events in Russia. Especially at a time when Yeltsin seemed vulnerable, such demands opened them to coun-ter-charges of imprudence or recklessness. Clinton campaigned suc-cessfully in places like the Midwest, trumpeting his commitment to careful yet certain enlargement. The president's stance left him broad latitude on this issue after his re-election in November. Thus the administration endorsed plans for a mid-1997 Alliance summit to announce the first new members, implying that Poland, Hungary and the Czech republic – if not yet the Baltics – could hope for admittance by 1999, the fiftieth anniversary of NATO's founding.

But while government officials and mainstream political leaders from both major parties have thus outbid each other in trying to show who could best implement plans for opening up NATO for new members, sustaining support for such plans in the United States may prove easier said than done. Since the early 1990s a coalition just as broadly diverse as that favouring enlargement has crystallized around the opposite pole. It includes those voicing nuanced doubts, tough questions or outright rejection.

Opponents have begun by drawing on the same main point as early administration sceptics. Concern about possible Russian aggression may not have been the only original motive behind enlargement, they have noted, but the thin credibility of any other arguments for this plan would inevitably lead advocates to fall back on 'bear-bait-ing'. Yet pushing NATO into the old Soviet sphere will exploit Mos-cow's Cold War humiliation and ostracize it from the Western democratic club, they have emphasized, which might in turn arouse nationalists and demoralize reformers, making failure, even revanchism, a self-fulfilling prophecy. Such reservations have helped to mobilize opponents ranging from arms control groups such as the Union of Concerned Scientists (UCS) and the Centre for Defence Information (CDI), to experts at establishment think tanks like the Council on

Foreign Relations (CFR) and Carnegie Endowment, to prominent retired US diplomats – from George Kennan to Paul Nitze – and the late Richard Nixon.

Beyond this common concern, sceptics have voiced varying, even contradictory fears about enlargement. Some, like retired Admiral Gene Carroll of the CDI or former Ambassador Jonathan Dean of the UCS, have evinced a general, long-standing wariness of putting military alliances front and centre in security policy. By contrast, those like Nitze or long-time hawk Fred Ikle have approached the issue from a purely power-politics perspective. Never having seen Eastern Europe as vital to US interests, they have cautioned against extending American pledges to a region long beset by political instability, nationality conflicts and weak economies. Sceptics have never seen much prospect of the West mounting a credible defence of the Visegrad states, let alone the Baltics. As to other advantages of enlargement, they have scoffed at treating the Alliance like 'a kindergarten for democracy' in Eastern Europe, a mission wrong for a military organization and likely to come at the expense of its main job of collective defence of the West. Such arguments have left even cornerstones of the American foreign policy establishment – Carnegie, Brookings, CFR – ambivalent or divided over the merits of enlargement. The latter's study group on European security, for example, avoided endorsing Alliance plans in 1995. At a forum in late 1996, members clearly sided with sceptic Michael Mandelbaum in his debate with the administration's spokesman, Richard Holbrooke.[22]

As if this coalition of sceptics were not diverse enough, it has come to include increasingly vocal anti-establishment analysts suspicious of post-Cold War US internationalism. The libertarian Cato Institute and journals like *The National Interest* have depicted enlargement as a risky, costly, needless plan that could draw America deeper into a region where it has no interests at stake and into conflicts that Europeans should be willing and able to resolve on their own. They have depicted Washington's support for the plan as the result of desperate efforts to find NATO some post-Cold War purpose by an elite too deeply invested in overseas involvement. At times even implying that the Alliance never really served US interests, some charge that it has become a costly irrelevance. While conceding that public opinion began backing enlargement because of general sympathy for both NATO and Eastern Europe, they have predicted growing opposition as debate intensifies over the plan's cost and any idea of extending US nuclear guarantees eastward.

Concerns about the Russian reaction and other uncertainties about enlargement have spilled over into the political realm, cutting across party or ideological lines. Among Democrats, the former Senator Sam Nunn, a respected defence expert with a long record of support for NATO, has voiced reservations – 'somebody had better be able to explain to the American people why, or at least why now' he declared in mid-1995 – as has another popular moderate colleague leaving Capitol Hill, Bill Bradley of New Jersey.[23] Other longtime liberal sceptics of NATO and Pentagon plans in Congress have grown even more adamantly opposed to enlargement.

Across the aisle, even many Republican conservatives who supported the Contract for America have evinced uncertainty about what they signed on to. While eager to depict the administration as soft on military issues and to placate constituents of East European descent, few have shown enthusiasm about extending US security guarantees. Such caution has been greatly reinforced by reluctance to resist the vocal, if still minority, 'America First' neo-isolationism on the political right. And leaders of the latter have left no doubt where they stand on enlargement. During his briefly successful presidential bid, for example, the columnist Patrick Buchanan mocked the idea of 'extending to Bratislava when it's obvious NATO won't even fight in Bosnia'.[24]

As with other post-Cold War foreign policy controversies (like the dispute over a North American Free Trade Agreement), executive and legislative leaders, as well as the foreign policy establishment, find their shared commitment to enlargement questioned by a broad array of longtime colleagues, defectors and mavericks. When the Senate meets to approve extending US security guarantees – in effect still a nuclear umbrella – deep into East Europe, mustering a two-thirds majority may prove difficult.

CONCLUSION

Some Cold War-era debates over NATO policy remained at the elite level, while others engaged broader passions, a notable case being the medium-range missile controversy. Yet such rows usually boiled down to differences over how best to confront a widely-perceived, seemingly constant Soviet threat, which tended to impose some clarity on the discussion: from issue to issue, the same participants could be identified as hawks, others as doves, and those differences in turn bore some connection to the overall left–right political dimension in each country.

In contrast, proposals for enlarging NATO functionally and geographically have aroused fewer passions. Moreover, attitudes among politicians and voters have remained vague or unstructured. Both leaders and the public traditionally take their cues on security issues from a small community of experts, but on this issue the specialists themselves have become divided over the Alliance's future into two odd, shaky camps. Moreover, even proponents have a difficult time making the case for either plan based on compelling (let alone urgent) security interests, while sceptics see no such stakes at all in either form of enlargement.

One implication of the unstructured, fluid nature of this debate is that the outcome in Europe will hinge very heavily on that in America: as the key to both forms of enlargement, Washington's decision and subsequent actions will ultimately either give life to both new ventures, slow them down or even conceivably reverse them. Just as likely, political debate in Europe, but above all in America – unstructured and loose as it is – may prove especially susceptible to perceptions of cost. Estimates of the price tag for both types of enlargement have naturally varied. Proponents at Rand contend that the same steps vital for enhancing NATO's out-of-area capabilities – more mobility, and above all airlift – will allow it to provide for a credible defence of new member states, obviating any need for major forward stationing of forces, let alone nuclear arms; they put the cost for including the Visegrad states at $42 billion. The Congressional Budget Office has suggested $60 billion to $125 billion over a fifteen-year period for overall enlargement, with the US covering about one-tenth of that bill.[25] Not surprisingly, sceptics have suggested that both understate the likely costs. And whatever the *actual* resource burden, American support for enlargement in the long term may also be affected by perceptions, including a suspicion that West European defence reductions will prevent them from paying their share, or an assumption that East European applicants are freeloading. Even something seemingly tangential, like transatlantic trade frictions, could also shape the overall climate of opinion about NATO, making it more difficult to sell the case for a greater US contribution.

In a discussion of foreign policy as unstructured as that over double enlargement, the outcome may also depend on how other developments affect perceptions of the possible *risks* involved. Such events could stem from regions in or beyond Europe:

The Balkans

In mid-1995 officials grumbled that discussing enlargement seemed premature, since differences over Bosnia might well kill the Alliance before it had a chance to grow. A year later the picture appeared very different. Tackling that crisis seemed to have helped overcome German qualms about out-of-area involvement, US reservations about an EU security identity, and French resistance to enhancing NATO's role. It led to a Western military presence beyond the Alliance area and even in candidate states like Hungary, while allowing for co-operation on the ground with Russia's military, perhaps a confidence-building measure. Yet from early on, few believed IFOR would be the final chapter, doubts confirmed in late 1996 by the creation of SFOR. Any major delay or complications in the final withdrawal of all Western forces in the late 1990s, to say nothing of Bosnia's possible relapse into bloody civil war after their departure, or simply a generally negative verdict on the mission's overall outcome, could risk re-igniting major intra-Alliance recriminations. Especially if accompanied by possible loss of US lives, that sort of legacy would also sour the climate for any future CJTF-style operations or even reverse progress on that front altogether.

Russia

By late 1996, Russian leaders – resigned, if not reconciled – said they would react 'pragmatically' rather than 'hysterically' to NATO membership for some East European states. Yeltsin's stance at his March 1997 Helsinki meeting with Clinton seemed to reflect a sense of resignation. The Alliance had won this grudging acquiescence by its pledge not to station nuclear weapons in any new member countries; some ambiguity about forward deployment of troops; presumed exclusion of the Baltic republics from any early stage of expansion; adjustment of two arms agreements; and offers of a charter (if not a formal treaty) for relations with Moscow that called for regular consultation. NATO leaders counted on these first steps toward enlargement going smoothly enough to allay remaining Russian doubt about Western intentions. They also hoped for signs of stability in Moscow, for progress toward reform, and for Yeltsin to stay in power – or at least (or perhaps even ideally) to make way for a healthy, less erratic moderate. If forthcoming, such trends also promised in turn to weaken Western concern – albeit also any sense of urgency – about enlargement.

Yet, alternatively, a hardline parliamentary backlash in Russia against early steps towards expansion, or deteriorating domestic conditions there, risked polarizing NATO's own internal debate. Some proponents of enlargement would see any such events in Moscow as grounds for haste and thus fall back on a politically easier but volatile case for 'containment'. Yet that argument in turn would risk splitting the shaky pro-enlargement coalition, antagonizing those – especially in Europe, but in the US as well – who prefer to see it as a form of 'inclusion' that might even serve Kremlin security concerns. Thus, well into any enlargement process, developments in Russia seemed certain to remain a key, perhaps decisive variable affecting possible later NATO steps, above all into the Baltic region, formerly Soviet territories.

The Middle East

The Gulf War offered a showcase for how effectively NATO members (and other) could co-operate out-of-area when they share common views of the interests involved. Yet this early 'coalition of the willing' was atypically convenient in the degree to which it united Western countries and in the relative ease with which military operations far afield could be handled. Consensus is likely to prove far more elusive in any future contingency involving, for example, Algeria, or above all Libya, Iran, Sudan, or terrorists vaguely linked to any of them. Past precedent and ongoing frictions over how best to handle such regimes suggest that Washington may be more ready to use force than its allies, as in 1996 when it punished Saddam Hussein's military for his incursions into northern Iraq. Such differences would either strain an Alliance now permitted, even mandated, to co-ordinate the West's response, or else prompt unilateral US action that would also risk generating antagonism on both sides of the Atlantic, a mood with potential costs for the new NATO.

European Integration

As so often in the past, European unity poses a quandary for the Atlantic Alliance. If monetary and political union, as well as a common foreign and security policy, proceed generally as planned, it could weaken the case of those in the US who complain that Europe's inability to speak with one voice permanently handicaps transatlantic co-operation. At the same time, such progress may nourish US unilateralism by creating an impression that the EU could handle the security of its eastern neighbours on its own and even perform most policing tasks elsewhere. On the other hand, if integration were to lose steam, or even go off-track altogether, supporters of expanding NATO's mandate and membership will claim vindication. Yet American sceptics in particular could see in that development only further reason for charging that the fecklessness and disunity of Washington's European partners militate against expanding the transatlantic Alliance's ranks and role.

By late 1996, NATO had made its initial commitments to both functional and geographical enlargement, even announcing plans to name some new members at a July 1997 summit meeting in Spain. Yet both steps promised to mark only the beginning, not the end, of a long process. Adapting the Alliance to its new geopolitical environment will thus remain a difficult challenge, testing Western leaders for years to come. How well they are able to sustain a solid political consensus for double enlargement, within key countries *and* across the Atlantic, will determine the scale and pace of this venture into uncharted territory.

NOTES

1. Joschka Fischer, '"Sicherheit in Europa ist ohne die USA nicht zu gewährleisten"', *Frankfurter Rundschau*, 8 June 1996, p. 14.
2. United States Information Agency (USA), 'The New European Security Architecture: Publics Assess the Building Blocks of European Security', September 1995. USIA conducted extensive surveys and focus groups in Western and East Central Europe, as well as the US and Russia in the spring of 1995.
3. 'Wooing the WEU', *Economist*, 4 March 1995.
4. Cited in William Drozdiak, 'US and Europe in Serious Rift Over Bosnia War', *Washington Post*, 27 November 1994.
5. Kohl's parliamentary floor leader and heir apparent Wolfgang Schäuble, 'Wir müssen verlässliche Partner sein', in CDU/CSU Bundestagsfraktion, *Stichworte der Woche*, 8 December 1995.
6. Fischer, 'Sicherheit in Europa'.
7. A RAND-sponsored survey cited in 'Das Bündnis mit Amerika auf festen Grund', in *Frankfurter Allgemeine Zeitung*, 8 March 1995.
8. Andreas Oldag, 'Das Konzept einer flexibleren NATO', *Süddeutsche Zeitung*, 3 June 1996.
9. Cited in *Frankfurter Allgemeine Zeitung*, 8 December 1995.
10. USIA data in 'The New European Security Architecture', pp. 10, 21.
11. CDU/CSU parliamentary leader Wolfgang Schäuble quoted in the *Frankfurter Allgemeine Zeitung*, 15 November 1996.

12. Volker Rühe, 'Europa und Nordamerika auf dem Weg ins 21. Jahrhundert', (speech presented at the Spring meeting of the North Atlantic Assembly, Budapest, 29 May 1995).

13. 'Rühe: Ost-Erweiterung der NATO noch vor dem Jahr 2000', *Frankfurter Allgemeine Zeitung*, 30 May 1995; Karsten Voigt, 'NATO Enlargement: Sustaining the Momentum', *NATO Review*, 44, no. 2 (March 1996), 16.

14. Green spokesman Helmut Lippelt, for example, has warned more reluctant party colleagues that upholding the 'purity' of anti-NATO dogma should not come at the expense of German-Polish relations. *Frankfurter Allgemeine Zeitung*, 21 June 1996.

15. USIA data in 'The New European Security Architecture', pp. 9, 21.

16. USIA data in 'The New European Security Architecture', p. 9.

17. Jim Hoagland, 'Kohl on the Campaign Trail', *Washington Post*, 30 May 1996.

18. Karl-Heinz Kamp, 'The Folly of Rapid NATO Expansion', *Foreign Policy*, 98 (Spring 1995), 116–29.

19. Cited in Bruce Clark, 'NATO Hopefuls Let Their Impatience Show', *Financial Times*, 7 May 1996.

20. Newt Gingrich, 'American Engagement in Europe', *Hudson Policy Bulletin*, no. 24 (July 1996), 2.

21. 'Dole: Widen Alliance Faster', *Washington Post*, 5 June 1996.

22. Richard Cohen, 'Endangered Expansion', *Washington Post*, 12 December 1996.

23. Cited in *The Economist*, 1 July 1995.

24. Cited in *The Economist*, 1 July 1995.

25. See the chapter by Ronald Asmus in this volume and data cited in *Washington Post*, 22 October 1996.

Index